THE HUNT

ANDY McNAB

THE HUNT

The True Story of the Secret Mission to Catch a Taliban Warlord

WELBECK

Published by Welbeck
An imprint of Welbeck Non-Fiction Limited,
part of Welbeck Publishing Group.
Based in London and Sydney
www.welbeckpublishing.com

First published by Welbeck in 2022

A CIP catalogue record for this book is available from the British Library

ISBN
Hardback – 9781802793499
Trade Paperback – 9781802793505
eBook – 9781802793512

Typeset by seagulls.net
Printed and bound in the UK

10 9 8 7 6 5 4 3 2 1

CONTENTS

Author's Note   vii

Prologue: The White Mountains, October 2001   1

Chapter One: Kandahar, February 2007   19

Chapter Two: FOB Juno, February 2007   51

Chapter Three: Deliberate Action   85

Chapter Four: Mullah Dadullah   103

Chapter Five: Orders   139

Chapter Six: Recce   159

Chapter Seven: Target Confirmed   177

Chapter Eight: The Plan   191

Chapter Nine: Battle Prep.   205

Chapter Ten: Contact   241

Chapter Eleven: Into the Breach   257

Chapter Twelve: Jackpot   277

Chapter Thirteen: Aftermath   293

Glossary   303

AUTHOR'S NOTE

Thousands of operations were conducted by UKSF (UK Special Forces) in the Afghanistan battlespace during the thirteen years British servicemen and women were engaged in combat there.

Many of these operations are still secret, known only by those who fought in, planned, or approved them – and none have equalled the fight that took place in southern Helmand Province in May 2007, striking at the Taliban's most ruthless yet skilled wartime leader, Mullah Dadullah. And so that's where I wanted to start this new series, recreating the stories of real-life Special Forces missions.

UKSF were represented in Afghanistan at that time by the SBS (Special Boat Service), the Royal Navy's equivalent force to the Special Air Service. (During that campaign, the SAS were deployed to Iraq.) After leaving the SAS, I had the privilege of visiting UK and US Forces in Afghanistan on several occasions and was on the ground with them during operations.

All Special Forces missions are difficult and dangerous, and that's why the job is given to them in the first place. For those not as familiar with the SBS as they are with the

SAS, it's easy to assume that the actions they undertook in Afghanistan were not as challenging, or as extreme, as those going on in Iraq at the time, but this is far from the case. As you'll read here, what the operators of C Squadron achieved was extraordinary, by any measure, and they have my total respect.

The ultimate success of Operation Tetris meant the death of a truly brutal man. As you'll discover, he thought nothing of throwing away people's lives, including those of his own countrymen and women. His sadistic pleasure in the torture and execution of those unlucky enough to fall into his hands would be enough to condemn him, but he planned to escalate the war against Britain, America and her allies not only across Afghanistan but also far beyond its borders. He needed to be stopped, before he could target people in Europe and elsewhere in the world.

The Hunt might focus on the SBS operators involved, but the planning, preparation and support drew in hundreds of specialists from many branches of the UK and US armed forces, and perhaps because of that the news of Operation Tetris spread quickly through the SF community.

The names of those involved have been changed, and of course details that would compromise other operations conducted by UKSF have been omitted. But the facts remain true to the extraordinary action undertaken at the very limit of the capability of Britain's Special Forces.

In the wake of Operation Tetris, the Americans wanted to award decorations to the SBS for their daring and determination under enemy fire. But in keeping with their practice of never acknowledging Special Forces operations of any sort, the British government refused them permission to give the SBS any honour that might have confirmed they had taken part in an attack on Mullah Dadullah.

This account is testament to their bravery.

Andy McNab CBE DCM MM

Prologue

The White Mountains, October 2001

What Jay would remember about his first time in Afghanistan was the cold. It wasn't the kind of chill that simply caused his muscles to shiver. It seemed to get into his teeth, and bones, and never gave him a moment's real rest. Jay had experienced the misery of nature as a shivering young recruit at Lympstone, the training depot of the Royal Marines, but the cold of the Afghan mountains was a constant, perilous sensation. With scorching heat in summer, and savage snows in winter, it was no wonder that this country was known as one of the most hostile places on earth. For thousands of years, great armies had come here, from Alexander the Great to the Soviet Union, and most had left with their tails between their legs, if they'd been allowed to leave at all. Afghanistan was a country where war was the norm, and survival was a daily battle. Even when the enemy was absent, the cold remained. Make the wrong decision here – disrespect the land – and the mountains would kill you as surely as any Taliban fighter.

Jay knew that many of his enemies had been fighting for almost as long as he'd been alive: first contesting the Soviet occupation of the country, and then battling the Northern Alliance to put the Taliban in power. Jay's life didn't have that kind of bloody background, but he firmly believed that he had the best military training in the world, and he had the best soldiers by his side. He held the rank of sergeant, but Jay was part of a unit where *everyone* was expected to think for themselves, show initiative, and be above ordinary in all aspects of soldiering, no matter the rank. Jay had proven himself once by becoming a Royal Marines Commando, and a second time by passing Special Forces Selection to join the elite Special Boat Service, but now, for the first time, he would be up against a real enemy, and the price of failure was not to be returned home or to his unit, but death: for Jay, or worse, for his comrades.

Many of his squadron had served in the Special Forces for several years, and they had been waiting patiently for a war like this. When he passed Selection, Jay couldn't have predicted that Al-Qaeda would attack America and destroy the Twin Towers. The footage of the attack had made him bitterly angry, and to be a part of the response against those responsible filled him with pride. Very few soldiers were part of the effort to take out the terrorists and the people who supported them, but Jay was one of them. Jay's civilian friends could not understand that he was grateful to be sent to war, but his team mates all understood. They had volunteered again and again to get into this position, and this was what they wanted more than anything else: a mission that mattered.

Jay took another breath of the cold, thin air and looked around him. A range of harsh, jagged peaks stretched away into the distance. Beneath them was a long, flat plain broken by the lines of high compound walls. Jay was too far away to see the details, but he knew that these compound walls were made of thick layers of mudbrick, a testament to the perpetual violence in the region.

The frost-dusted slope that Jay stood on was part of a range of mountains known as Spīn Ghar, which meant the White Mountains, for obvious, snowy reasons. They were located in Afghanistan's east, and the border to Pakistan ran down the middle of the range, but the idea of a national boundary meant little here, and tribe and sect were far more important to the locals. The high mountain passes had long been both a route for smugglers and a refuge for fighters, and it was in places like this that men like Jay would have to root out those who supported the attacks of 9/11, and trap them if they tried to flee south into Pakistan. Easier said than done when the mountainsides were steep and often frozen, and the air was thinner and lacked the oxygen that Jay was used to. Part of Special Forces Selection took place on "the hills" for a reason, but the mountains of Wales did not compare to the peaks of Spīn Ghar, the highest of which was over five times that of Pen Y Fan, the famous mountain where British forces are sent to test their mettle.

Jay turned and looked behind him, seeing some of his comrades follow up the slope. Though not born to this region, the SBS men were operators through and through, and they had adapted to this harsh terrain with no more than a few wry grumbles. The truth was that they all welcomed the opportunity to test themselves, and relished the fact that they were on the hunt.

It didn't feel strange to Jay that this was, in fact, the essence of his mission. He was a hunter, and though he had never shot an animal in his life, hunting the enemy felt like the most natural thing in the world. He didn't know why, and he didn't need to. As Jay watched the other five men of the patrol snake their way along the cover of the mountain-side, he just knew in his gut that there was no place in the world he would rather be.

• • •

When people think about Special Forces missions, they usually think of raids, and hostage rescues, but less often do they think about deliberate, methodical patrols through mountains or jungle, or days on end spent immobile watching a house or a pass for one moment that can be missed in a second of lost focus. Jay was determined that he would not be responsible for allowing any of the terrorist group to escape into Pakistan, where diplomacy meant that his team could not follow. Like soldiers who had fought in Northern Ireland, Vietnam or countless other conflicts, Jay had been given a set of rules within which he must fight his war. The same was not true for his enemy, and Jay didn't think too much about that: it was enough to know that being taken alive was not an option.

It was no surprise to Jay that when there was even a sniff of Osama bin Laden, the man behind 9/11, the American Special Forces rushed to that area like wolves. He could only imagine how he'd feel if thousands of his countrymen had been killed in London, and so Jay fully understood why the Americans would want to be the ones to kill or capture Al-Qaeda's leader. Sometimes it felt like the American command – beneath which the SBS contingent fell for this operation – often forgot about the Brits at their disposal, and days had passed without patrols, let alone contact with the enemy, which Jay was yet to experience.

Clearly Jay wasn't the only one who was champing at the bit, and someone with a rank a lot higher than sergeant had convinced the American command to put the SBS to more frequent use. So it was that Jay found himself in the White Mountains, patrolling the slopes for signs of enemy occupation, and feeling the cold in his lungs with every breath of the thin air. Sometimes, he even worried that his fingers would be too stiff from the cold to pull the trigger. The only thing to do to keep warm was to move, but movement draws the eye, and enemy fire. There was nothing else to do but suck it up, and that didn't bother Jay; he hadn't joined the Special Forces for an easy life.

Clearly his enemy had their own toughness. The men that Jay's patrol were looking for didn't just visit the mountains, but often lived on them – or rather, *in* them – for extended periods of time. There were caves in the White Mountains, and while some occurred naturally, many had been expanded drastically in the fight against the Soviets, giving the mujahideen, as the Afghan fighters were known, places to plan, prepare and carry out operations against invaders. They were important sites to store weapons, and house men and equipment. You can't beat an enemy if you don't know where he is, and by going subterranean, Al-Qaeda and the Taliban were using nature to their advantage, and making NATO's job of destroying them a lot harder.

Jay had been surprised at just how many caves his patrol had found, often discovering them by following faint trails over the stony ground, and through sparse woodland: the stubborn trees somehow clinging onto life in the inhospitable terrain. The patrol had found stores for war, and destroyed them using explosives, but the enemy had been really elusive. Though Jay and his comrades moved tactically, and operated stealthily, he could not shake the thought that the enemy seemed to be one step ahead.

Jay knew that this wouldn't last forever. His squadron had trained too hard, and given too much for the enemy to escape. Jay and the patrol would keep hunting. Sooner or later, the enemy would make a fatal mistake.

● ● ●

It happened on another crisp, cold day, when the sky was pale blue and cloudless.

Jay's patrol was above the forest line: a height too cold for even the hardy trees to survive. They were moving along one side of a mountain pass, using cover where they could: boulders, scrub bushes and stunted trees. It was a hard, bleak landscape, but someone had made it their temporary home.

Mike, a fair-haired Scot, was studying a small ledge in the hillside. As some men of the patrol kept their distance and provided security, the patrol commander closed up to his point man to hear what he had to say.

"They had a tarp or something here to make a shelter," Mike said, indicating the holes in the ground which would have housed the structure's poles. The point man then stood, and indicated where ropes had cut into the bark of a tree. "They tied it off here," he said, and the patrol commander, Ken, nodded in agreement. Both men had grown up on British council estates, but by applying themselves to their trade they had come to be able to recognise, sign and track the enemy in the mountains of Afghanistan.

Ken was the Squadron Sergeant Major (SSM) leading the patrol. That wasn't usual, but the patrol commander had gone over badly on his ankle on the last patrol, and clearly Ken wasn't going to miss a chance to get in at the sharp end. He'd taken the injured man's place, and that meant that Jay was no longer the senior rank. Jay could have taken the role of patrol 2 I/C, but he didn't want to disturb the team's order any more than it had been, and so he had stepped back for a few days. As much as Jay was proud of his professionalism, he was not controlled by his ego: maybe all that surfing in Cornwall had something to do with it.

The SSM was another man who let his actions, not his mouth, do the talking for him. Unlike the caricatures of that rank, he was calm, and quiet, referring to the other men by first names, or nicknames, which was the norm in the SBS. Right now, with the shelter found, Ken didn't need to say anything to his blokes. Just a look was enough to communicate that they were drawing closer to the enemy.

Ken had barely given Mike the order to continue the patrol when the sound of gunfire suddenly crashed out along the pass. The steep mountainsides and stone funnelled the noise outwards and upwards, and though Jay could tell from the volume that it wasn't right on top of him, the

7

crashing noise made it difficult to place the distance and location of the firing point exactly. The buzz of adrenaline pumped quickly into his veins, but Jay and the other members of the patrol had drilled thousands of times for this moment, and so the excitement of the gunfire did not get the better of them.

When it was clear that no rounds were hitting the ground around him, and no one in the patrol was hit. Though gunfire was echoing along the pass, that didn't necessarily mean it was aimed at Jay's patrol. If they could avoid a firefight, then they would do so: there was no telling how many of the enemy were in the mountains, and though Jay and the others carried Bergens and webbing heavy with ammunition, there was no such thing as too many rounds, particularly when you are operating in a six-man patrol on one of the most dangerous borders on earth. There would be no engagement unless necessary.

"Does anyone see the firing point?" Ken called out, not a hint of stress in his voice.

Jay looked over, and then through, his weapon sight, looking for anything that might give the enemy away, such as smoke, or muzzle flash, or movement. Truth be told, he still wasn't convinced that the fire had been aimed at their patrol, but the next heavy burst put an end to that doubt, rounds whooshing overhead and smashing into rocks with heavy thuds. These sounds were not the angry wasps that many soldiers talked about, but the bigger rounds of a heavier calibre weapon.

"Dushka!" Jay called out, meaning they were on the end of a 12.7mm DShK machine gun. It was the kind of weapon that could ruin your day in a hurry, but Jay wasn't put off by that. The DShK had to be fired from a platform, like a vehicle or tripod, and it would be very hard to move it in terrain like this. The patrol could fix it, flank it and destroy it, but first they'd have to find the weapon and its gunner.

"Can you see it?" Ken shouted to him.

"No," Jay replied, feeling a little frustration, but forcing himself to stay methodical in scanning his arcs.

Jay kept searching for the firing point as another burst hit the mountainside, followed a second later by the cough-cough-cough of the DShK as the noise of the firing reached the ears of the patrol – the target. From the time between the rounds going overhead, and the weapon's report, Jay could tell that it was neither on top of them, nor at great distance, and he adjusted his scanning accordingly. Many belt-fed weapons like the DShK use tracer rounds, but none had come at them, and Jay quickly wondered if this was deliberately done to help conceal their position. If this was the enemy's plan, then it didn't work.

"Enemy. Right, two hundred!" Will, a Liverpudlian and one of the patrol's light machine gunners called out. "Two hundred!" he shouted, giving the rest of his team the distance to the enemy in metres. "Watch my tracer!"

Suddenly, bursts of fire sounded off to Jay's left, and he watched as Will adjusted his fire until his red tracer was hitting and bouncing off a V-shaped rock formation about two football fields' distance from them, on the other side of the pass. With such a rocky, desolate battlespace, Will had used his tracer to quickly bring the rest of the team onto the enemy.

"2 I/C, take over," Ken shouted, leaving the job of supp-ressing the enemy in the hands of his second in command. Once the patrol came under fire, the patrol commander would have sent a "contact, wait out" on his radio to alert command that they had come into contact with the enemy. Now, Ken would follow with a more detailed report giving where and when the contact had happened, what the enemy was, what they were doing and what Ken planned to do about it.

Jay followed Will's tracer, checked his sights were set to the correct range, and started to return fire at a slow and deliberate rate. After every few shots he would get low and move into another firing position: staying too long in one spot was inviting the enemy gunners to lay their weapons onto him.

His contact report sent, Ken could make his plan and decide what action the patrol would take. Jay knew that there was a good chance they would stand off and use air assets to smash the target. He also knew that there was a chance the patrol could withdraw out of the killing zone, but he didn't want to do that, and neither did his patrol commander.

"We're going to take the position!" Ken shouted along the line of men, his voice hard but calm, the mark of a professional in the battlespace. "Gary, you and the two guns stay here and give fire support, deliberate rate. Don't let the fuckers get their heads up, or bug out. Mike, Jay, on me. Dump your Bergens and fix fucking bayonets."

Not the textbook way to give the order, but Jay didn't waste a second in carrying it out. He had already shrugged off his heavy pack, and now his left hand drew his bayonet from its place on his webbing, and attached it to the end of his rifle. With the blade fixed, Jay was no longer thinking about the cold of Afghanistan: the only thing on his mind was killing the enemy, and surviving the next few minutes.

"Follow me," Ken said, choosing the route himself. He used folds in the ground to give them cover, and led Jay and Mike through boulders on the mountainside. No doubt this was why he had ordered bayonets fixed so early: in this kind of terrain, the enemy could appear from anywhere.

Bursts of fire continued to crash through the pass – they were the light machine guns of the fire support group (FSG), who fired in a steady rhythm. No wild bursts, but a rhythmic fire as one gun aimed, fired, and then waited for the other to do the same. Their job was to keep the enemy pinned down, and that could be achieved by short, accurate bursts. In the meantime, Ken would lead his team close enough to where they could assault, and fight through, the enemy position.

After following a low, stone wall erected by some shepherd centuries ago, Ken turned to Jay.

"Jay, you go down here as point of fire." He ordered, having chosen a position that would let his operator fire onto the enemy position from a flank. Now, under fire from two directions, the enemy were truly fixed.

Jay wasted no time in getting rounds down. He didn't think about the fact that today was his first time in real contact. He just sighted in on the barrel of the enemy machine gun, putting rounds inches from where the faces of the Taliban must be. He couldn't see them behind the rock, but Jay's slow, deliberate fire from his carbine would help keep them in position until Ken finished his approach and launched his assault.

Occasionally the DShK would fire, but it was clear that the SBS patrol had won the fire fight, and that the initiative was theirs. Jay heard Ken get onto the radio to his 2 I/C.

"Two One Delta, Two One Charlie, you got eyes on us, over?"

"Yeah, roger," his second in command replied. "You're good to launch from there. Firing point is thirty metres south of you. You won't get into our beaten zone so we can fire you in if you want, over," he finished, assuring Ken that his pair would not come into friendly fire as they assault the position.

"No need to fire us in. Standby to give rapid fire on my command. We'll throw grenades on the position then move without fire. I don't want a ricochet from our guns hitting us."

"Yeah, roger, standing by."

Ken looked his grenadier in the eye. "Ready?" he asked, but it was a rhetorical question. The Squadron Sergeant Major would never have taken the men on patrol unless he had full faith in them. On hearing Ken's radio message, Mike had pulled a grenade in anticipation of the order. Ken grinned and pulled his own from his kit: the long–time soldier wasn't about to miss the chance to lob a grenade at the enemy. His rifle slung and holding the grenade in one hand, Ken used the other to push a pressel [button] for his radio to transmit:

"Rapid fire, rapid fire, over."

There was no need for the FSG to reply on the radio. The increased machine gun fire did that for them, burst after burst hammering in and around the rocks that sheltered the enemy and the DShK. Jay picked up his own rate of fire, checking over his sights to make sure there was no chance the assault team would run into his arcs of fire.

He needn't have worried. Ken and his grenadier raced a short distance along the slope, then launched their grenades. A second later they were down and in cover.

The *CRUMP-CRUMP* of the detonations rolled across the mountainside.

"Cease fire," Ken ordered on the radio, but the guns and Jay had already gone silent. Every round counted, and none could be wasted. Ken's men understood that, and had ceased firing as soon as they saw the grenades explode. Later, one of the men would tell Jay that he saw a figure momentarily kicked into the air by the blast between the rocks.

Jay kept his weapon trained on the enemy position as Ken and Mike approached it, and disappeared into the rocks. A single shot rang out, which meant that at least one of the enemy had tried to fight on after the grenades. A couple of seconds later Ken's voice shouted: "Re–org, re–org!" It was time to re–organise the patrol. On hearing the command Jay sprang from his position, changing magazines as he moved and following the route that Ken had used into the rocks – there was no telling if the enemy had laid out mines, and so the proven route was the safest, though not fully certain, way of joining his team.

As Jay arrived, followed not long after by the 2 I/C and the machine gunners, they were put into all-round defence by Ken. They had cleared one position, but there could be more enemy in depth, or even behind where they had fought: these mountains were multi-dimensional – that's why it was called the battlespace – and this wasn't the time to switch off and let their guard down.

For the first time in Afghanistan, Jay saw the enemy, and they didn't make a pretty sight. There were two bodies, cut up badly by shrapnel and splinters, both of the men's faces fixed into grimaces as their bodies had lost the fight to survive.

Ken was finishing up sending his contact report, no trace in his voice or manner to suggest that he had just assaulted an enemy position with grenades and fixed bayonets.

"Jay," the patrol 2 I/C called over, "what's your ammo state?"

Jay knew the question would be coming and replied instantly, giving the amount of ammunition he had left in quantities of full magazines, rather than individual rounds. He'd gone through under two mags in the contact: enough to keep the enemy's head down, and do the job without overkill.

The grenadier had frisked what was left of the bodies for anything that might be of use: papers, ID, phones. Anything they found they'd piled up to one side, and a couple of the lads were leafing through the documents, trying to decipher anything of value: sometimes, information taken on one position or person could lead straight into a team's next move, but that didn't look like it would be the case here. There was a banged-up AK-47 dumped alongside the DShK's ammunition boxes, while the heavy machine gun itself had been hit by the grenade Ken had lobbed, leaving one tripod leg bent and its optics damaged.

"That's a fucking big gun to be shooting at a few people," Paul said grinning. The good-natured frogman had joined the squadron only two years ago, but he was showing a lot of promise. Like the rest of the patrol, Paul was in a very good mood after coming through a fight on the winning side. "They must have been waiting for some vehicles to come through the pass," he added.

"Then why open up on us?" Mike asked. "We might never have seen them."

Jay thought he had an answer to that: maybe the Taliban fighters thought that they could be heroes, and it would be them going through the SBS patrol's belongings, and not the other way around.

Happy that the danger had passed, Ken reduced the all-round defence down to a sentry front and rear. Jay wasn't one of them, and so while keeping a sharp eye out for disturbed earth and trip wires, he moved towards the far end of the V-shaped space. There was a sharp drop down the hillside, and then beyond that the mountain range climbed higher and extended away. The peaks in the distance were all white, heavily covered in snow, but Jay's attention was drawn to something much closer, and he began to study the opposite slope.

"What were they protecting?" Gary wondered out loud behind him.

"Fuck knows," Ken shrugged. "All we've found here are these ammo boxes and a few personal items." He gestured towards the olive-drab containers thrown to one side. "Most of the ammo boxes were empty. They were probably pre-recording targets," he shrugged, meaning that the gunners had test-fired bursts for future reference. By bringing the fire "on" to a reference point, and recording the sight and tripod settings, the gunners could then quickly and accurately hit targets without the need to first find their range, and make their adjustments, while under fire.

"Well if that's what they were doing, they did a shit job," Gary laughed, and he was right. A properly laid-on gun should have caused casualties in the patrol, but by the time the Taliban gunners were getting close with their fire, the SBS operators had already brought their own weapons into action, and from then on there was only ever going to be one result. "Maybe we came out onto higher ground than they expected," Gary went on. "They probably thought we'd be coming out of the treeline."

Jay looked at the two dead men, then back out to the slope. "I think they were here to hold us up," he said, and even though he was a newer member of the squadron, the other men listened to his explanation of why.

"One hundred metres, reference the lone tree on the opposite slope to us," Jay said, using the flat of his hand to indicate across the pass. "Come two knuckles right of the lone tree and there's a track leading down towards the treeline."

Ken and a couple of the others followed Jay's target indication. "Seen," Ken said, meaning that he had picked up sight of the track himself. He looked over to Jay, indicating that the younger operator should continue. Ken was a good leader like that, always looking for his men to find the answers rather than giving them.

"It's hard to move a weapon like this in this terrain," Jay said with a glance to the bulky and heavy DShK, "and if they knew there were patrols out looking for them, maybe these two were dicked to wait here and fight a delaying action so that the others could get out of the area."

Ken looked at the two bodies. "Dicked" meant that they would have been ordered to fight and die here, but the Squadron Sergeant Major wasn't so sure of that. "They probably volunteered for it," he said, "guaranteed ticket to heaven and all that." For a moment he looked around the mountainside, stroked the stubble on his chin, then came to a decision.

"If there was a cave nearby they wouldn't have contacted us like this. If they've all fucked off and left these two useless twats here to slow us down, then there's not a lot we can do here. Let's get a wet and some scran in us and then we'll RTB," Ken said, meaning that they would eat and drink, and then return to base.

Jay sat down in the weak Afghan sunshine. The activity of the contact had warmed him up but the cold was back, and making its presence known. Still, the two dead fighters were a reminder that things could be a lot worse, and Jay enjoyed his "hot wet": a term that the men used for hot drinks that came in the ration packs. Usually, one man in the patrol would "brew up" or "get the wets on", and then that mug would be passed around the rest of the men. Jay made sure to add plenty of sugar to the drink, every calorie important in the mountains, and he ate a chocolate bar that was rock hard from the cold. The fact that there were bodies a few metres away didn't bother him, and Jay didn't give it much thought: this was war.

Once his patrol had something warm inside of them Ken ordered the DShK to be stripped and its working parts taken with them, and confirmed the route that his point man would use to get them to the Helicopter Landing Site (HLS) for extraction.

"Alright," Ken said, "let's get moving."

Before Jay took his place in the patrol, he found himself drawn to the bodies of the enemy. He felt no remorse for their deaths – the things they would do to him if he was captured didn't bear thinking about – but Jay couldn't help but think about the fight ahead in this new war. These two men had poor clothing against the cold, a few tins of ammunition and little training, but they had belief, and that had given them the courage to stay behind for a fight to the death. How many more men like this were willing to die for the Taliban and Al-Qaeda?

With the clarity that comes from facing death and coming through alive, Jay realised that this was going to be a long war.

His first time in Afghanistan would not be his last.

CHAPTER ONE

Kandahar, February 2007

Jay wasn't wrong: not only had the Global War on Terror opened new battlefronts around the world – most spectacularly with the invasion of Iraq – but the fight in Afghanistan had dragged on just like Jay had predicted. In 2001 it had seemed as though Osama bin Laden had been cornered in Tora Bora, but for some reason that had never been explained to Jay's satisfaction, a section of border had been left free of coalition troops, and Al-Qaeda's leader had slipped through the mountains into Pakistan. For a man like Jay, failure did not sit well with him, and he could only imagine how the American SOF (Special Operations Forces) units felt about having their number one enemy slip from their grasp.

Al-Qaeda lived on. In fact, they were turning much of the world bloody with their brutal tactics, such as suicide bombings and publicised beheadings, but the war had grown bigger than them, and they were far from the only enemy. As well as other terrorist organisations and militias, the American-led coalition was fighting the Taliban that they had ousted from power: the two men that Jay had seen killed in the mountains were far from the only Taliban willing to die for their cause. Thousands of British soldiers were now deployed to the country's Helmand Province, and shot and shell were flying in both directions. Towns like Sangin and Musa Qala were becoming household names in British homes, the evening news showing footage of intense combat that the soldiers had filmed on digital cameras and helmet cams.

Helmand Province was half the area of England, but with only two per cent of the population size it often seemed deserted. There were mud-brick compounds in the desert, easily visible due to their thick, high walls, but few people ventured into the mountains that towered over the plains. The province's built-up areas were concentrated along its rivers, where irrigation made the land a carpet of bright green fields and orchards. It was a region infamous for its poppy production, the flower that is used to produce opiates, but unlike the red poppy that Jay wore in November to remember fallen service personnel, the poppies of Helmand had white and pink petals. Helmand was as beautiful as it was deadly, and Jay reckoned that it would be an outdoorsman's paradise if it were ever at peace.

The dirt of Helmand seemed like a million miles away from where Jay was now, sitting on a picnic bench with a Tim Hortons coffee in his hand. "The boardwalk" was a strip mall on a raised and covered wooden platform, with different shops separated in portacabins: there was everything from Afghan rugs, to "Gucci kit" to the world-famous Tim Hortons donuts that Jay had just put away.

It was not Jay's first time sitting at the picnic table, but it was the first time of this tour, and it had become something of a ritual. With a few other members of the headshed (nickname for anyone in authority), Jay made up the advance party of C Squadron, SBS. They had come in ahead of the Troops to do the part of war that no one likes to think about: paperwork, admin and briefings.

It didn't bother Jay. Promotion to SSM had been an honour, and though he would always prefer to be in the field, he didn't shy away, or try and offload the paperwork side of Special Forces soldiering. He was a team player, and a professional: that meant doing every aspect of his job to the best of his ability.

Jay took another swig of the Tim Hortons coffee – not bad – and looked at the assortment of NATO military members who were going from shop to shop. He recognised groups of young fighting men, lads barely out of their teens who were laughing and joking: they had the smiles of soldiers who had just left fighting, and were going home. Here and there were groups of Royal Marines, their green lids worn with pride. Jay spotted the red and white hackles of the Fusiliers, and the cap badges of various support arms, and uniforms of different nationalities. Many were young, but Jay also spotted older soldiers with rank: it was 3 Commando Brigade, and they'd been carrying the weight of the winter's fighting. Jay knew a lot of their senior NCOs from his time as a young Royal. They were mates and comrades, and that was the case for many of the SBS men in C Squadron. Although any British Army soldier could attempt Selection, the Royal Engineers, Paras and a few other regiments tended to make up the bulk of the SAS. When operating with, or in the area of an infantry battlegroup, it might be that there were no personal connections between the infanteers and the "Blades" from Hereford. But when the SBS were deployed with fighting formations of Royal Marines, there was always familiarity between some senior non-coms. Many had gone through the Commando Course together, and that was a long-lasting camaraderie.

War also forged the strongest of bonds, and Jay could see it in these groups of young men who were on their way home for R&R. They had been through some of Britain's hardest fighting since Korea, and they had paid a price: mates sent home without limbs, without eyesight, or in a casket. Jay saw that a group of three Royal Regiment of Fusiliers junior ranks were looking for a table to eat their massive tray of donuts, but all of the picnic benches were taken.

"Squeeze in here lads," Jay said.

The truth was that there was no need to squeeze. Jay was built like a rugby number 8 but that still left a lot of space at the table. The infantry lads paused nonetheless. They recognised an operator when they saw one: Jay was wearing DPM bottoms, a North Face fleece and a baseball cap. He was twice the age of the young soldiers, and that meant he had a lot more rank.

"You sure, sir?" The lance corporal asked.

"Yeah, take a seat."

The soldiers did, and looked a bit sheepish. They'd just been fighting tooth and nail with the Taliban, but they were awed by Jay. They didn't know exactly what his job was, or what unit he was attached to, but they could smell a man who was at the top of their profession.

"You want a donut, sir?" The youngest soldier asked in a thick Geordie accent. Jay doubted he could be more than 18.

Jay wasn't hungry but he took one with a grateful smile. Nothing put people at ease like breaking bread. "My name's Jay," he said, then shook the lads' hands. The Fusiliers were lean and hungry, whittled into shape by a summer of war.

"You lads on your way home?" Jay asked, and when they replied that they were, he asked where those homes were. One of the men was returning to a child he had never met.

"They couldn't get you home for the birth?"

"I didn't ask," the lad shrugged. "We needed every man we had. It would have been jack to leave them."

Jay liked these men. People could say what they wanted about the PlayStation generation, but there were still young British soldiers out there who were doing their country proud. "Whereabouts were you in Helmand?"

"Sangin, sir," the lance jack smiled wryly. "Sorry... Sangin, *Jay*. We bounced around before that, but that's where we did our last fighting. We went to Bastion for a bit after that, but fuck all happens there."

"What was Sangin like?" Jay asked.

"It was pretty mad like," the lance jack said, and the other two laughed. Jay smiled. Weeks of Taliban attacks, mortar attacks, throwing grenades back and forth, and danger-close airstrikes: yeah, that did sound pretty mad like.

"You lads have done a cracking job," Jay said, and he could see that they took pride in that. Jay wasn't some grey old general that they didn't care about, but a hard looking operator: his opinion meant a lot to the young infanteers.

23

Jay looked at the empty tray of donuts and got to his feet. "Let me replen that," he said. The lads protested but Jay returned a couple of minutes later with a fresh batch. He did not sit down, and instead offered his hand. The young Fusiliers stood to shake it.

"Take one for the road, sir?" they asked him.

"I'm good, lads. Stay safe."

They laughed at that: it had become the term soldiers used as "See yer" in this war. But what could ever compare to trouble after the times they had just been through?

Jay turned down the boardwalk, and checked his watch. He still had some time to kill until his next meeting, and so he went back to looking out the corner of his eye at the other people on the boardwalk, most of whom gave the big man a wide berth. There were a few other men in civilian clothes, contractors from America and Britain. There were members of several air forces, and some were so much on the fat side that Jay wondered at what – if anything – their fitness test standards must be. As a young Commando he had been thrashed constantly with PT, and as an SBS operator he had continued that trend, driven on not by an instructor but by the strong voice in his head. Unlike some soldiers, Jay didn't let the sight of fat military members get him angry, but he couldn't understand an unfit military person's mindset: why wouldn't someone want to be the best that they could be?

As Jay walked through the base, he couldn't help thinking about the history of the war in Afghanistan, and how it was going. KAF (Kandahar Airfield) had been secured by American Marines a few months after Jay had seen his first dead enemy in the White Mountains. Although that day had been a win for Jay and the patrol, and many large battles were won by Special Forces, it was hard to see that deployment as a total success: Osama bin Laden was still alive, and the war had dragged on. If the aim of the deployment had been to come to Afghanistan, rout Al-Qaeda and put an end to Islamic Jihad, then it had failed. Five years later, the violence was only escalating as our casualty count increased.

Following the attacks on the Twin Towers in September 2001, the limited surface-to-air missile capability of the Taliban was destroyed to make way for air assets to start flying in kit and people. That opened the skies for ops, and by the end of the month, the first US troops were flown in, and members of UKSF were deployed alongside them.

But Osama bin Laden escaped through the net thrown around the Tora Bora mountain range, and fled the country into Pakistan. Jay couldn't understand why sections of the cordon had not been held by NATO SF, or US Marines, but whatever the reason, Al-Qaeda exploited the gap, and its leader escaped. The Taliban leadership followed soon after, and were cleared out of Afghan mid-December 2001. An interim government was established and then, in October 2004, there were national elections and Hamid Karzai was elected President.

That was the easy part, Jay thought to himself, casting his mind back to a briefing that they had received in Poole, home of the SBS. It had been given by an army staff officer who was built like a toothpick, but the man had a surprisingly commanding voice that held their attention.

• • •

"Anyone telling you that President Karzai has the full support of the country is full of shit," the Intelligence Officer told the assembled audience of C Squadron, who sat listening in the camp's theatre. "All of the institutions of the country, such as the police, are riddled with corruption. There is very little legal trade coming out of Afghanistan. The government receives very little income from taxation, which prevents them from putting the police, and the Afghan Army, on to a proper footing. To be honest, even if they did get more money, it would just be embezzled, as is happening with the international aid that's coming to the country by the bucketful. It's not that there isn't the money being sent to help Afghanistan, but we can't easily get back what is being stolen. Our choice is to either deal with this government, or the Taliban."

From his position at the front of the room, Jay looked over towards Manc, one of his senior NCOs. Manc had grown up in one of the most impoverished parts of the UK, and his dad had decided that Labour didn't go far enough. Manc had inherited a lot of that far-left thinking, leading to many "spirited" debates in the sergeants' mess, but if Jay had expected Manc to pipe up he needn't have worried: the sergeant was busily taking notes.

"They get a bit of money from gemstone mining in the Tajik area, here," the officer said, using a mouse pointer to indicate an area of a map on a projector, "up near the border with Tajikistan, but nothing like the amount they could get if they could mine effectively. Their main income comes from the movement of goods across the borders and around the country. However, the Afghan police tend to set up roadblocks and extract taxes of their own when they feel like it, and most of the border towns have warlords who control what comes and goes across the border they manage, and they take their share for that service. The Americans are angrier about this than we are. I think we knew a bit more about what it was going to be like than they did, thanks to the old empire. The US came in expecting to find a modern state that they could engage with, once the Taliban had been driven out. What they encountered really shocked them. Meanwhile, the Taliban started to regroup over the border in Pakistan, and it's very likely that the corruption and lack of central authority from the Kabul government gave the Taliban legitimacy in some of the areas they have re-entered."

Jay looked around at the men listening intently. Normally briefings were a bit dry, but this was great, and the officer had captured his audience well. Talk of gems and money and corruption and drugs always went down well with the audience.

"The Americans, and us, and other allies, have remained in Afghanistan as part of the International Security Assistance Force, or ISAF," the officer continued. "The country has been divided into five separate commands, spread across the regions." He turned back to point at the various areas on the map, each marked out by thick red lines. "These are managed by NATO in conjunction with ISAF. The north is managed by the Germans, and the Italians are leading in the west. The Americans are managing the central zone, around Kabul, and the eastern area that runs up to the Pakistan border. They're having a hard time of it there.

"That leaves the south." The officer clicked onto another map, a large-scale one covering the southern part of the country, outlined in a thick yellow line. "That means the provinces of Nimruz, Helmand and Kandahar. Regional Command South is currently under the command of the Canadians. Later this year it will be the Dutch. Next year it will be Britain's turn. Helmand, as you all know, is the area where the Parachute Regiment, along with other elements of the Army, operate. Later this year, it'll be the turn of the Royal Marines. This is the Afghan part of Baluchistan, primarily an area for the Pashtun tribes, and they have no interest in the rules that are laid down by their own government, let alone anything that we might propose. The border with Pakistan, which is over 2,200 kilometres long, means nothing to them, and they cross it at will. It's mostly mountainous, interspersed with a bit of sand and rock. The area over the border in Pakistan to one side is the remaining part of Baluchistan, and to the other it's what we used to call the North–West Frontier, now the Khyber Pakhtunkhwa. The region is lawless and consists of seven tribal agencies, not one of whom thinks the Pakistani government has any right to control their lives, any more than those on the Afghan side of the border think Kabul's in charge. Tribal rules and traditions take priority over every-thing there, and if there are Al-Qaeda or Taliban among them, they will never tell us. For these reasons, the region is largely left alone, and not patrolled by the Pakistanis."

The officer paused to take a sip of his tea. It must have hit the spot, because he took another two before continuing.

"I don't know where you men have been before, so forgive me if any of this is teaching you to suck eggs. I have been to Helmand myself and I can tell you that it is largely a very primitive place, with high rates of illiteracy among the population. There are only four other places in the world where the statistics around poverty and illiteracy are worse: Number one, the Royal Marines. Only joking, only joking. But yes, only around twenty per cent of Helmand's population can read and write. Unemployment runs at about forty per cent. For comparison, UK unemployment is about five per cent right now. As you might expect, over half of their population live in poverty. The per capita GDP is around one thousand US dollars. Again, for comparison, here in the UK it's about fifty times that."

"Not in the forces it isn't," came a shout from the back and the officer laughed.

"Maybe I shouldn't have told you about the gemstone mines?" he grinned, and was rewarded with a laugh. The last time Jay had seen his audience this happy was for a briefing about an upcoming exercise to San Diego. Helmand was hardly California, but it did have something that the sandy beaches did not: an enemy to fight.

"Now, I tell you those things for background," the officer said, a little more gravely now, "but of course the truth of the matter is that you are not going to be a part of lowering corruption, or raising literacy rates. At least not directly. You're going to Afghanistan to fight the Taliban, so let's talk about them."

He clicked the mouse, and a picture of hard looking, bearded men came onto the screen, armed with an assortment of small arms and RPGs.

"The Taliban, who had been in charge in Helmand, and continue to hold sway in the region, were awful rulers. They have left the people there in a bad state, made them very insular, and very suspicious of strangers. There's an old saying, 'You cannot buy the loyalty of an Afghan – you can only rent it.' You might not find that to be true in the north, I wouldn't know. Kabul certainly feels differently to the rest of the country. But it's certainly true of the south, and the person who befriends you today might be the one who stabs you in the back tomorrow. It is a very difficult environment to operate in, and a very dangerous one too."

He stopped, and looked about again. "What I'll tell you now is an open secret. One of those things that we all know is going on, but that politicians can't talk about openly. A large part of the problem in Afghanistan stems from the Pakistan side of the border. The ISI, or Inter-Services Intelligence, is Pakistan's main intelligence agency, and although officially Pakistan supports the US, a number of ISI agents still aid the Taliban. We don't know how many, and we don't know the extent of their assistance, but we do know that the Taliban co–ordinate the insurgency from within Pakistan borders, and use the area to resupply and even recruit from. The aid supplied to them by the ISI could be in materiel, or it could be in intelligence, or possibly both. Add that into the mix and you can see why it's such a dangerous environment."

The officer studied the room. "I don't suppose many of you are old enough to have served in Northern Ireland. Well, that is probably for the best, as Afghanistan is a very different beast in many ways. One of which is the international aspect of the mission. As you all know, this is going to be a highly unusual deployment. You are going to be working closely with the Americans, as part of the newly formed Combined Joint Special Operations Task Force [CJSOTF]. There are a number of roles that will be carried out under that umbrella and most of them won't concern you. I'm sure your CO will be talking to you about your role. I will be working there too, as part of CJSOTF's remit is to train the Afghan Army forces, particularly in developing a special operations capability. Once their troops are at a suitable level, they will be accompanying you on tasks, as it is believed that operations will be more successful if they are seen to be led by Afghans. They will be trained how to conduct both offensive and reconnaissance operations and once you are in Afghanistan, and once the Afghans themselves are up to speed and everyone is confident about their abilities and discipline, you will be working out how to operate with them alongside you."

There was some restlessness among the gathered men in the room at the idea of working alongside Afghans. One of the reasons they had put themselves through Selection was so that they would only work with the best. Jay caught the officer's eye, and addressed the room:

"Lads, let's remember that every successful counterinsurgency has relied on Special Forces working alongside indigenous forces. We're going out there to win a war, and we won't be working with dross. The Afghan Commandos will be trained by Brits, and look: if the Afghans weren't warriors, then we wouldn't be into year five of a war, would we? These lads know how to fight. It's in their blood."

Jay looked back to the officer, who nodded his thanks for the interjection. The words had reached the men, and they had understood and accepted Jay's logic.

"The use of SFSG and the Afghan task force will free this squadron up to do what you all do best," the officer told the men. "A conventional army is always going to be wrong-footed by the Taliban, because they will never be stupid enough to come out and meet the British Army on our terms: at least, not after the pasting they've had this summer. We've already seen the change in tactics. They will stay in their small units, they will stay concealed within their caves and their networks of supporters, conducting their raids across the border. They will mount an ambush rather than an attack. If they do attack it will be fast and mobile, because they are not bogged down with lots of kit or lots of protocols. So this is where what you all do comes in. To play them at their game, to confront them where they least expect it, back way behind the lines. Your actions could prove devastating to the Taliban, because you can target them precisely and without the collateral damage from regular Army attacks."

He turned and gestured at the expanse of empty ground indicated on a map of Helmand. "Behind the lines will be dangerous, obviously. You will have to assume that everyone you see is likely to pass knowledge of your presence to the enemy. So be careful, and observant when travelling in these regions. You will have access to support and this is where the SFSG's other role can come into play, acting to assist as well as taking the weight of training off your shoulders."

The officer met a few of the men with his eyes, and held them. He wanted his point to carry home...

"You are all about to embark on a very, very tough tour. The men you are fighting have no regard for their own safety. They will not surrender. Your job, when you are out there, will be to work alongside the Americans, their intelligence networks as well as their Special Forces, and the SFSG. You will be the tip of the spear, as you will be on operations in an offensive capacity for the duration of the deployment. Be prepared for the most intense and exhausting period of your lives. Don't underestimate your enemy, especially their desire to die in battle. You may have heard or read this, but some rifle companies on previous tours have had to fix bayonets in the fight – it's been that fierce."

Jay saw a few of his lads smile: fighting with bayonets would be a dream come true for them. He understood the enthusiasm but hoped they didn't get what they wished for. Things between steel and men can go either way.

"Make no mistake about the Taliban," the officer finished, "they will use innocent civilians to hide behind. They will use them to stop you from firing on them, with the aim of showing their bodies to the media so that it will seem that you have willingly shot at women, and children. If you fire back, you will kill innocent people. Civilian lives will be lost on this tour, no matter how hard you try to avoid it: the Taliban will make sure it happens. They are ruthless, gentlemen. Fucking ruthless."

• • •

Thinking back to that day in Poole, Jay had walked the distance of the airbase without even thinking about it. He was close to the flight line now, where the buzz of helicopters and roar of jets filled the air. Jay took a seat on the lip of a thick concrete blast wall and watched the aircraft come and go, wondering about where they were heading: were the helicopters delivering mail, or collecting casualties? Was the fast jet heading out to take aerial photos, or drop bombs? Jay's favourite jets were the American A-10s. Designed to be a tankbuster, the aircraft with its 30mm cannon was achieving legendary status amongst British troops for its close support missions, and the skill of its pilots. Hearing an A-10 fire for the first time was a moment that no soldier would forget.

Sitting with his back against the shaded side of the concrete, Jay started to think about the men he had been sent here to kill. The truth was that – on his first tour – he had little idea about the enemy, and for good reason: they'd needed to get on the ground as soon as possible. For this deployment there had been time to really tailor training, and briefings, and Jay thought back again to the old intelligence officer with a toothpick physique, and the commanding voice, and what he had said about the Taliban's ways of war...

• • •

"There have been instances of finding children with their arms tied behind their backs among the victims of an ISAF strike," the Intelligence Officer told C Squadron. "They were not there by accident. The Taliban abducted them, abducted their families, held them against their will, and drew fire upon their own positions. They do not care about life; yours, theirs or the ordinary Afghan.

"You are going out to Afghanistan to kill the enemy, and to protect the lives of your comrades, and of the Afghan civilians. It is not always possible to do all of those at the same time, and the Taliban will do whatever they can to put civilian blood on ISAF hands."

His words hung heavily in the air as he looked about the room once more.

"So who are the enemy? Where did they come from? What do they want? Well, the Taliban are relatively new players on the international stage. They only began as an organisation in 1994. Initially it was formed by a group of Pashtun religious students led by Mullah Mohammad Omar. The religious students were called 'Talibs' in the local language, which is where the group gets its name. The religious seminaries preached a hard-line form of the Sunni Islam doctrine, and some of their initial funding came from Saudi Arabia. However, once their influence started to grow, a new backer came on the scene. The Pakistani intelligence agency, the ISI, that I mentioned before, was instrumental in the formation of the Taliban. They wanted a buffer zone between Pakistan and the chaotic situation in Afghanistan that had come about as a result of the Soviet withdrawal from the country in 1989 and the resultant civil war between the various factions in play, the Mujahideen, the Northern Alliance."

The officer paused for a moment, as though expecting questions. None came. The assembled operators were paying rapt attention. Contrary to how they were often portrayed in movies, these Special Forces operators knew how to pay attention to a briefing. They were here to listen and learn, not arse around. This wasn't a profession where mistakes meant the share price would fall. It meant you got dead.

"The ISI helped build the Taliban from a rural insurgency made up of these Sunni Islamic fundamentalists," the intelligence expert went on. "They turned what was basically a

35

Pashtun militia into something more structured and better supported. They began to expand deeper into the country from their bases in the border areas, in the mountains. The appeal of the Taliban to the local people came not so much from its hard-line religion, or its identity, but from its policies. As they planned to impose the Sharia code, the Taliban announced that they were going to stop the endless violence, the anarchy and the revenge-killings that were taking place all over the country. People wanted that security, so the movement spread quickly, largely through the open spaces of the south-west, and by September 1995 they'd captured the province of Herat, bordering Iran on the west of the country. Within a year they'd taken Kabul, overthrowing the President who'd been one of the Mujahideen that had opposed the Soviets. Two years later they held almost all of Afghanistan."

He paused briefly. "I should add that Pakistan disputes some of what I've just said," he smiled, clearly not believing a word of it.

"The government in Lahore repeatedly denies that there is any institutional support for the Taliban in the country, but they were one of only three countries – Saudi Arabia and the United Arab Emirates were the other two – to recognise the Taliban as the legitimate government when they seized power, and they were the last of those countries to end diplomatic ties after 9/11."

The officer scratched at his chin for a moment. "Look, let's not kid ourselves that the Taliban only came to power because they were bloodthirsty arseholes. In a country that had lived through years of Soviet occupation and the ferocious internal wars that had followed, the Taliban's message of peace and stability proved popular to many people. Remember that two million Afghans died in the Soviet occupation. That kind of suffering will make a person open to solutions they may not consider under other circumstances, and the Taliban did reduce the levels of violence. They made the place generally safer for those who abided by their rules, and stopped the corruption endemic in all the country's institutions, and this was all a lot of Afghans were asking for. The Taliban could never have risen to power, and held onto it, if no one wanted them there."

He picked up a remote for the projector and clicked through a few photos: they weren't pretty.

"But, like many governments that rose to power with the use of force, they ruled with a cruel, iron fist. The Taliban would stone people to death, publicly execute them for adultery, and amputate limbs from thieves. Women were made to wear full burkas, and were confined to the home with no rights against their husbands, who could pretty much do with them as they wished. Infant mortality was higher than anywhere else in the world. Girls over ten years old were no longer allowed to go to school, is this all clear, and the Taliban banned pretty much everything, including films, TV, music, dancing – you name it, they were against it. Men had to grow beards, and were beaten if they cut them short or shaved them. People stopped going out at prayer time because if they did, they were beaten for not being at prayer. The Taliban's religious police would go about with batons and iron cables ready to enact punishment on anyone they deemed deserved it, whether or not there was any evidence of guilt.

"The basic, brutal governance the Taliban brought stopped some of the worst excesses of the past few years, but it introduced a whole new level of incompetence to government. The ideology of the Taliban is incapable of improving the lives of Afghans in any meaningful way, because they will always prioritise their religious beliefs over anything that comes from the outside world. For instance, they have, and do oppose vaccination programmes, like polio."

The Intelligence Officer shook his head, struggling to understand who would put a child through such suffering.

"The Taliban weren't prepared to stop in the territories that welcomed them," he went on. "Just before the start of Enduring Freedom in 2001, the Taliban had assembled a force to work alongside Al-Qaeda to take their Islamic radicalism all around the country, and even across borders into neighbouring countries. As well as Pashtuns, and those of other tribes from the borders, they had Pakistanis, Uzbeks from the Islamic Movement of Uzbekistan, Arabs, Chechens, Kashmiris, Chinese and even Filipinos fighting with them."

For the first time, a hand was raised from C Squadron's ranks. It belonged to Paul, 1 Troop's sergeant.

"Sir," he said, respectfully addressing a visitor who may not be used to the lax forms of address in the Special Forces, "reference the Chechens. Do we have solid intelligence that there are hardened Chechen Muj in Afghan, or is this just something the Taliban put out to ride the reputation that the Chechens got from fighting the Russians recently?"

"I can't give you a hundred per cent either way on it, I'm afraid. The Taliban use out of area fighters, and Chechnya is a poor part of the world with an abundance of men who are experienced in war, and in particular, jihad. I think it is a safe assumption to say that some of them have made the trip to Afghanistan. It wouldn't be particularly hard for them. We do know that the Uzbek militants have been working with the Taliban and with Al-Qaeda since the late 1990s. They have formed a top–level bodyguard and strike force, because they've usually been better educated than their Afghan equivalents, and they've also had extensive Soviet military training. As Russian speakers, maybe they confuse signals intelligence into thinking they're Chechens. But, if I was a betting man, I'd say there are Chechens in Afghanistan. In what strength, I don't know. Any other questions so far?"

No hands came up. "OK, then. So, the Taliban you'll face in Afghanistan can be broken down into different tiers. First there's the hardcore group of students from the madrassas who believe they're fighting a holy war – they're diehard warriors who are the most important grouping in the Taliban. They are sometimes referred to as *Aslee*, or 'real' Taliban. The leadership cadre is strongly linked to this group.

"The next two largest groups couldn't be more different. Let's look at the dedicated group first, which is itself made up of three distinct elements. There's the foreign jihadists we've just spoken about, often battle-hardened fighters who've joined the Taliban to carry on the fight against the West. Alongside them are the foreign volunteers who are untrained but committed to jihad, and usually mentored by the more experienced foreigners. And then there's the trained Afghan fighters, who came out of the civil wars, and whose base is the villages and small towns throughout Helmand. They are motivated strongly by their loyalty to their family, and to their tribe, and they are called *Daakhelee* Taliban; they are frequently incited to join the fight by the drug warlords who employ them, and their motive is less about religion, and more to do with attacking those they perceive as invaders, which can be anyone from the West, but also someone from elsewhere in Afghanistan. They are sometimes motivated by fears of their livelihood – the poppy fields – being taken away from them. Or, by hatred of the Afghan National Police, who are not liked in the region, as some of them are closer to bandits than police. These are all Taliban who will rarely be captured alive, and they will fight on to the end.

"The final tier of Taliban is what we call the ten-dollar Taliban, usually local people who are hired to fight alongside them, wave a gun about in a show of force, or sometimes those who act as dickers." [Dicker was a term that came from "keeping dick" – having someone on lookout when a crime was being committed – and was one of those words that had passed out of use in society, but hung around in military parlance.]

"These ten-dollar Taliban have had little training and almost no exposure to war. They're usually poor, and often paid in drugs. Sometimes they'll be the ones to place an Improvised Explosive Device (IED) after some basic instruction. The ten dollars are usually the ones to get killed first by ISAF. Thankfully, they show little or no commitment to the cause when things go against them, unless they've got one of the upper–tier groups stood behind them with a weapon. They probably account for about half of the Taliban. A large problem with them is that, like most of the Taliban, they wear no uniform. So, if things are going badly in a fight, they put their weapon into a hole somewhere, wander off, and go from fighter to civilian just like that.

"The dead ones often vanish quickly, too. Muslim burial laws emphasise speed of burial and preparation of the body. They will rarely leave the dead out for long periods of time. Expect them to send young boys out to collect them, with an adult directing from a distance."

This soured faces in the room. Using kids for dirty deeds was not something that was approved of by these men.

"Now, onto their leadership. After NATO kicked the Taliban out in December 2001, most of their leadership went south, and re-established themselves in the Pakistan border territories. Quetta, Peshawar and Miran Shah all became their new homes, with well over a million Afghan refugees and others turning up there, too. The ISI, and others in Pakistan, re-established lines of communication with the Taliban. Their shared ideologies and religious beliefs, aided by well-established friendships made in the decade before, made such a reorganisation possible. It is surprising that the more secular elements of Pakistan society can co-exist with the more extreme elements of the Taliban, but they have found a way to accommodate each other out of necessity.

"Quetta, in Pakistan, is where the leadership re-emerged. The religious schools that had spawned the Taliban back in the early 90s started churning out new recruits. The madrassas take the young boys away from their families, and with their blessing, I should add. The youths are then only given the point of view of their teachers, and intellectual dissent does not exist. A bit like the forces, really."

A few of the men chuckled at that, and the officer smiled at his own joke. "The young recruits never hear anyone telling them to think or act differently. Jihad against the infidel Americans and British is the only option open to them. Given that many of the Taliban commanders themselves went to these madrassas, the links between the young and old are very strong."

"You could say that, sir," Jay grinned. Operators from Poole would often return to take up senior positions in the Commando units, and there they would inspire a new generation to push themselves for Special Forces Selection.

"I keep talking about 'the Taliban' as if they're one group," the officer addressed C Squadron, "and when you're in the battlespace that's pretty much how it is, but I must point out that the group itself is fractured and that this is very apparent now in the tactics the Taliban are employing out in the field. There are a number of networks that work together against the Kabul government and the ISAF forces. As well as the Taliban, and what's left of Al-Qaeda, there's the Haqqani group; Jaish-i-Muslimeen; and other smaller extremist groups like Hezb-e-Islami. And I'm not yet mentioning the drug warlords who control the southern areas of Helmand through their militias. There's in-fighting between a lot of these groups – we've heard rumours that the Kandahar element of the Taliban is in dispute with the non-Kandahar element. What that means is that, while they may agree on general aims, they're often not able to cooperate on the ground or conduct operations together. The groups operating within Pakistan, and of course Al-Qaeda, are a different level of threat altogether.

"These connections are often shown in their propaganda more than in the battlespace. There are elements of the Taliban that are now using DVDs and the internet to distribute and promote their message of a global Christian war against Islam. This has wider implications, as it suggests they are no longer confining their campaign to the internal insurgency in Afghanistan, but have an eye on a wider jihad against the West. Some of the videos they've produced suggest an on-going solidarity with other jihadist movements around the world.

"Clearly there are two levels of danger here. One is that the Taliban start to emulate Al-Qaeda, and draw in disparate terrorist groups to their cause. The other is that they start to export their fight to the cities of Europe, and further afield. It could, of course, be no more than a ruse to force us to tie up some of our resources in reacting to something that's never going to happen. The good news is that we know that there's a large section of the Taliban who are very strongly opposed to this approach. Unlike Al-Qaeda, if we can take out a Taliban leader who pushes for global jihad, there's a good chance they will be replaced by someone who does not." The officer exhaled: "Shall we have a break for a brew, Sergeant Major?"

"Sounds good, sir," Jay said, turning to the squadron. "Fifteen minutes, gents. Grab a wet, grab some air."

The men filed out, did what they needed to do, and then the seats of the theatre filled up minutes before the time was up. The Intelligence Officer was surprised by this, and said so quietly to Jay.

"With all respect to them, Sir, this isn't an ordinary line unit. Everyone's here because they volunteered again and

43

again, and met the standards. No one wants to fuck up when the dream tour is on the line."

"Is that what this is?"

"Of course, sir. You said it yourself. The Taliban are a strong enemy who are holding back the people of Afghanistan. There's no one we'd rather be going up against."

The officer smiled, but his eyes looked a little nervous. Though both men wore the same uniform, there was something about the men at the tip of the spear that unsettled those in the supporting roles. "Right then, I'll crack on," he said to Jay, then turned back to the audience.

"Let's talk money, gents. The Taliban is becoming very wealthy. The drug warlords I've mentioned earlier are obviously opposed to the Kabul government, and its western backers. They don't want to have any restrictions on the growing, processing and transportation of poppies and opium. The Taliban act like an extortion racket, and take a cut, but they don't want the poppy trade to end as it's helping to fund their war, and there are plenty of people in government willing to turn a blind eye. Corruption extends right through Afghan society. A governor in Helmand was found in possession of *nine tons* of opium. *That* is the level of corruption that we are facing.

"The Taliban tax the farmers growing the poppies. They provide the smuggling route to get it across the border, and the protection too. Afghanistan's heroin production is enormous. So enormous that it's estimated that 90% of all the illegal heroin in the world comes from here. The harvest price of a kilo of opium is about a hundred US dollars, so you can imagine the figures we're talking about here."

The officer clicked through some photos on the projector: bale after bale of seized drugs.

"And it's not just the opium that brings in the money. The Taliban make money from kidnappings, usually Westerners. And also from illegal mining across the country – both in controlling the extraction themselves, and in extorting money from those that do; marble and precious metals are common products. All those goods have to get out of the country somehow, and the Taliban generates money from Helmand's smuggling operations. There's no doubt they are taking some of the reconstruction money the Americans are putting into the country. They take in revenue from the madrassas, and donations from families and powerful, rich donors who share their religious beliefs. They receive donations from abroad, including Iran, Pakistan, Saudi Arabia, as well as support from within Afghanistan. No one now believes that the Taliban are doing all of this while hiding out in caves in the mountains. They have the cooperation of some – maybe many – within Pakistan's banking community, and probably the UAE as well."

The officer stopped, and looked at his watch. Turning to Jay, he said, "I'm coming to my final few points. Just a few more minutes."

"No rush, sir. If it's important, we want to hear it."

The older man nodded his thanks. "Money is what the Taliban use to arm themselves," he told C Squadron. "Given the history of the country, there's lots of old Soviet weaponry floating about there, and you are likely to see some things that belong in a museum, but the enemy also spends lots of money on acquiring guns, mines, mortars, rockets, and all kinds of material from buyers around the world, most of it Soviet design." He took a deep breath.

"I'm going to read you a poem."

Jay caught sight of a few eyebrows raising before the men gathered themselves back into neutral expressions.

The officer cleared his throat and read aloud:

"When you're wounded and left on Afghanistan's plains,

And the women come out to cut up what remains,

Jest roll to your rifle and blow out your brains

An' go to your Gawd like a soldier.

This was the last verse of a poem written by Rudyard Kipling, published in 1890," continued the Intelligence Officer. "It may be over a hundred years old, but the prospects for a wounded British soldier in Afghanistan have not improved. I don't think I'm about to tell you anything you don't already know, but I'll say it anyway.

"Do not get captured. It will not end well for you. The Taliban routinely torture their prisoners before mutilating and then killing them. As Special Forces soldiers, you can expect the most hideous deaths that the enemy can dream up.

"Torture and mutilation are things the Taliban have been doing for a long time. They did it to their former Prime Minister, back in the 1990s. The things they do are so bad that most Muslims find them repulsive. They torture people, beat them, disembowel them, then drag the body around on a rope. Some people suffer through being skinned alive, having their eyes cut out, or being cut open, throat to groin. I've heard of them beheading people by pulling a thin wire through the neck, which isn't quick and is, I imagine, extremely painful. Other ways of killing people are no less barbaric. They have been known to cut the skin off a man's back, exposing the lungs from behind, and leaving them like that, in the open, to die. They videotaped themselves killing Russian soldiers that way when the Soviets invaded, and sent the tapes to Moscow."

The room was silent. Jay looked round; these were all tough men, not afraid of physical threats or of violence, he knew that, but this was something else. As trained commandos, they saw the enemy as just that – the enemy – and no more. Not as something to take vengeance upon. Torturing someone for fun... that was really, really sick.

"If you're dead and fall into their hands, they will mutilate your body. They'll drag it behind trucks. Maybe hang it up in public. Shoot, or chop it to pieces."

The officer paused, and exhaled. Jay wondered if the man had seen evidence of this first hand, but even reading reports of atrocities could wear a person down.

"No one in this room joined for that kind of death, but we all know that it's a possibility when we sign on the dotted line. Well, the civilians of Afghanistan made no such choice, but it is them who suffer the most at the hands of the Taliban.

"We've had information that the worst of these crimes are often carried out by the foreign fighters within the Taliban ranks, particularly those who have joined for religious reasons. The Taliban themselves have also committed extensive massacres of populations, and the town of Mazar-e-Sharif, in the far north of the country, near the Uzbekistan border, was the site of horrendous atrocities on both sides during the Taliban take-over of the country in the late 1990s.

There are reports of men being thrown down wells, and the top bulldozed over, leaving them to die in the water. And of men being herded into metal containers which were then sealed shut and abandoned. In 1998, thousands of civilians were massacred in a two-day rampage by the Taliban through the town. Afghans were killed in the street, and in their homes. Patients in hospitals were shot in their beds. Estimates of the dead range from 2,000 to 8,000. The Taliban shot at anything and anyone, but in particular they targeted the ethnic Hazaras, raping the women and murdering the men. One of the things that made it a particularly horrible crime in the eyes of the locals was that the Taliban refused to let anyone bury the bodies, which were left lying out to rot in the heat, and were eaten by dogs for six days. This is very much against Muslim beliefs. In 2001, further south in the country, in Yakaolang, nearly 300 Hazara men, women, and children were killed by the Taliban under the command of the extremist leader Commander Dadullah."

The officer clicked the PowerPoint remote, and the projector cast a photo onto the large screen: he was a scowling man, with hard features and pitiless eyes.

"This is Dadullah. You will be hearing more about him, I'm sure, because he is the man behind a new threat from the Taliban: the use of suicide bombers. Suicide bombings are familiar events in Iraq. Not so much in Afghanistan, but it's started to happen here too, with attacks on ISAF forces, Afghan government forces and even Afghan civilians. These are something we're monitoring very closely at the moment, as they pose a very real problem to ISAF right now. If it expands into a regular thing, across Afghanistan, it could become a lot worse. It's increasingly common in the south-ern areas of the country and our intelligence tells us that it is this Commander Dadullah who is the organiser and instiga-tor of these attacks. In 2002, there were no suicide bombings in the country; in 2005, there were seventeen. There have already been more than double that this year already.

"Now, you could say that this is an act of desperation, that our tactics are succeeding if the enemy is reduced to this. However, I'm sure you'll agree with me that this sort of analysis is of no comfort to a soldier in the battlespace. This is a move by the enemy that we need to stop as soon as possible."

The officer stopped and took a long look at the men of C Squadron, like he was committing their faces to memory. Perhaps – as an expert on the place they were going, and the enemy they were facing – he did not expect them all to make it home.

"Thank you for your patience, gentlemen. I've bombarded you with a lot of information, but as Sun Tzu said, *know your enemy*. Your Squadron Commander and Sergeant Major have a secure email address for me. If I can be of any assistance, please do not hesitate to get in touch, but trust me when I tell you that the intelligence sources out there are the best that the world has to offer. That's all I have to say. Thank you, and good luck."

When he turned to face Jay, he saw that the big Sergeant Major was waiting for him with a handshake: "Thank you, sir. We appreciate your time today."

"Not at all, Sergeant Major," he replied, and then shook the firm hand, and smiled warmly, adding, "Stay safe."

CHAPTER TWO

FOB Juno, February 2007

Jay watched the Apaches circling in the distance, then spotted the Chinook as it appeared over the horizon, heading for the Helicopter Landing Site (HLS) at the Forward Operating Base (FOB). For the next six months, this patch of ground would be the place where his men ferried in and out of Deliberate Action (DA) missions: door kicking was a more unofficial way of putting it.

Having arrived with the advance party, Jay had been at the HLS a lot as C Squadron's men and equipment had come trickling in. He could have sent a delegate in his place to greet the helicopters, but Jay knew this would be a tough tour. Without arrogance, he knew that his men trusted him. He wanted his face to be the first one that his men saw when they touched down in their new home. For many of them, the next four months would define their lives.

The thump of helicopter blades was getting closer. The Chinooks were the workhorses of the Afghan campaign. About thirty metres long, and seven metres tall, they could fly at 160 knots. They were built as troop carriers, carrying anything up to 55 personnel, though this was rarely achieved when the men had to carry everything that they needed for fighting. The big machines were flown by two pilots, with two to three aircrew acting as loadmasters and gunners for the Chinook's formidable weapons: two miniguns, and an M60D machine gun. Unlike the infantry and Special Forces units, the flight crews were a mix of men and women, and the door gunner on Jay's flight to Juno had been a cheerful woman in her early twenties who was all smiles and jokes before take off. Then, during the flight, she'd been all business, constantly scanning the ground for danger, and looking for targets for her minigun.

The RAF aircrew had been highly efficient, and the Chinooks were airborne as soon as the last man had wedged himself into his seat. Tightly packed, everyone's weapon was held pointing downward between their knees, and with their gear stacked in front of them so there was no room to shift about during the short flight, they were off. Jay's aircraft's engines throbbed, and the airframe shook as it lifted up, dust whirling around outside. The tail ramp was kept open and Jay was grateful for the cool air that blew in. He could see the vast camp disappearing from view as they headed north-west, up into the slopes of the hills that formed the barrier to the desert that spread across the southern part of the country.

The view from the Chinook had been spectacular, and Jay envied the crew who sat on the ramp, clipped onto the machine by a thick strap, their legs hanging out the back. The flat desert had quickly given way to twisted folds of hills, a darker brown than the sandy valley floor. In the distance, Jay had made out the green zone that lay alongside the winding Helmand River.

That had been the first of many lifts for C Squadron. There would be raids and resupplies, but today, the incoming cargo was not crates of weapons and equipment, or lean-looking operators, but a British politician with a team of aides and press in tow. Jay had been in the Royal Marines and SBS long enough to know the civvies in charge loved a good visit to the troops, and he didn't think it was just for a photo op: politicians got a little weak at the knees for their Special Forces, and who didn't like handling weapons, and getting some rounds down on the range?

That was what Jay had planned for the visitors today: show them the kit, introduce them to a few of the men, and let them do a little shooting on the FOB's range. It was a bit of a hassle considering the operational load that they had on, but Jay could trust his sergeants to admin their Troops. As much as he'd rather be spending his day with his squadron, it fell on the Sergeant Major to do the honours today.

"Welcome to FOB Juno," Jay said, shaking the minister's hand. After introducing himself to the minister's aides, and the members of the press, Jay gave a wink and smile to the security detachment: they were from C Squadron. A few of them had volunteered for the duty, knowing it would look good when they got out onto "the circuit": private security and bodyguarding. A couple of the other close protection team had just drawn short straws.

"Good to meet you, Sergeant Major," the politician said, his eyes drawn to a makeshift sign that read *Welcome to the*

GAFA. "I thought we were coming to FOB Juno?" the minister asked, confused.

"You're in the right place, sir. The Royal Marines came up with GAFA. It means the Great Afghan Fuck All."

The minister laughed. "Ha! Well I can see why. A bit bleak around here, isn't it?"

Like many of the Forward Operating Bases in Helmand, Juno had been set up in the brown zone, far from habitation. That made it easy to secure, but it also felt like living on the surface of another planet.

"We've got some kit displays set up, if you'd like to follow me?"

"Brilliant. Yes, please, lead on, Sergeant Major."

"How was your flight into Afghanistan?" Jay asked, walking at the front with the minister, the trail of his entourage following on behind, and that flock watched by the close protection team: even in a FOB they would not let their guard down.

"A little on the hairy side, for a civilian at least. Lots of twisting and turning. They told me the plane was fine, and it was as a defence against surface to air missiles, but I'm not sure I found that any more reassuring," the minister said with a smile. "I don't expect this is your first time here?"

"No sir," Jay replied. The minister was cleared for the highest levels of intelligence – he was one of the people running the war, after all – and so Jay continued with his voice low enough so that the conversation was theirs alone.

"Some of us were out in 2001. We had a few lads at the Taliban uprising at the fort at Qala-i-Janghi."

"Gosh, that must have been a heck of the fight. Six days, wasn't it?"

Jay nodded. "It was a well-made fort."

"Ah yes, they don't make them like they used to."

Jay was warming to the minister, and gave a short smile of his own. "I'm not sure Juno will last a hundred years. Some of the walls in that fort were sixty foot wide and thirty foot deep."

The minister looked at Jay: was he speaking from experience? "How did it all start?"

"Towards the end of November 2001, over 400 foreign Taliban who'd surrendered to the Allied forces were transferred there for it to be used as a prison."

"Hmm, yes. I suppose the only difference between a prison and a fort is which way the guards are facing."

"That's right. Well, the CIA decided to interview the prisoners but some of the fighters had smuggled weapons in, and they overpowered the CIA and their Northern Alliance guards, killing one of the Americans. Two small teams, including an eight-man SBS team, took guard on the fort's walls and managed to keep the armed insurgents at bay. A CIA case officer and a German TV crew were trapped inside, and so every airstrike had to be pinpoint. The SBS team put down the uprising and recovered the body of the American."

Jay went on and explained that the SBS had fought alongside the SAS and American SF in the attempt to pin down Osama bin Laden, and the rest of the Al-Qaeda leadership, in the Tora Bora mountain. He left out that – much to the frustration of the men on the ground – the most wanted man in the world had been left to slip through a gap in the White

Mountains and into Pakistan. Since then, the SBS had been in the country a few times, but never in great numbers. The SAS had enough on their plates in Iraq, and it was decided at some senior level to push the war in Afghanistan onto the SBS. The deployment of a full squadron at this point in the war, now that the British were expanding their role in Helmand Province, was a statement of intent; Special Forces were going to be used in a far more kinetic way than previously. "Kinetic" was the military way of saying "shoot and blow things up".

Jay saw the minister's eyes light up as he spotted the weapon and kit displays that were set up for the visit. Jay took a quick look at the members of the press, and was happy to see that none of them had cameras in their hands: they'd been briefed, and they had listened. That wasn't always the case, and Jay was glad that he didn't have to play "nasty Sergeant Major" and take their toys away.

"Ladies and Gentlemen, before we take a look at the kit and weapon systems, I want to just give you a brief background on who we are, and what we do. I'm afraid that everything I tell you know is already in the public domain, so there will be no juicy headlines."

A few of the press smiled at that. The old hands among them knew how it worked with the Special Forces community: do right by them, and they would do right by you. Cross them once, and there would be no second chances, and definitely no second visits.

"My name is Jay, and I'm the Squadron Sergeant Major of C Squadron. These are a few of my men. They all volunteered for this duty instead of sunbathing, didn't you lads?"

Jay's lads chuckled: no one wanted to get dicked for this kind of duty, but bone tasks were an inescapable part of military life no matter the unit.

"There are four squadrons in the SBS," Jay continued. "Z, X, M and C. M Squadron works on Marine Counter Terrorism operations, which can take the form of boarding anything from a cruise liner to an oil rig. In peacetime, every squadron does a rotation in that task, depending on need and what else was going on.

"X Squadron handle marine-based insertions and extractions, using small boats or inflatable canoes that can be taken close to an enemy's coastline in a submarine. They carry out recce missions along the sea's edge, a bit inland, or up through the river networks. This is all classic SBS stuff, the sort of warfare the unit was invented for back in the Second World War."

"Was the Cockleshell Heroes an SBS raid?" a reporter asked.

"The movie was a fictionalised story of real events," Jay answered, having been asked this question at least a hundred times in his career. "It's definitely the kind of mission the SBS in the Second World War would undertake, but that particular mission was carried out by Royal Marine Commandos. In fact, most men in the SBS come from the Royal Marines."

"Do you do the same Selection as the SAS?" another reporter asked, and Jay nodded.

"We run a joint Selection, all the way through. Any other questions at this point?" But there were none, and so he continued.

"C Squadron would usually carry out the same kind of missions as X, but I don't think we'll be doing many marine-based insertions and extractions out here in the desert," he said, smiling for the guests. "Finally, Z Squadron is responsible for underwater insertions, attacks, and underwater vehicles.

"Each squadron is broken down into four sixteen-man Troops, but the reality is that we are rarely at full strength. That's just the nature of the beast when you have a long, arduous selection process, and then an arduous training and operational cycle. People get injured in training far more often than they do on operations. We have people away on long courses, such as languages, and medical training. Then there are people on leave, and the million little tasks that come down to you when you're in Special Forces."

"Such as showing civilians around your base," the minister said, smiling wryly, and Jay couldn't help a grin of his own.

"Let's take a look at the kit. I'll hand you over to the capable hands of one of my sergeants, Paul."

Paul stepped forward. He was average looking with a bit of a receding hairline, but he was one of the most respected NCOs in the Corps. Jay's lads always joked that while some of the squadron looked like they belonged in Hollywood, others were only suitable for roles in *Lord of the Rings*. Good looks and muscles counted for nothing unless a Special Forces candidate had the right stuff between his ears, and in his heart.

"If you all would close in around me I'll show you what we use to do our job out here."

First was the basics: Global Armour PASCUT helmets, their plate carriers (both light and full variations), knee pads, elbow pads, gloves and boots. Paul gave them a chance to feel the weight.

"They're a lot lighter than what we've got," a reporter said, "do they have ballistic protection?"

Paul nodded. "Our friends in America's Delta Force used to wear skateboard helmets until the Battle of Mogadishu, when they found out that they needed ballistic protection as well as something that wasn't bulky and awkward. This kind of helmet is the result of that. The best of both worlds."

They didn't spend much time looking at webbing, chest rigs, vests, belts and pouches, either. Only the ghillie suits for the snipers and for long-range recce patrols seemed to draw their interest, and Jay smiled to himself: everyone loved snipers.

"What's the longest sniper kill?" someone asked Paul.

"There are a couple of Canadian snipers with kills over 2 kilometres. Both were out here in 2002."

"What about from our side?"

Paul smiled cryptically. "Special Forces don't really publish that kind of information."

Next was the part that the visitors always loved: weapons.

Jay watched as his men showed the visitors the ropes. The operators handled the weapons like they were part of their own bodies. The civilians looked awkward and ungainly. The difference in ability was simply down to tens of thousands of hours of training.

C Squadron had brought an array of weapons with them to Helmand, but the staple was the Diemaco Colt L119A1 C8 assault rifle, each with SOPMOD – Special Operations Peculiar Modification – items. The C8 was the Special Forces weapon of choice mainly because of its size. C8s were relatively light-weight, and compact for carrying in confined spaces such as their Supacats (a type of all-terrain vehicle) or on helicopters, yet powerful enough to engage with targets in ranges up to a couple of hundred metres. There were downsides to the weapon: its recoil was stronger than on full-length rifles, and it was prone to stoppages caused by overheating if overused. But these issues were nothing when put against its versatil-ity, because it could be modified so easily with the Picatinny rail system that allowed various attachments to be mounted or removed both on top and below the barrel.

"The C8 is a versatile weapon that has proved itself in SF hands both in Afghanistan and in Iraq," Paul told the squad-ron's guests. "It fires a 5.56x45mm NATO-calibre round from a 30-round magazine and has a range of 600 metres. The UKSF close-quarter battle version of the C8 could be fitted with a shorter barrel length, 25cm as opposed to 39 cm long. The telescopic stock, together with the shorter barrel, comes in handier when we're cramped in a helicopter together. The heavier, longer barrel is preferred for engage-ments carried out at longer distance. For instance, if I was firing out at the desert from the sangar at the main gate, I'd want the long barrel. If I was clearing all of the buildings here, I'd want the shorter one."

SOPMOD items were laid out on a table. First up were the sights. A rail attached to the top of the barrel, replac-ing the carrying handle, provided a loading system for the sights they used. Jay was used to working with the Trijicon

ACOG x4 optical sight, and the Aimpoint red dot sight when required. He'd also used the AN/PEQ-2 laser sight, which was regarded as standard for use in darkness. However, EOTECH Holographic Weapon Sights (HWS) were also on their lists, as these worked best in CQB situations, such as room-to-room clearances once they were inside buildings. The EOTECH HWS, unlike the Aimpoint red dot sight, did not require the operator to press his eye to the sight in order to see where the laser sight was indicating on a target, which immediately improved peripheral vision in the battlespace. Additionally, the EOTECH HWS placed its red dot within a reticle, but the holographic sight meant that the image was visible at a number of angles, so that the operator didn't have to align themselves with the sight in order to shoot on target – as long as the reticle lined up, they could use the weapon much faster than when having to glue a sight to their eyes. This, in addition to the improved peripheral vision around the sight, gave the operator a wider field of view of the target area. Of course, the red dot and the reticle was only visible to the user, the target saw nothing, and remained ignorant until the round hit them.

Paul had been working with the EOTECH HWS up at the firing range, and he ran through what he'd learned when working with it. "It's great when you're moving or trying to shoot from a tight angle," he said. "Not having to pin it to your face to see clearly makes all the difference. Plus, you can get it dirty and it still works. I smeared some mud over the front and it worked fine. The manufacturer claims it still works even if the glass is cracked, but I wasn't going to break it to test that, so we'll have to take that on trust.

It also comes with a switch-to-side magnifier that means you can increase the optic by three times, and then switch it away quickly if you're moving into a room and want to use the CQB sight. So, yeah, I was impressed with it, I'm all for it – it makes a big difference."

One item of standard kit that would be attached to the weapon was the Knight's Quick Detachable sound suppressor, consistently reliable and efficient, and used by everyone in the squadron. Additional equipment that could be fitted to the Picatinny rails on and under the carbine included: an underslung H&K AG-C grenade launcher; an underslung twelve-gauge shotgun; SureFire tactical lights, which could work with night-vision googles; and folding fore grips, which could fold out into mini bipods for greater stability.

Next, Paul showed the guests the SIG Sauer P226 pistol in its SERPA holster. Everyone in the squadron carried one at all times. "A weapon like this is a back-up, for the moments when you can't use your primary weapon. This might be because your primary has a stoppage for whatever reason, or the environment is so tight, such as a tunnel or tight bunker, that there isn't the room to use your primary." Paul moved on then to camouflaged, long-barrel rifles.

"Right, let's talk sniper rifles. This is the Accuracy International L118A1. Like it says on the tin, it's a very accurate piece of kit. Gleaming, really. It's got a very smooth action, it's easy to move with when you stalk, and it's well suited to open ranges, or more built-up areas. Right, if you will all follow me to this cabin, I'll show you our night-vision capability."

Paul stopped outside the cabin and lifted a pair of NVGs from a table: "These are the PVS-21 Low Profile Night

Vision Goggles. Night-vision capability has come on a long way in such a short space of time. These are light, and adaptable when switching from dark to light, so the operator doesn't suffer 'white-outs'. This means that the goggles can be used with the Aimpoint and EOTECH sights without having to rely on the laser illuminator. Would anyone like to try them?"

A few hands went up. One after the other, Paul fitted the NVGs on a guest's head, then showed them into a darkened cabin. After the minister had his turn, he walked over to Jay.

"Is there anything else you need, Sergeant Major? Kit? Weapons?"

"We've got everything we need, thank you." Unlike much of the military, requests for kit and equipment in the Special Forces were accepted more often than not. C Squadron had their tools. Now, they just needed to be pointed in the direction of the problem.

The first part of the day's visit finished with a look at C Squadron's vehicles: camouflaged dirt bikes and Supacats that bristled with belt-fed weapons of all kinds.

"Are they bomb proof?" a reporter asked Paul, and the sergeant gave a soldier's patient smile.

"Depends how big the bomb is."

"They'll give protection against mines," Jay said, leaving out that he was referring to anti-personnel mines. Due to the wheel placement, an anti-tank mine would go off almost directly under the driver and commander. At the very least they would be thrown into the air like rag dolls: there was no roof on the Supacats, which was a good thing when you were launched hurtling towards the sky.

After eating lunch with them in Juno's "galley", as the cook house was known, Jay, Paul, and a few other members of C Squadron took the guests to the FOB's range. The OC joined them, fresh off the back of briefings, and took over the job of shadowing the minister. Jay didn't mind. He was itching to get back to business, and he was relieved to hear that the Apaches would soon be back on station to watch the Chinook safely back to Bastion.

"Nice to meet you, sir," he said to the minister as the helicopter crew span up its engines.

"Best of luck, Sergeant Major. Give them hell."

It was a cheesy line, but well intentioned, and Joy nodded his thanks.

"We will. Stay safe."

As the guardian Apaches circled the desert looking for trouble, the heavy Chinook lifted into the air, and lumbered off across the desert.

"Thank fuck for that," Paul grinned beside Jay. "Can we get started on the Taliban now?"

Jay chuckled. "You're keen, mate."

"I didn't come out here for the bar scene, Jay."

"Fair one. Well these lads we're meeting tonight are the right people to talk to about Terry." The OC had told Jay that some important Americans were coming in to camp.

Paul cocked an eyebrow. "Gen?"

"Yeah. They call themselves Gray Fox rather than CIA, but…" Jay shrugged.

"Proper spooks then?" Paul asked, meaning that the men were the kind to run deniable ops, and those that pushed the boundaries.

"Very spooky."

"Hmm. You reckon they could hack some servers and get me Nelly Furtado's number?"

Jay laughed. Paul had been obsessed with the singer back in Poole, but since they'd got to the desert the obsession had gone up to another level. "What?" he asked. Paul had a funny look on his face.

"Feels like a long time since we first came out here, doesn't it?"

"It does mate. And at the same time it feels like yesterday, do you know what I mean?"

Paul nodded. He had been a promising member of the squadron at that time, and he had lived up to it, rising quicker than most to the rank he held now. "You never forget your first time, as they say. You reckon those two Terry are still where we left them?"

Jay shrugged. "I don't think they were walking that off." He had respect for his enemy, but no soldier at war could be too sensitive to the human side of conflict. Start thinking too much about who you're killing, and you might never pull the trigger.

"Fuck 'em." Paul said. "Big boy rules, isn't it? They started a scrap, we came for a scrap, we won the day. If they'd been better with that Dushka they'd probably have our heads on a mantlepiece."

"Who'd want your banging head as a decoration?" Jay teased his mate. "An oil painting you are not, mate."

"Fucking hell, I didn't realise we had Jimmy Carr on the tour. I'm surprised you can still talk after having that politician's..."

Paul didn't get a chance to finish. A voice boomed out across the HLS:

"Oi! You two! Get your fucking hands out of your pockets!"

Jay slowly turned his head. He wasn't going to tell the person to fuck off: a look would do the job. But then, when he saw the man behind the voice, Jay broke into a massive smile: "Tommy!"

As tough and reliable as an entrenching tool, SSM Tommy Bryce was at the end of a long career in the Royal Marines. So long, in fact, that he had been an instructor to many of C Squadron when they'd gone through their Commando training at Lympstone. They may be Special Forces now, but their careers had started under his watchful gaze, and with the encouragement of his size 11s.

"What you think of Helmand so far?" Jay asked, once he'd introduced Paul.

"I prefer it to Iraq. There's some proper infanteering to be had here."

"Bollocks. As if you didn't get any of that in the Iraq invasion."

"Well, yeah, but that was different. Living in your NBC suit and worrying about gas attacks all the time. The tankees and the pilots got the best of the Iraq invasion, Jay, but this place is an infantryman's wet dream. All those years crawling up ice cold streams in Brecon is about to pay off."

SSM Bryce put his hand on Jay's shoulder. They had come across each other a lot over the years, and some of the wilder sergeants' mess do's had a way of bringing people together: or creating rivalries for life. Fortunately, this was not one of them.

"We won the fucking lottery, Jay. Not many sergeant majors will get the kind of ops that we're about to be getting. I don't need to know the ins and outs of yours, and I'm not asking, but we've all been watching Task Force Black over in Iraq. Looks like things are about to get as serious out here."

"I've been meaning to come over and see you," Jay said, "but we had visitors today."

"You fucking Barry Bigtimer," Bryce joked, "I noticed they didn't want to come over and see my lads."

"Probably worried you'd make them do a joining run," Paul said, and Bryce gave a belly laugh. Joining runs were a form of initiation for new Royal Marines when they reached their unit. Apparently, they were a thing of the past, but each of the three NCOs had been through one. They were certainly nights that they would never forget.

"We've got a while until our next timing," Jay said to Paul. "We can come over to your lines now if you're not busy, Tommy?"

"What do you think I was doing looking for you at the HLS, you fucking rock stars? Come on, I'll show you around. But don't put ideas in my lads' heads about Selection," he joked, "everyone wants to be an operator in this war. I don't know what all the fuss is about. Rab jackets? Salomon boots? What's wrong with what Harry Pusser's gave us?"

Bryce was having fun playing up to a Royal Marine caricature. Unlike the Special Forces unit, which wore a mix of civvie and issued gear, the attitude of the Royal Marines was that if the military wanted you to wear it, they'd issue it. There was no scrim-netting on the helmets like the paras, or mixed patterns of camouflage like the line infantry units who had been fighting in Helmand. The Bootnecks wore what they were given by Harry Pussers, who was to the Royal Navy and Royal Marines what Tommy Atkins was to the British Army.

They walked on through Juno. A few soldiers were caught off guard, but most men on the camp were salty enough to recognise who was coming, and slip away behind the HESCO HESCO (rapidly deployable barrier system) bastions: a sergeant major can't give you jobs if he can't find you.

Bryce led them into the fenced-off, and guarded, British enclave, a space about the size of a football pitch, with the tents wedged closely together. Jay looked up and down the narrow passageway between the tents, taking in the distant view of the desert in one direction and the steep hillside on the other.

"Does the view cost extra?" Paul asked.

"No, but being upwind from the porta-shitters does," Bryce said. "SFSG headshed is over here. I'll make the introductions."

Jay had already met dozens and dozens of people so far in this early phase of the deployment, but it was one thing to meet someone at a briefing, and another to have an old friend make the introductions over a hot wet. After some chat, informal plans were made for joint training between the two units and their Afghan allies.

"We've got a good OC," Jay told Bryce privately. "Major Wood. If we bring him good plans, he signs off on them. He's not one of those who fucks with things just to put his own fingerprints on it. How about at your end?"

"We've got a good lot," Bryce said, and Jay breathed an internal sigh of relief. There would be times when the units would be relying on each other. The less friction in their own chain of commands, the better.

"And what about the Afghans?"

"Fucking hell," Bryce snorted, "it's like herding cats. You think you've got through to them about skills, drills, rates of fire, etc, then the first RPG comes flying over from Terry and it's game over."

"They don't want to fight?"

"No, no, the fucking opposite, Jay. They're mental. Standing in the open, no cover, ripping mags off, Lebanon unload style. It's a hell of a thing to see, to be honest, but it's not going to win a war. If we can get them a bit more disciplined, and keep their natural courage, they'll fight well."

"Nice one." Jay's internal body clock told him to check the one on his wrist. "I've got to shoot, Brycey."

"Hot date?" the bootneck smiled, offering his hand in farewell.

Jay took it, and shook. "You could say that."

• • •

Jay met the OC at the FOB's command building. Major Jeremy Wood was a shade over two metres tall with a triathlete's physique, and little wonder: his hobby was competing in Ironman competitions. He was a couple of years younger than Jay, and had served in the SBS for about the same amount of time, though much of that had been posted out in various duties. The two men respected each other, but they kept the relationship a working one. Maybe, when retirement came in the not too distant future, Jay could see himself sitting down with "the boss" and chatting on a purely man to man basis. For now, rank and station was observed, if not as rigorously as most units.

Over the last few days, Jay and the OC had been meeting signals, ISTAR, JTACs, and members of the Int Corps, all of whom were British. Now, Jay was about to meet two men who had flown into the camp in the back of an American Blackhawk. They were to be C Squadron's liaison officers to Gray Fox: this elite American intelligence organisation, usually referred to as "the Activity", was going to change how the SBS went about their appointed tasks in the country.

The two Americans, both dressed in plain civilian clothing you would find in an outdoor pursuits catalogue, introduced themselves as Scott and Richard. Scott was the taller of the two and was an archetypal American; blond, blue-eyed and with a broad smile, he was a muscular plank of Californian woods and sunshine. How he'd coped out in the field, when he stood out so obviously as an American, Jay could only guess. Richard was the taciturn one, shorter and darker, with a thin moustache and a semi-permanent slouch, as if he spent his life hunched over a computer.

After a few pleasantries to get to know each other, the OC got down to business. He reiterated that the SBS were in theatre as part of Task Force 42 with the sole aim of working through high-value targets on the Joint Special Operations Command's (JSOC) Joint Prioritized Effects List (JPEL). To the operators of C Squadron this was known as the Capture-or-Kill list: Taliban commanders deemed to be directing the offensive against ISAF and the troops in the country, and who therefore needed to be hunted, and either taken prisoner, or "neutralised".

Jay knew something of Gray Fox: he'd had dealings with an earlier incarnation of the group, if only indirectly, when they had been operating in Afghanistan in the early days. The TV pictures of the Twin Towers in New York falling to the ground had galvanised thousands of Americans into joining their armed forces, wishing to strike back at those who'd attacked them. For some already in service, they knew the moment they saw those images where they'd be going, and what they'd be doing. Experts within the CIA and other government agencies were buying equipment and arranging flights within hours to northern Afghanistan, and making contact with anti-Taliban forces among the Northern Alliance mujahideen.

Among those early entrants into Afghanistan were Gray Fox operators. They worked with the US Special Forces teams, intercepting enemy communications and conducting intelligence-led operations with members of the SF units. They were involved in the large-scale attacks of Operation Anaconda in March 2002, and the subsequent operations in clearing the Shah-i-Khot valley, and Gray Fox had operated in the country ever since.

Scott launched into his explanation of their role, saying that they were there to assist in "operational preparation of the battlespace", using HUMINT [Human Intelligence] and SIGINT [Signals Intelligence] assets. Like any secretive agency – and few were as secretive as "the Activity" – exactly who was providing the HUMINT was a closely guarded secret. Jay knew that this was as it should be. Someone on the ground, acting as the Agency's eyes and ears – possibly even joining enemy organisations to provide intelligence against them – was incredibly vulnerable.

How Gray Fox obtained their SIGINT was also top secret, but Jay had a high clearance, and the Americans wanted the men carrying out the raids to have confidence in their Int: they gave an explanation to Jay in a way where nothing could be compromised.

The Major and Jay then outlined what they knew of the ISTAR systems operating in Helmand. They were well aware of the benefits it brought not just to them and their squadron, but also to the SFSG. Indeed, to all the various elements of the British armed forces in the region. There were manned RAF Nimrods, with infra-red vision, and Sniper Advanced Targeting Pods, fitted to RAF Tornados that could send back video in real-time to a man on the ground. There were also different kinds of unmanned aircraft, from the MQ-1A Predator drone, which undertook long-distance surveillance and could fire Hellfire missiles, if they were carried, down to the miniature UAV, the Desert Hawk, used for closer aerial surveillance. On the ground, there was MSTAR, the Man-portable Surveillance and Target Acquisition Radar, which could be set up in three minutes, and with a range for detecting targets up to forty kilometres. Light Electronic Warfare Teams – LEWTs – could listen in to the Taliban's unsecured communications on the I-COM radios that the enemy used, and they could also jam the Taliban's signals, making it impossible for them to communicate.

"As you probably know," Richard said, "we're using a lot more unmanned surveillance these days. We're developing a way of running surveillance from multiple aircraft over a twenty-four-hour period, so as to follow a target and build up a picture of their contacts and the places they go to, without them being aware of it. If we follow a number of targets, and they intersect at places, then we can see patterns of connection that might suggest a cell or even a larger network of insurgents. They might lead us to safe houses, weapons dumps, all sorts of things.

"Obviously, Scott and I aren't doing all of that ourselves, but we have access to it, and to some of the other surveillance methods you guys aren't using yet. Once the Unblinking Eye, a surveillance aircraft, has picked up, say, a vehicle that's being used by suspected terrorists, then we have methods of following that vehicle without being seen to follow it."

"That's all brilliant," Jay spoke up, "but it also sounds a bit too good to be true. What are some of the difficulties out here, intelligence-wise?"

Richard smiled. "The main problem is it's so backward in this country that there isn't much of a telecommunications network. So we have to be a bit more creative than just doing a lot of manual scanning of frequencies because we don't do that here. So, it's all about the satellite signals, and what we can learn from them. Cell phones are good, same with their walkie-talkies – we can listen to conversations in real-time, using the satellites they bounce off. We've got location finders hidden inside SIM cards that we put into a Taliban commander's phone."

Jay asked him how they'd got hold of that phone, and didn't take offence when Scott shrugged with, "above my paygrade". It clearly wasn't, but it was a polite way of saying that he couldn't give that information out.

"Now," Richard continued, "even if the guy's smart enough to turn off location services and maybe turn off the phone to prevent it sending a signal, we're still reading a location because the SIM's drawing enough power from the phone to let us see where it is.

"We've started a programme, CCTTL, or Continuous Clandestine Tagging Tracking and Locating, which works as a long-range facial recognition programme. That's not so useful out here in the sticks. What works better here is to tag the Taliban's trucks. We've got some RFID [Radio Frequency Identification], trackers we can stick on vehicles; they're passive so someone scanning the car to check won't find anything showing up. That is, until the radar searching for them gets within 20km of the vehicle, maybe from a drone so high up in the sky it's pretty much invisible to the naked eye, and then the RFID card starts pinging its position. We've also got NightMarks, a clear liquid that can't be seen in normal light but shows up under NVGs, so you can tag someone without them knowing and then follow them. What we are developing now is a way of using that idea – a liquid tag – but building some sort of signal into it so that, just like with the RFID trackers, a drone or a plane can follow an individual from a distance. Part of its effectiveness is that the suspect wouldn't know it's on them, so wouldn't be looking for anyone or anything following them. All of this takes time, you know, so we're patient."

"OK," Scott interrupted. He'd obviously decided that was it for now. "I think Richard's given you enough of an idea about how we go about getting the information you guys need for the JPEL."

Jay nodded. The Capture-or-Kill list would be what drove every one of C Squadron's actions on this tour. No one ever got to see the full list, just the names that they wanted you to go after, but from the way it was spoken about, Jay guessed that it had to be a hell of a length.

"We're working on a list for your guys right now," Scott continued. "Between us and the teams attached to the other Advance Force Operations [AFOs] we're tracing hundreds of Taliban, and trying to get a fix on any one of them to pass on to you."

Just as the Taliban themselves were divided into group-ings – top-level, medium, low-level – so too was the JPEL. Normally, the British were simply dispatched after the MVTs on the list. The HVTs were usually considered the business of the American Tier 1 units – Delta Force, and Seal Team 6 – but right now those forces were being kept busy by the number of targets they were having to chase after in the centre and the north of the country. British Special Forces had been doing a great job of working on HVTs in Iraq: now their role was about to be expanded in Afghanistan.

"Top of the list for us right now is this guy," Scott uncov-ered a pin board on the wall. In the centre was a photograph of a man in a black turban, showing him glaring at something on the ground. Around the edge of the photograph, pinned to the board, were printed sheets, transcripts, coordinates, dates – Scott dropped the sheet back down before Jay could read anything on there. "His name is Mullah Dadullah. A big fish, and a Grade A piece of shit."

"He's one of those natural born psychos who passes his sick shit off in the name of religion," Richard added.

"I've heard the name a few times now," Jay said. "Can you tell us anything about him?"

Scott shook his head in apology. "Not right now, but we're putting together a file for you guys. You'll have something on him soon, I promise."

For a moment Jay held the man's look. You could never be certain with the spooks, but Jay thought he saw something in the American's eyes that told him Dadullah wasn't just a big fish; he was *the* big fish, and C Squadron had been brought here to catch him.

• • •

FOB Juno was built on a much smaller scale than Camp Bastion, or Kandahar Airfield. It took no time at all for the men to get used to their living quarters, such as they were, and to tour the different sections. These were fenced off from each other, which slowed down progress when moving about, but they were needed for security: it was accepted that, given the chance, a unit would help itself to another's kit.

Everywhere in Juno was covered with dust and sand, and equipment and weapons gained a film of dust almost immediately. There was the British accommodation section, with a gym area for "OP Massive", as lifting weights was known. A number of portacabins held the Command structure, management and planning, with a rudimentary medical bay for holding a couple of patients before a helicopter transfer back to the hospital at Bastion, and the life-saving medical staff there. There was a third section for workshops, maintenance buildings and the vehicle store, and then there was the Afghan Army section, which most Brits stayed away from. Finally there was the HLS, and an L-shaped entrance at the front gate: drivers had to negotiate past thick walls of HESCO bastions, under the watchful eye of Afghan Army guards. There were also sangars at each corner of the FOB. Earth banks, created by the digging of ditches ahead of winter rain, formed lips around each encampment within the larger FOB.

High up on the steep hill beside the base was an observation point allowing for distant views across the desert: an impressive sight of low, bare, jagged hills, and flat, featureless sand. It was a fair climb, and Jay wanted to stretch his legs: there was only so much paperwork that he could take.

Sam was a corporal in 1 Troop and an old friend of Jay's from the Commando they had both served in. Back then, Jay had been a section commander in a Close Combat Platoon when Sam had arrived as a "nod". He knew all about Jay's high standards, and so it came of no surprise to Sam that, rather than have a cushy walk, Jay wanted to do the climb up to the OP with Bergens and carbines.

"I bet you make your wife and kid do this on holiday," Sam joked as they sweated their way up the heights.

"My daughter doesn't complain as much as you."

"Not to your face," Sam said, smiling. "Have you been phoning home much?"

"A few times. Finding a gap between briefings when the time zones work is a pain in the arse."

"I told my missus I'll call her when I'm on my way home for R&R. It's what works for us. Always has."

"Well yeah, because she just moves her other fella in."

Sam laughed, and took no offence. "She wants me home in one piece, and the best way for me to do that, and get the lads back that way, is to focus all in on this tour, and nothing else. I don't need to hear about the bills or if the neighbour's being a dickhead, and she doesn't need to hear me talk about work, not that there would be much I'm allowed to tell her." Sam wiped sweat from his eyes. "The rate we're going to be working at, four months is going to go fucking fast, mate."

Jay wasn't so sure about that. There was a fine line between time going quickly when you're busy, and feeling like it's stretching into eternity, but he understood Sam's point about not calling home. Everyone in the squadron was different with how they chose to deal with relationships while on tour. A lot of the younger lads were free and single, and would often give their phone credits to mates with kids. Some people wanted to check in with their parents now and then. Some others had come from bad homes, and were happy to never speak to their parents again. For Jay, he knew this would likely be his last deployment, and it was the one with the most responsibility. It sounded like a harsh thing to say, but his men came before his family right now. If they didn't, then he shouldn't be here. Once he took off the uniform he could right any wrongs, but for now, he needed to be all in on his job.

"Almost at the top," he said.

Sam grinned as they cleared the crest and took in the view. "Oh, yeah, mega. More sand."

"There's hills too," Jay said.

"Hills made of sand."

The ridges looked like rolling swell in the sea of the desert. There was no sign of anything green. No sign that anything could live out here, but Jay knew that wasn't true. He wasn't one for fawning over celebrities, but Jay could admit to himself that he was a fan of Sir David Attenborough. He'd seen all of his documentaries, eagerly anticipating the ones that he'd asked his wife to record while he was away on exercise, or ops. Jay particularly loved the episodes that were set in harsh environments, like tundra, or desert. He admired the toughness of the animals, and respected the patience and diligence of the camera crew. Like a sniper, they might wait days for their shot. They were Jay's kind of people.

"Bit mental, isn't it?" Sam asked.

"What?"

"Life. A week ago I was getting a carvery with the missus, and now I'm on Tatooine to shoot bad guys in the face."

Jay placed his Bergen down and laid his carbine on top of it. He pulled a water bottle and took a swig. Under almost any other circumstance he would have held it out to Sam first, but with the risk of stomach bugs high, the men had been told not to share food or water unless it was absolutely necessary. Diarrhoea and vomiting could rip through a unit, and a severe case could mean hospital. Even a mild case meant a lot of misery and, more importantly, take troops out of the line.

"How's your lads?" Jay asked Sam, meaning the men in his team, and Troop.

"Champing at the bit mate."

"No jitters?"

"Fuck no. They were born for this."

That was all Jay needed to know. He trusted Sam to know his men.

Jay turned and looked at the lonely observation post. "How'd you fancy doing some stag up here then?"

"I've wanked in worse places."

"Fuck's sake, no wonder you don't call home." Jay put his carbine across the toes of his boots, lifted his Bergen back on, then took the weapon back into his hands. When Sam had done the same, Jay took one last look across the desert.

"Get your lads in the briefing area at 1900, mate. I think it's time we got out of camp."

• • •

No unit could win a war alone. It didn't matter how many HVTs C Squadron killed or captured if the infantry didn't do their job of patrolling the towns. It didn't matter how well the infantry patrolled if the artillery and air support dropped their fire on the wrong positions. It didn't matter how well the artillery or pilots could fire if logistics didn't bring the ammunition out to them. It didn't matter how well logistics could resupply if the engineers didn't maintain an airbase in the desert. It didn't matter how well the airbase was maintained if no aircraft flew into it. On and on it went. There were thousands of military personnel in Helmand with hundreds of jobs, but it didn't end there. The mission was supported not only from the British mainland, but British and NATO bases around the world. Fighting the war was a global undertaking, and Jay understood that, but there wasn't much he could do about most of it. What he *could* control was the working relationship between C Squadron and the SFSG detachment. To that end, Jay and Bryce, the SFSG's senior enlisted, took a plan to their officers for a series of joint exercises in the desert. After some work from the ops staff, the plans were good to go.

The Major, his junior officers and Jay spent the next couple of days working on the exercises, planning the different kinds of scenarios that could arise on the tour: compound clearing, contact in the desert, mine strikes, casualty evacuations, and more. The exercises were conducted dry at first, then with live ammunition, and culminated in one long day where all the pieces were put together. Jay would have been shocked to find any of his guys lacking in their drills, and he didn't. The exercise was a nice way to knock off the dust of travel, though, and by the end of the package, both SFSG and C Squadron felt happy knowing that the other unit had their back.

"What do you reckon, Jay?" SSM Bryce asked Jay after the final live fire exercise: an SBS raid on a compound, while SFSG had provided fire support against "enemy positions", and all on the back of a rigorous insertion that involved moves both on vehicle, and on foot.

"You've trained your lads well," Jay said, which was the truth.

"We've had Hereford and Poole helping to bring us up to speed. And some of these lads, they've seen action, Jay. Proper action. Some of them were up in Baghdad. They'd worked with Delta, Seals, Rangers, Hereford. They might not be badged but there's a lot of talent and experience here."

"I don't doubt that at all mate," Jay agreed. "I've heard from some of the Hereford lads about the scraps they had over there. They spoke highly of the SFSG boys. Even the ones from the RAF Reg."

Bryce laughed. "Turns out that even the crabs have some good lads. I never thought I'd see the day when we had boot-necks, pongos and crabs in one unit but here we are, and I like it, to be honest. Our lads are a bit more mature, not that the Paras aren't either but, well... they're Paras, aren't they?"

Now it was Jay's turn to laugh. He knew what the Commando was saying. There was a certain... esprit de corps about the Paras. They worked hard to earn their maroon beret, and the regiment had an excellent reputation for getting the job done and fighting against the odds. A lot of British army units had long and proud histories – much of them far more storied than the Paras, which was less than a hundred years old – but Paras were told from Day One of Basic that they were different, and they were special. They weren't even to socialise with the "crap hats" as any non-Paras were called, although they made an exception to this rule, referring to Commandos as "Cabbage Heads". (Elite soldiers who hadn't come from "The Reg" were respectfully known as "Super Hats".)

Jay turned back to Bryce, but saw that his friend was absorbed in watching his men cleaning their weapons and kit after the exercise. It wasn't the clichéd angry sergeant major look in his eyes, but a fatherly one, and Jay reckoned he knew that Bryce was thinking: the next time that his men fired their weapons, it would be at an enemy shooting back. In a war that showed no signs of relenting, would all of Bryce's men return alive, or in one piece? Jay knew that the odds were against it.

He put out his hand: "Anytime you need us mate, you shout."

Bryce took it, and shook. "Same to you, mate. Fucking smash them."

• • •

The next day, four members of the Special Reconnaissance Regiment arrived at the compound. Their role was primarily intelligence gathering, and shortly after they appeared and caught up with the SBS lads they knew, the four men disappeared into the secured CONEX [converted shipping container] belonging to Gray Fox. They left again sometime in the night.

The two Americans – Richard and Scott – kept largely to themselves, rarely venturing outside their air-conditioned sardine can. Jay assumed that was down to their workload rather than any aversion to him and his frogmen. Sometimes, those that directed the blade could be a little wary of those who carried it.

Jay met regularly with the OC. It was like waiting for the kick off in a big game, now. They'd done everything they could to prepare. They just needed tasking. And then, finally, the OC was not alone when Jay came to see him.

"Jay," Scott said, smiling. "We've got your first target."

CHAPTER THREE

Deliberate Action

The roar of rotor blades chopped through the sky, hot air and the smell of the Chinook's fuel washing over Jay as he sat by the helicopter's open ramp, and watched Helmand roll by underneath in the bright green shades of his night-vision goggles. Turning his head back into the cabin, he saw the blacked-out faces of his men, weapons between their legs. It was the kind of scene they put in movies and video games, but there was nothing playful about Jay and his men's intentions: they were flying into their first raid of the tour, and their intention was to capture or kill the enemy.

Their prize was a Medium Value Target (MVT), and intelligence reckoned he was housed in a compound on the outskirts of Sangin, where British soldiers had been fighting tooth and nail with the Taliban. Jay had taken part of the squadron for this job, while the rest had gone on a joint operation with American Navy Seals further north.

The MVT was supposedly only lightly guarded and the operation wasn't expected to be a difficult one, but no operation was ever simple. It only takes one enemy fighter, and one round fired from a decades' old bolt-action rifle to be deadly, but through experience Jay knew how to push apprehension aside: his best chance of bringing all of his lads back in one piece was to remain calm, and so that's what he did. No need to overcomplicate things. Just tell your mind what to think, and your body what to do. Jay would never have even got as far as passing Selection if he hadn't been able to do such things.

And C Squadron's men weren't going in half-arsed. Intelligence had provided more than just a compound location: there were aerial maps to plan routes and cordons, and video and photo taken around the compound itself. Jay didn't know who was behind the camera, but guessed it was an Afghan who could move around Sangin with more freedom than a Westerner in disguise. He didn't spend any time thinking about what would happen to such an agent if they were caught: considering the Taliban would kill a girl for going to school, what they'd do to an enemy wasn't the kind of thing that Jay wanted to direct his focus onto. Much better to put that energy towards thinking of ways to kill *them* instead.

After they'd been briefed, the men had prepped their kit and ate some hot scran. Some lads ate more than others, but they all ate something. Nerves weren't going to get the best of men who had sacrificed so much to be here. There are a lot of people in the world who would fight *not* to go on a helicopter flying into danger, but these were the men who would fight to be *on it*. No one wanted to be left behind. Everyone wanted to be out there and doing their job. They were professionals whose business was war. It was that simple.

The big Chinook helicopters were like buses, ferrying the Special Forces troops around Helmand, and the lads had started hearing war stories – "dits", they called them – about the helicopter crews from the others at Juno. How some pilots would put down their human cargo in exactly the right spot, close to cover, so they couldn't be targeted when debussing. How they'd hover above ground to block the Taliban shooting at soldiers, returning fire with the fearsome minigun poking out the side door behind the pilot's cabin, giving the soldiers a chance to regroup. And then there were those who dropped down out of the sky to pick up wounded in the middle of a firefight, seemingly oblivious of the danger, as if stopping a taxi at the side of the road. The pilots, aircrewmen and mechanics were as overworked as everyone in the country, but they flew and flew and flew.

Jay and his men were in the hands of those crews now, but they were capable hands, putting Jay and his men down in a field with little more than a bump. Jay made a point of being the first down the ramp into the night, counting his men off as they took up arcs and prepared to fire back if the landing site was hot.

No sign of the enemy. Everyone accounted for. Jay communicated with the crew, and then the massive heli was lifting, battering Jay with its powerful rotor wash. In what felt like just a few seconds the sky was empty, and the fields and compounds were silent but for the barking of dogs.

Jay gave the word and the point man moved off. There was a threat of IEDs and mines, but it was a low one. The enemy tended to concentrate such things in choke points on supply routes, and – at this stage of the war at least – the enemy seemed to be content with trying to drive the British out with small arms, mortars and RPGs. Over in Iraq, IEDs were killing and maiming British forces on a weekly basis, and Jay knew it was only a matter of time until similar tactics were adopted here. Tonight, however, he was confident that the enemy wouldn't have placed the devices out in this part of town so far from supply routes and British patrol bases. Even if they had, the detonators were often taken out of the devices so as not to kill their own men or locals, then replaced when coalition forces were spotted headed in that direction. By arriving at night and from the air, the SBS had reduced that risk dramatically, and Jay wished that the conventional forces fighting here weren't forced to take the same tracks and the same risk. It was for those soldiers that his men were risking their lives tonight. Jay and his men would hit where others couldn't, taking out bomb makers, mortar teams, snipers and commanders who had British blood on their hands.

And the British were not fighting alone. They were here to support the Afghan government, and to that end this raid was being supported by Afghan Special Forces. These men were violently anti-Taliban and were risking their lives – and the lives of their families – because they believed in a future for Afghanistan where there was the freedom to vote, education, and where they could share the freedoms that so many in the West took for granted. These Afghan commandos were tough, courageous and fearsome. They weren't trained to the same standards as the SBS, but they were born warriors.

The moon was lost from sight as the raiding party entered the rabbit warren of Sangin's mud walls. This labyrinth was what the Taliban used to ambush British patrols, but at night the Special Forces task force was turning the tables.

It didn't take long for the silent snake of the raiding men to wind its way through the alleyways, and coil itself around the target compound. Some were looking in, others out, ready to deter any counterattack or fire that came from other compounds. There was an Afghan team who would enter the target compound, but not until Jay's men had killed or captured their man.

Jay melted into the deep shadow of the compound wall, listening to the whispers on the radio. His door-kicking days were behind him, and command and control was his role in this raid: get people in the right places, at the right time, and kill or capture the right bad guys. Jay knew his men didn't need someone watching over their shoulder, and his style was to be as hands off as possible, only stepping in when needed. That was how he'd been mentored, and it had made him a good soldier. Because Jay rarely raised his voice, or barked a command, it carried all the more weight when he did.

Beside Jay, Sam laid a ladder against the wall. It made no noise, the metal padded with hessian and tape. Then Sam moved onto it until his goggles were barely peeking above the lip. Sam gestured with his hand, clenching his fist twice (indicating two buildings to the left), and one to the right. He raised a straight finger to indicate one figure was visible, down by the right-hand side. The enemy were fully unaware, and they were about to be given a rude awakening.

Everyone was in position, and Jay looked at his watch: 0158. A few dogs were barking in the distance. There was the hum of insects in the air. High above them was the distant drone of aircraft on station, the never-ending succession of jets waiting to support soldiers fighting on the ground thousands of feet below.

Jay spoke quietly into his radio: "Standby, standby…"

At the end of the second word, two shotgun blasts shattered the night, blowing the metal gate off its hinges. One team would be entering there, and Jay saw Sam's shape slip up and over the wall, leading another assault team. Jay followed, hugging the wall to avoid any fire that might come blazing out into the night.

As Jay cleared the wall he heard the dull *crack-crack* of Sam's carbine as he double-tapped the Taliban guard who had been moving towards the direction of the gate. Jay ignored the dropped body and instead looked over to where his men were racing through the open gate towards the main building in the compound.

Movement drew Jay's eye to one of the outbuildings: it was an opening door. Through his night vision Jay saw a man bringing an AK47 into his shoulder, but he didn't ever get a chance to fire it. Through thousands of hours of training, Jay's reaction was as instinctual as breathing. He saw the figure, saw the weapon in his hands, and fired a double tap into the centre of mass. Sam and the other operator close to Jay did the same. A second after throwing open the door, the Taliban fighter dropped to the ground with six rounds through his chest.

Leaving two men to watch for squirters – people trying to slip out and escape – Jay moved himself to the entry position on the target building, where his operators were now going room to room. He heard a couple of cracks, and a few moments later one of his men appeared, leading a figure. Jay knew straight away that the captive was not the man that they had come for. In fact, he was not a man at all.

"No weapons on him but he's fighting age."

Jay looked the scared boy over. He was probably shy of 15, but that was certainly old enough to hold a weapon in Afghanistan. "We'll hand him over to the Afghans," he said. Even if the kid had no part in the fight, they had just killed every adult in the compound. The kid was now an orphan, but that wasn't a part of the war that Jay had to worry about. His men were his concern, and he oversaw their search of the target building, and the bodies.

Jay used his torch to get a look at them. There was nothing beautiful about death, and both men stared at the sky with glassy eyes and open mouths. For a moment, Jay was reminded of the two Taliban who had fought to the death in Spīn Ghar, and his first taste of combat.

"Find anything useful?" Jay asked one of his NCOs.

"Picked up a bunch of paperwork for the green slime to work through, but no weapons or drug caches."

The green slime were the Intelligence Corps. Their bright green berets made it so easy for the military to come up with a name for them.

"Alright, this will have to do. Photograph, print and swab the bodies, then we're gone."

Sangin was a hostile town, and no doubt enemy commanders were rousing men from their sleep and forming a counterattack. The longer they lingered, the higher the chance they would have to fight their way out.

"Jay," said the soldier who had taken the kid to the Afghans. "They said it wasn't his dad we were after. The kid was drugged up, not in shock. He was a fucking sex slave."

Jay could tell that his operator was fighting the urge to kick the bodies on the floor, but professionalism won out over human instinct. Still, for a split-second Jay entertained the hope that the enemy had died more slowly, but quickly squashed it. A wounded enemy was a danger to his men. A dead one was not.

"I hope the dogs find them before their mates do," his soldier said. Afghan street dogs were big and hungry, and a lot of stories had filtered back from British soldiers about what would happen if Taliban dead were left out in the battlespace.

"We did what we came for," Jay said, "let's get back to the HLS before all of Sangin shows up."

• • •

This was the beginning of three months of unrelenting night-time actions that were to dominate C Squadron's deployment in Afghanistan. With almost no break between each operation, elements from – if not all of – the squadron would leave base every day, and return in the early hours of the following morning to rest and recuperate for a short while before setting off on another mission.

The operators of C Squadron had dreamed of nights like these, and they got so many that they began to blur into one. Moments stood out, though. They remembered the shots that they'd taken. The closest of calls. Compound clearance meant close-quarter fighting, but some kills were closer than others. There were mistakes, justifiable ones, but dead was dead. On those days Jay felt the old saying that there was no glory in war, but on others it was hard not to feel the pride and the excitement that came from being a Special Forces unit on the hunt. They took bomb makers out of play. They lifted commanders to hand over for interrogation. They were cutting heads off of snakes, but more snakes were rising in their place. This was expected. Jay and his men had to keep the pressure on until the Afghans decided they wanted to support the Western-backed government. There would never be a shortage of targets, but if the locals threw everything behind ISAF, then the Taliban's insurgency would be fucked.

Setbacks occurred. One insertion by two Chinooks was ambushed, so the heli which had already emptied its load of men placed itself in between the enemy force and the remaining Chinook, which was still offloading, and was hit. A couple of the men were injured, but not too seriously, so they were airlifted back to Bastion but were able to return to the line a few days later. The damaged Chinook was destroyed by an American AC-130 Spectre gunship, to prevent any of its equipment falling into Taliban hands. The Spectre gunship was a fearsome weapons platform. Essentially, it was the well-known Hercules with a fuck ton of weapons along its port side, including miniguns, cannons and a howitzer. The Spectre would go into a left bank to bring its weapons to bear, and then smash them as it circled above like a hungry eagle. Equipped with powerful thermal vision, the gunners in the sky could pick off the smallest of targets.

After a few months, Jay returned home for some R&R. Everyone in the squadron was rotated home at different intervals, to give them all a break while keeping the pressure on the enemy during the deployment. Jay didn't want to leave his men behind, but he knew he needed the break. He worried about what might go wrong while he was on leave and, sure enough, the worst happened while he was away. On a night-time operation in the Sangin valley, two members of C Squadron were killed when they came under attack during the extraction. Their deaths were incredibly tough for the squadron. It was a tight-knit unit where everyone knew each other, and their families. Jay was there to see their flag-draped coffins off the aircraft at RAF Brize Norton. The next day, he boarded a flight back out to Afghanistan. That was how it went during war. Live men fly into the country, and the fallen fly out. Jay was under no illusions about how dangerous C Squadron's job was, but a part of him had always believed that he could bring everyone home alive. He wasn't a man to lose his temper or be controlled by emotion, but losing your brothers will test any man's limits.

When Jay returned from the UK, he had a job to do in lifting everyone's spirits. He didn't want to put anyone on the spot, or interrupt their downtime – after all, he was a part of the hierarchy, and men needed time away from senior NCOs and officers to blow off steam – but Jay knew that no Royal could go long without a wet, and so he positioned himself tactically close to the kettle. Over the course of the day he made dozens of brews, and the lads knew they had a choice: go back to their pits, or "swing a lantern" with the SSM. Many chose to stay and chat, and Jay let them lead the stories of the job that got more exaggerated as time went on. The lads were rightfully proud of the work they'd been doing, and understandably reticent to talk about any feeling, other than that of being happy to smash Terry.

"Everything good?" Jay would ask them, and the replies were all the same:

"Sweet as."

"No dramas."

"Living the dream."

And Jay believed them. Losing brothers was hard, but it was a part of war, and his men knew that. They dealt with it the best way they knew how: by applying themselves to their task, and taking the war into the enemy's backyard.

There was a purpose to every raid, and that helped a man's mindset. There wasn't the endless, seemingly pointless patrolling that many infantry units go through, and the SBS Squadron were always on the attack, which is an incredible mental advantage when at war. They weren't waiting to be ambushed: *they* were the ones taking the enemy by surprise.

Jay felt for the conventional units, which included the Royal Marine Commando unit he had once been a part of. Some of the men that he had gone through the Commando Course with were now senior NCOs leading young men in war, and Jay would do everything he could to support them.

It was a gruelling spring. Hot days and dust sometimes gave way to bitter cold and slippery mud. With fixed bayonets the British forces fought in close combat to clear enemy areas, but there weren't enough men to hold the areas that were taken, and the enemy would simply spring up elsewhere. This made the work undertaken by the SFSG and other mentoring teams even more vital. Britain could not stay here forever, and creating a viable fighting force of

Afghans was the only hope. For now, the Afghan Army was kept upright by the actions of the British. It came at a bloody cost, both to them, the civilian population, and the enemy.

But the Taliban showed no signs of surrender, and Terry was grudgingly respected by the Brits. Even if you hated what they stood for, you had to give it to the man who comes to a fight knowing he is minutes away from being on the end of an Apache's Hellfire missile, or an A-10 gun run. The Taliban died in their hundreds, but there was no shortage of volunteers to continue the fight. And, as they had done against the Soviet invaders, the Afghans and the international jihadists studied their foe, and adapted their tactics.

Each night-time operation became harder and harder to undertake, the difficulties greater than the weeks, or even days, before. Occasionally, C Squadron would be called in to work alongside the Americans. The US part of the Task Force was primarily made up of a Navy SEAL detachment, a company-sized Rangers Quick Reaction Force, and the substantial air assets from 160th Special Operations Aviation Regiment (SOAR), nicknamed the Night Stalkers. Sometimes SFSG were involved, accompanying C Squadron on an op, and setting up cordons to prevent counter attack and squirters. SFSG would usually be accompanied by the Afghan Army. The idea was to make more show of an Afghan presence in these operations, so that the locals would feel that they'd consented to these night-time assaults. Although many locals had no love for the Taliban, the rain of coalition bombs had made them at best wary of ISAF forces.

This was just one way in which the Squadron was changing its tactics, but change didn't have to come from up top.

Everyone in the SBS had a voice, and it was encouraged to take nothing for granted. "Is there a faster way to do this? What if we try that?" Jay encouraged his men to speak openly, always listening even if he didn't agree with what they had to say.

One common theme seemed to be that – while the men enjoyed the direct action raids – they believed there was a better way of taking a war to the enemy. Counter insurgency forms much of the basis for Special Forces work, and successful campaigns of the past had all involved living with the locals, enlisting local volunteers, and creating a local solution to the problem of the enemy. Jay took this up the chain of command.

"It's what's worked for us in other campaigns, Boss" Jay said to the OC. "We'll never win this war without the locals onside. Right now we come in at night, leave in the dark, and the only thing the locals see of us is the bodies we leave behind. I know we do these ops for a reason, but could we break away part of the squadron to do hearts and minds?"

The OC agreed with Jay's "if it ain't broke, don't fix it" attitude towards counter-insurgency tactics developed by the Brits, but their commands came from JSOC, and the American ethos seemed far more aligned towards "cut the head off the snake", rather than "break bread with the locals".

"Right now, the lads never even get to see the people they're fighting for," Jay said. "We're here for the Afghans, right, Boss? So let's talk to them, and let them see we're on their side."

"I'll certainly pass this up and do my best, Jay," the OC promised.

"Thanks, Boss."

"Before you go, there's something that I wanted to talk to you about."

Jay felt like this could be a long conversation, and took a seat.

"Latest intelligence from the Americans has found out a lot more about the Taliban leadership groups in Quetta and what's been going on there. As you recall from the briefing we had back in Poole, when the Taliban were kicked out of Afghanistan the leaders slowly made their way out of the country to Pakistan, and ended up in Quetta, and after a couple of years organised themselves again. They aren't welcomed by the Pakistani government, officially, but they appear to be protected by the ISI, and so they can operate there with impunity. They recruit from the refugee camps, and many of the local mullahs rally behind them, claiming that dying while fighting for the Taliban guarantees you a trip to Paradise. Anyone who opposes them, including high-ranking mullahs, gets taken out."

Jay saw where the OC was going, and put the pieces together himself. "Someone's orchestrating this, then?" he said, and the OC nodded. Jay thought for a second, then pulled the name from their intelligence briefings: "Mullah Dadullah?" Gray Fox were targeting him, a big fish in a pond full of piranhas. "He's the one with a fondness for suicide bombings, isn't he?" Jay asked.

"Yep, the Grade A piece of shit," the OC confirmed. "JSOC are hugely concerned at the exponential numbers of suicide bombings that have taken place this year. Intelligence has traced the bombing campaign as the work of Dadullah, and at the moment they're trying to uncover as much as they can about what he's up to, and what he's planning. Here's the text from the most recent briefing note I've received."

Jay took the paper from the OC's hand and started reading: a high-level meeting had been held in Quetta, where six suicide bombers were given orders for an operation in northern Afghanistan. Two persons have been given targets in Kunduz, two in Mazar-e-Sharif and the last two are said to come to Faryab. These meetings took place once every month, and there were usually about twenty people present. The place for the meeting alternated between Quetta and villages, no further details given, on the border between Pakistan and Afghanistan. The top four people in these meetings were Mullah Omar's representative (whoever that may be), Osama bin Laden, Mullah Baradar the "co-founder of the Taliban" and Mullah Dadullah.

Jay looked up from the paper. "Some company he keeps. Please tell me we get to go after this bastard?"

"Be a nice one to bag, wouldn't he?" the officer smiled. "We can really make a difference by nailing someone like him, Jay. Iraq has turned into a total fucking blood bath. We still have a chance here to smash the Taliban and give the people a better life, but that gets a lot harder if suicide bombers are walking into mosques and markets everyday and blowing dozens of people apart."

Jay exhaled. "As much as I'd love for us to get this shit-head, Boss, is it not something that can be done with a drone strike? It's not like they don't do them in Pakistan."

"There's definitely the will to do that, but not the way. Getting good intelligence has proven impossible. First, they paid local agents to find him, and pass information along. What came back was along the lines of, 'Mullah Dadullah's house is in the third street off the right-hand-side of the main road running south in the old part of Quetta.' Then they sent CIA officers from the Islamabad station to Quetta, with ISI men in tow, and they'd try and find this house and realise that it was a mosque – which was why Taliban were going in there regularly. They studied satellite photography, really detailed pictures, but the place is a rabbit warren and very little could be discerned from above like that – you'd have to have a specific address to work from and then use that as a target. So the Gray Fox people can get signals intelligence, and photographic intelligence, but just not on-the-ground intelligence. And, as you know, if you can't be sure, well, then you're buggered."

"Don't they have any good agents in Quetta?" Jay asked, surprised.

The OC shook his head. "I think they've found getting people to do that is very hard for them. We have an advantage in Britain, with British-born Pakistanis who can play that role for us, when required, but the US would struggle. It's got to be one of the toughest jobs, hasn't it, being an agent in the Taliban and ISI's backyard."

Tough was one way of putting it, Jay thought. It sounded like a one-way ticket to a public beheading.

"Can we at least get a heads up on him coming into Afghanistan, and take him out here?"

"That's the hope," the OC confirmed. "If he does come over he'll be well protected. This guy is a massive part of their war effort, Jay. If we take him out, we save a lot of Afghan and ISAF lives."

The tone of the statement let Jay know that the conversation had reached its conclusion. "When he comes, we'll be ready," he promised.

Jay left the OC's office and went to his own. He was a hunter, and he had his prey. It was time to start learning everything he could about the murderous Mullah Dadullah.

CHAPTER FOUR

Mullah Dadullah

Alone in his office, Jay sat down and began to read over the package that the squadron had been handed on Mullah Dadullah.

He was an Afghan, born in late 1966 in the town of Deh Rawood, in the province of Uruzgan. Uruzgan was in the centre of the country, and bordered Kandahar and Helmand to the south. From the Kakar tribe, Dadullah was Afghan through and through, and his later home was part of "Loy Kandahar" – greater Kandahar. Kandahar was the capital of the Afghan Empire from 1747–1776; the city was originally named Alexandria after one of its many invaders, but one of the few who had found something coming close to a successful campaign – Alexander the Great.

As a child, Dadullah went to Pakistan to study, but when the Soviets invaded Afghanistan in 1979, the young teenager joined the jihadists in opposing the Moscow-installed regime. By the time that the defeated Russians withdrew a decade later, Dadullah was an accomplished student of war. He then returned to Pakistan to continue his religious education, but the drums of war began to beat again in 1994, and Dadullah returned to Afghanistan to join the Taliban movement.

Only a year after returning to his native soil, Dadullah trod on a Soviet landmine: over ten years after the war had ended, his enemy had finally got to him, but Dadullah survived with the loss of his leg which, according to one of the mullah's chroniclers, "preceded him to Paradise". Dadullah was taken to hospital in Pakistan and fitted with a new prosthetic leg. He then returned to command, and take a position as one of the Taliban's three defence ministers.

After losing his leg, Dadullah became Dadullah Lang, "The Lame". It is likely that he chose the nickname himself, to associate himself with one of history's more famous disabled warriors, the Tartar conqueror, Timur Lang or "The Lame". Better known in the West as Tamerlane, the merciless Mongol conqueror from the fourteenth century rampaged through what would later become Iran and Afghanistan, his armies killing many millions of people, all while calling himself the "Sword of Islam". No doubt Mullah Dadullah would have liked to have made the association in people's minds. Perhaps he had an eye for publicity, and a skill at creating myth and legend. He was certainly as bloodthirsty as the Mongol conqueror.

Dadullah always wore his beard long, as the Taliban prescribed. He had two wives, and three children, all of whom lived in Quetta, Pakistan. His features, according to the same enthusiastic chronicler, were "sharply chiselled" as befits someone from the wild central highlands of his home province. The man was prone to mood swings: he could be cheerful, and then suddenly go into a wild rage which could last for hours. No one in his circle would question, or challenge him, for fear of provoking these rages.

As a leader, Dadullah was clearly determined and ferocious. He often led his men into a fight from the front, and no one was allowed to retreat. There was a story that he once shot a man in the leg when he tried to move back from the front line, presumably because he, Dadullah, was fighting with one real leg, along with his prosthetic limb. From then on, no one ever tried to retreat without a direct order from the commander himself.

The Taliban decided to use this intensity as part of their propaganda, to the point where it was felt that even *believing* Dadullah was leading the opposing force was a way of undermining the morale of their enemies. Before America's Operation Enduring Freedom began, a member of the Taliban described how Dadullah was always willing to lead each operation himself, alongside "his men on the front line and dashing into the offensive as the first person over the ridge". Jay wondered how a one-legged man would dash anywhere, but such was propaganda.

Dadullah put up with no issues that were not important. He was deeply religious and often spoke about how he was fighting for Islam. He made decisions summarily. "If anyone strayed or said something stupid, he would throw his leg at them," said another Helmandi who knew him (the "Helmandi brigade" were core Taliban, from their heartlands in the south of the country, and used as shock troops). This particular Helmandi, however, was not a fan of the commander, describing him as "Not merciful. Not kind."

105

This, Jay thought to himself, was exactly the kind of thing his men needed to know. Out on the ground, living amongst the populace, they could find such divisions in the enemy ranks, then exploit them. He read over the paragraph again, and smiled: Jay knew more than a few NCOs who would have loved to throw a leg at him as a young recruit. Instead, Jay had had to duck a rock or two in his time. He turned back to his pile of papers, and continued pulling Dadullah's story from the sources:

Once the Soviets had left Afghanistan, the resistance had split along tribal and political lines, and the Taliban had gone on the offensive against the mujahideen who opposed them. Many of the mujahideen occupied the northern part of the country and, when the disparate groups joined forces, became known as the Northern Alliance. Their leader was Ahmad Shah Massoud, known as the "Lion of Panjshir".

By now a trusted ally of Mullah Omar, the Taliban's ultimate leader, Dadullah was placed in charge of over 6,000 men in the northern province of Kunduz. He found himself facing Shah Massoud on a few occasions over the year-long campaign, and the Northern Alliance leader was thought to respect his opponent. If so, the respect was not mutual. Dadullah had become more extreme in his attitudes, becoming merciless, ruthless and pious. A lethal combination.

Dadullah backed up his attitude with results. He succeeded in defeating the huge forces ranged against him: not just Massoud's men, but also the Hezb-i-Islami (an Islamist group primarily fighting the Soviets), led by former Prime Minister of Afghanistan, Gulbuddin Hekmatyar. In a country of shifting allegiances, and multiple factions –

each of whom believed themselves to be the true saviours of Afghanistan – the Taliban began to emerge as a dominant force, and much of that was down to Madullah's generalship. These victories, and his loyalty to Mullah Omar, were to pay dividends.

Hekmatyar continued to influence politics in Kabul from his home in exile in Iran, but Shah Massoud's defeat precipitated a greater disaster for his country. On 9th September 2001, the Lion of Panjshir was assassinated by Al-Qaeda. By eliminating the staunch enemy of the Taliban, Osama bin Laden hoped to cement his support from their leaders in the years to follow: two days later, Al-Qaeda attacked the World Trade Center, and decades of the Global War On Terror had begun.

Against this larger background of alliances and global jihad, Dadullah demonstrated his ruthlessness at home. Both the Hazara and the Tajiks called Dadullah the "Black Mullah", as they believed he had a black heart. This was evident in how he would treat the people who had housed the Taliban's opponents. Once, when he had taken control of the town of Bamiyan and other towns in the neighbouring Parwan province, Dadullah sent his men in to murder the civilians living in the town that had protected the opposing force. Hundreds of Hazara were killed in a three-day orgy of horror. Men were killed indiscriminately in Parwan. Two attackers, possibly seeking revenge for the slaughter of the Hazaras, lobbed a couple of grenades into the house where Dadullah was living, but failed to hurt their target. After finding out who they were, Dadullah had them hung on lampposts at a main roundabout, in full view of the community.

Dadullah would also kill anyone that he regarded as a traitor to Islam, which included working for the newly installed, American-backed government. Dadullah would make an example of them with horrible executions. The "traitors" were beheaded, and photographs of their corpses placed on display in local bazaars. He made sure the photographs were placed in the streets where their families lived.

Though this was being done "in the name of Islam", these acts tended to repel even the most fervent Muslims. Many actions of Dadullah's would be condemned by fellow Taliban leaders, and eventually, Mullah Omar ordered Dadullah to step down from his position. It's said that upon hearing this, Dadullah handed him his AK-47, and his prosthetic leg, and told him, "If you no longer need me, I no longer need these."

"Dramatic twat..." Jay uttered to himself. He took a sip of his wet. Outside he could hear a few Marines laughing and joking. He wanted to take a break from reading through the evil bastard's background, but it was precisely because Dadullah was so ruthless in war that Jay needed to know all he could about the man. He took another long, fortifying sip of his tea, then kept going.

As it became clear that America and her allies were coming after Taliban as well as Al-Qaeda, their headshed realised that Dadullah was just the kind of merciless leader they needed in the war against the world's only superpower. Dadullah joined the Taliban's ten-man rahbari Quetta shura, or leadership council, and publicity statements released in Pakistan declared that he was back to commanding men on the front lines.

Jay leafed through photos of the Quetta shura. He knew an old veteran when he was looking at one, and this council heavily carried the scars of war. It was hard to imagine a British cabinet officer these days even having served in the military, but the Taliban's ten men were missing eyes, legs and fingers from their war against the Soviet invaders, and the later civil war.

When America entered the war, they immediately set about supporting the Northern Alliance. The sides had been evenly matched in the past, but now Western Special Forces were on hand, and the air power that they could bring to bear proved a deciding factor in any pitched battle.

Dadullah was sent to fight and faced a new opponent among the allies of the Northern Alliance. General Abdul Rashid Dostum was a controversial figure, believed to have been behind the deaths of hundreds of Taliban in a number of atrocities. Things didn't look good for Dadullah when his men found themselves surrounded by Dostum's forces, but the wily leader escaped the noose. Other Taliban leaders negoti-ated a surrender which Dostum immediately ignored, handing the captives over to American forces, and a future in black sites and internment facilities. If Dadullah had been a part of that surrender, he'd likely be wearing an orange jumpsuit in Guantanamo Bay instead of remaining on C Squadron's radar.

Despite the defeat, Dadullah's escape only added to his legend. He and his men kidnapped one of Dostum's depu-ties, and used him as a human shield to get away to the south, releasing him when they got to Kandahar.

At least, that was the story put out by the Taliban. Other sources disputed this version of events. Far from the

Hollywood-style image of a man using a hostage to escape certain capture, these sources suggested that Dadullah went about it in a grubbier, less violent way. He simply paid his way out, handing over $150,000 to one of the Northern Alliance commanders, and abandoned his troops to get the fuck out of Dodge.

Whichever story was true, Dadullah had escaped Afghan and American clutches. With the Taliban reeling in Afghanistan, he crossed the border into Pakistan, and to Quetta, where the leadership was regrouping. Many others were making a similar journey, including leaders such as Jalaluddin Haqqani; his Haqqani network was heavily funded by the CIA during the Russian occupation, but went on to become one of the most violent, semi-autonomous elements within the Taliban. In Quetta there were also thousands of fighters and religious scholars who claimed they were taking refuge, known as *hajrat*, in the same way that the Prophet Mohammed had taken refuge in Medina during the early days of Islam.

After this huge resettlement, Dadullah found himself appointed to a key role. He would, over the years, slowly carve out his own unique brand of terror. These extreme acts forced the Taliban to either endorse what he was doing, or oppose him. His tactics divided the leadership, but he was beloved by the rank and file.

General Stanley McChrystal said that, "As the Taliban regrouped after 2001, Dadullah helped make them into a twenty-first-century insurgency." The Pakistanis, on the other hand, would later claim that Dadullah never operated out of Quetta but instead crossed the border back into Kandahar to carry out his activities.

Starved of resources, and with the leadership in disarray or missing altogether, the Taliban's coalition of extremists began arguing with each other who was best placed to represent the jihad against the invaders.

In areas where the Pakistani authorities had a measure of control over the people of a territory, there was a degree of stability. In other regions, though, where the police and other representatives of the Pakistani government were not welcome, the extremists acted as bandits and set up their own areas of influence. Nowhere was this more evident than in South Waziristan, a rugged landscape of steep mountains and green valleys. Here the groups in the region had enemies on all sides, not just the Americans and the coalition forces across the border in Afghanistan, or the Pakistani authorities to the south, but they also fought each other. Uzbeks of the Islamic Movement of Uzbekistan, who had fled from the north, were in opposition to the local Taliban. The Haqqani network resisted the Pakistani authorities. There had been an influx of Pakistani jihadis from all over the country into both North and South Waziristan, as well as the "foreign" jihadis, and there were now thousands of militants (some estimates suggested as many as 40,000) ready to be organised – if only someone could take command of the situation.

In 2003, Mullah Omar – who had gone into hiding after the coalition forces moved into Afghanistan – re-established the Taliban under the Quetta shura. He was aiming to reset the organisation in the face of their expulsion from Afghanistan, and to try and pull the various strands of the Taliban together. As part of that task, Dadullah was assigned a number of roles. As a diplomat, he was asked to make overtures to the disparate groups fighting in South Waziristan, and bring them closer to the Quetta shura. Dadullah's notoriety and reputation as a ferocious military commander would prove key to these appeals. Once he had succeeded there, Omar expected Dadullah to lead the Taliban's resistance to the coalition forces in Helmand.

It turned out that Dadullah had already begun looking for ways to restart the fight in Helmand. On his brief visits in and out of the country, as the Taliban sought to rebuild its networks in the province, he was lauded by his subordinates and followers. Following their disappearance from the country at the end of 2001, the warlords and drug gangs, funded by the vast profits of the opium trade, and in the absence of any recognised central authority in Kabul, had taken charge of the southern parts of Helmand. Their wealth was a source of envy for Dadullah. Trying to find ways of re-asserting the Taliban's authority in the area, while trying to gain funding for recruits, their weapons and supplies, became an issue that often put Dadullah at odds with Omar's closest deputy, Mullah Baradar.

In the chaotic years after 2001, Baradar never let his grip on power slip, and opposed anyone who might threaten him. Seasoned Taliban commentators in Pakistan noted how his rivals seemed to fall by the wayside, either by being imprisoned by the Pakistanis or by being killed by the Americans. Dadullah privately despised his caution and lack of aggression, while Baradar was opposed to what he saw as Dadullah's failure to see the larger picture. Almost certainly, it didn't help that they came from two different tribes of the same district in Uruzgan. Even before Omar had told

Dadullah to start building up forces in Helmand, Dadullah had asked Baradar for funds to start rearming. This apparent caution of Baradar's annoyed Dadullah, and the fact that Baradar assumed Omar's role in his absence probably wasn't welcomed by his rival. Baradar openly loathed Dadullah's brutality, and thought it was too soon to try and restart the insurgency. Baradar told Dadullah to forget about fighting for a while, and to go to a madrassa to spend some time studying in peace.

This was advice, rather than an order: at least the way Dadullah saw it. He ignored it, and set about trying to raise funds himself, travelling back into Afghanistan regularly, recruiting and reorganising. Leaders who were normally loyal to Baradar started asking Dadullah for advice and assistance instead. Baradar told Dadullah to stop acting independently in this way. Dadullah's reply was short, and to the point:

"Let me do what I want – I'll arm all of Afghanistan!"

But this stubborn approach that appealed to the fighters did not work on Baradar. Eventually, in an effort to get him to open the purse, Dadullah relented. He stepped up his plans for the proposed diplomatic visit to the disparate groups in South Waziristan, designed to encourage them to join with the Taliban. He realised just how important this trip was, coinciding as it did with the build-up of Taliban forces in Helmand. There was an expectation that this offensive would change their fortunes, and if he were able to stop the squabbling between the different factions, Dadullah could bring additional resources into the fight. It's possible he also saw an opportunity to expand his power base, by encouraging loyalty from other powerful figures, and it's highly probable that he'd grown to like being greeted as a hero whenever he travelled into insurgent communities.

The scheming Dadullah reckoned that if he succeeded in the diplomatic mission, then he would be in a better negotiating position to increase his resources – and influence – in Helmand.

While the leaders in South Waziristan may not have been receptive to many in the Taliban, they agreed to meet Dadullah because of his reputation; and, of course, because Dadullah came as the personal messenger of Mullah Omar himself, even bringing letters to be read to the various faction leaders. Dadullah met with many powerful men, including Tohir Yo'ldosh, who represented the Uzbeks; Sheikh Essa, of Al-Qaeda; Abdullah Mehsud, of the Pakistani Taliban; and Abdul Khaliq Haqqani, from North Waziristan.

Mullah Omar's message was, unsurprisingly, an instruction that they should abandon the fights they'd picked and instead focus on the battle to regain control of Afghanistan. According to sources, it is believed that his message included this call to action: "Immediately stop attacks on Pakistani security forces. This will lead to chaos and cannot be termed as Islamic Jihad… Jihad is being waged in Afghanistan so leave your places and come to Afghanistan to join the Jihad against the Americans and its infidel allies."

In the murky world of Afghan/Pakistani insurgency politics, nothing was as divisive as the idea that they should unite against a common foe. There were as many ideas of how to achieve their aims as there were splinter factions. The variations on where an Islamic state, following Sharia law, should be instilled, included: all over Pakistan, in

Afghanistan, in the areas they already held, in the ex-Soviet territories to the north of Afghanistan, further afield and across the entire Middle East, or perhaps wherever someone felt like it should be, depending on their mood that day. But the charisma of Mullah Omar, and the single-minded adherence to his doctrines that Dadullah represented, over-came these objections. Despite their personal differences, almost all of the disparate forces united in agreement, and the Taliban began to re-group en masse.

The militants came together in the wooded valleys close to the border, and started training. They prepared to cross into Afghanistan, and join the fight that Dadullah was preparing in Helmand province.

He returned to Quetta in triumph. The mission had been an unqualified success. Not only had he brought tens of thousands of militants into the Taliban's fight, but he had also strengthened his own position as a senior member of the Quetta shura. He started to act with even more assurance in his approach to the forthcoming insurgency in Helmand. He had great plans for a new campaign in Helmand against the coalition, and in particular the British, who were about to take up the role of patrolling there. The fight was coming together on both sides.

Initially, Dadullah's focus in Helmand was to carry on the task of rebuilding the Taliban's networks in their famil-iar locations, and to restore their influence over the local people. Then he planned to increase the reach of the Taliban into the places that were beyond their traditional base. To do this, he would need the support of the other commanders from Helmand who had fled south after 2001. Among them, of course, was Mullah Baradar, but also Mullah Akhtar Muhammad Osmani (who had controlled Sangin, and had become treasurer of the Taliban), Akhtar Mohammad Mansour, (also from Kandahar, and who would go on to lead the Taliban after Mullah Omar's death), and Mullah Naim, from Garmsir.

Dadullah's relationship with Baradar was clearly complicated. On the one hand, as a warrior, he felt constrained by the more cautious Baradar; on the other, as a leader responsible for the well-being of his men, he needed his cooperation. So when Baradar passed on to him Omar's instructions to prepare for an offensive in Helmand, Dadullah was happy to take those instructions, but he still preferred to operate away from Baradar's supervision. Some say that Omar didn't actually issue orders, but instead sent morale-boosting messages, which suggests that maybe the planned offensive came from Baradar himself.

It didn't help that, as well as being at odds with Baradar, Dadullah disliked Mullah Osmani, the former controller of Sangin. As military commander, Dadullah had immense sway over the military operations across the whole of the south of the country, and how they would be carried out, but only in an operational sense. Much strategic influence still rested with the exiled leaders. Dadullah wanted more control, and more power, and this put him into opposition with at least two of the more senior members of the Quetta shura.

One certain way for Dadullah to have influence was to control the largest number of fighters. So, whenever it was possible for him to do so, Dadullah travelled into Afghanistan himself, knowing full well what effect his appearance had on recruitment. One Taliban commander said, "We went to a meeting at night... and I couldn't believe what I saw: my top commander... Mullah Dadullah! He was my idol; his name meant victory for us."

While Dadullah did gain more independence, Omar continued to control him and his more dangerous ideas. As long as he could focus Dadullah's ferocity on the insurgency, and not on his fellow shura members, then he could give him a free hand. The first steps had been taken, and the reformed insurgent cadres, that had dissipated in the wake of the Taliban's collapse, were now being reactivated and rearming all across the province.

The regions Dadullah was targeting were a mix of those he knew well, such as western Kandahar and his birthplace in Uruzgan, as well as those where the reach of the government in Kabul was limited, such as Zabul. Dadullah needed to push Taliban support as far north, and as close to the city of Kandahar, as he could: if they could establish a strong base in Kandahar, then the outlying provinces would see them as a viable alternative to the Kabul government, and support them accordingly. He was patient, because time was on their side, as the political wrangling in Kabul – and the failure of the government to deal with corruption – only made things harder for the authorities. Waiting would make things easier.

To force their way up the centre of Helmand, through Garmsir and on to Lashkar Gah and then the city of Kandahar, the Taliban had to push up from the southern and south-eastern border and travel across the desert before reaching the Helmand River at a bend that the British referred to as "Fish

Hook". Then they'd need to take the small towns that ran alongside the river in the green zone and make their way north. To do so, they needed a toehold at the border with Pakistan which would allow them to travel freely north into Afghanistan, and to transport materiel as they did so.

In late 2004, the Afghan border police were almost the only thing standing in their way, so Dadullah's forces started attacking the border police in the town of Bahram Chah, the site of a large bazaar where poppy-smuggling across the border was its biggest earner.

Bahram Chah was an unmonitored crossing point for motor and foot traffic between Pakistan and Afghanistan. Unmonitored, that is, by either the Pakistani or Afghan governments. Local groups – controlled by the warlords and drug gangs – have a very clear idea of who was coming or going, and the tax they had to pay – which went straight into the pockets of the gangsters who controlled them. As it was the most used route for drug trafficking in Afghanistan, a lot of money went through, which meant a lot of "tax". In the years before the drug trade, the mujahideen had used it as a route to transport military equipment in both directions without being observed by the Soviets or the government. No doubt American intelligence agencies had been delighted to receive samples of the latest Russian military technology that had travelled through Bahram Chah on its way out to Pakistan, before being flown back to the US for analysis. Now, though, Bahram Chah was about to become an insurgent stronghold, an irritant to the Americans and their allies.

Dadullah's plan to take it was relentless. The beleaguered police force of Bahram Chah was ambushed, shot at, and its vehicles bombed on an almost daily basis by Dadullah's men. With their headquarters a hundred and sixty kilometres to the north, in Safar, resupply along the mined and ambushed roads was almost impossible.

The police retreated into their bases in the centre of Bahram Chah, far from the edges of the town and from exposure to the Taliban who freely roamed the hills and flat plains around it. In early spring 2005, Afghan tribal politics, and drug money, came into play. After the civil war, one warlord's group had taken control of the police, and their rivals dispersed. The local governor, not a part of the successful clique, wanted his cut of the drug money proceeds, and although he had control of the country around Bahram Chah, what remained of the police force held sway over the border town. Using the pretext of a United Nations disarmament programme, and at the district governor's urging, the border police – resented and unsupported by the locals, as they were not from the area – were dissolved. The police chief resigned and promptly took the side of the Taliban, whose return to the area promised "stability" to the locals. Further efforts by the governor and his coterie to take control of the town – and, more importantly, the money that flowed through it – failed, as the Taliban's resistance grew.

Dadullah held the town and, in the process, succeeded in opening up the gateway to Helmand. Now the Taliban had a route to the north, and a safe point to bring reinforcements and supplies one way, and transport wounded back to Dalbandin or Chagai in Pakistan for treatment. Leaders like Dadullah could move back and forth to Quetta without having to face a difficult trek over mountain passes. Junior

Taliban would travel so often that it became almost like a weekly commute for them, gathering in groups of ten to fifteen and riding across on motorbikes.

Once he was able to call southern Helmand "his" territory, Dadullah started issuing proclamations. "My most lovely activity," Dadullah declared, was "the jihad and fighting the heretics face-to-face"; but, he said, he would target not only the infidel invaders, but also any Afghans who cooperated with them. A warning was issued to all government officials, and also to international aid workers, that they too would be targeted by the Taliban.

Some of the actions taken were intimidatory, such as "night letters" written to some government workers, accusing them of being collaborators, or worse, spies. Some actions were more violent, and a number of district governors were assassinated. Teachers were also targeted. Schools were attacked and burned down (over twenty schools in Kandahar were wrecked in the space of four months, and two hundred more shut down), and, in one particularly grisly case, a teacher was beheaded in front of his own class. A one hundred-strong religious council that openly aligned with the government was also attacked: more than seventy members were killed.

These actions were designed to demonstrate that the Taliban were back in Helmand, and once the message had spread, more people, including from the surrounding countryside, started flocking to the organisation. These increasing numbers of raw recruits allowed Dadullah to introduce new elements to his training camps. These give an indication to his thinking, and how it separated him from the other leaders in the shura. Dadullah had looked abroad, and made contact with Iraqi terrorist groups, who sent him their most experienced Iraqi insurgents to help train the Taliban's new cadres. The recruits were trained not just in the tactics they'd need to oppose the Americans, but also the new technologies available to them in the battlespace – primarily ways to design and place IEDs. For those unable to attend the training camps, DVDs were provided so that they could learn to carry out acts of terror from the comfort of their own homes.

While there had been many victories on the path to Helmand, things didn't go all Dadullah's way. In 2004, on the Pakistani side of the border, he made the mistake of targeting the wrong person in an IED attack. The target was a member of Pakistan's parliament, an MP for the Jamiat Ulema-e-Islam party, and an open opponent of the Taliban in Balochistan. Dadullah was sentenced to life in prison, but he was sentenced in absentia, having already crossed the border into Afghanistan. He remained in hiding there for a few months until the authorities in Pakistan forgot all about him, and no doubt the right deals had been struck. Then he returned and carried on exactly as had before. Dadullah was in place and ready for their Spring offensive.

Mullah Omar's plan required that Dadullah push his troops against the established NATO bases in places like Sangin, and Kajaki, and to try to regain towns on the upper reaches of the Helmand River, and the mountainous area surrounding it.

Dadullah's return "was like the arrival of rain after five years of drought", according to a local commander. Local bazaars became transit points for Taliban rearming and supplies; and Dadullah returned to Pakistan to run the campaign from there. By now, Dadullah claimed, he had over 12,000 men under his command, though observers thought it was actually about a third of that number.

On the night of Friday 3rd February 2006, the Taliban Spring offensive ordered by Mullah Omar finally began, following several months' preparation. After his successful trip to South Waziristan, Mullah Dadullah not only had the backing of the Quetta shura, but also a boost to his own confidence and position.

The targets were the towns of Musa Qala, Sangin and Now Zad. Initially, the Taliban had tremendous success, facing not the well-trained NATO troops but the Afghan National Army (ANA). The ANA had courage but they were raw and ill-equipped. Some fought hard, while others simply walked away from their positions. They sold their uniforms and their weapons at the local bazaars, and then climbed into taxis and spent the proceeds on getting as far away from the battles as they could. Nearly 85% of the ANA disappeared this way. The Afghan National Police also suffered losses, both from defectors and casualties. Across Helmand, ten district police chiefs and district governors, as well as another one hundred and fifty police officers, were killed.

In May 2006, Dadullah was interviewed on the Al Jazeera network. He told the journalist that he intended to recapture Kandahar and Lashkar Gah, two key cities at the northern edge of the deserts, and strongholds on the main roads up to the capital, Kabul. He said that once the south had fallen to the Taliban, the rest of the country was then opened up to them. In June, he opened the second front, with five hundred men attacking ISAF forces at Garmsir, the gateway to Lashkar Gah. Dadullah himself came to visit the fight, observing, issuing directives and liaising with his local commanders.

By now, NATO had started their response to the Taliban insurgency, and a flood of troops descended into Helmand. Operation Mountain Thrust brought together nearly 3,500 British and 4,500 US and Canadian troops. This was alongside smaller contingents from other NATO countries, extensive air support and 3,500 newly trained ANA soldiers. According to reports, Dadullah himself sometimes took part in the almost daily fights with the Canadians in the districts to the west of Kandahar. IEDs and mines were laid on all the major roads. The Taliban became bold, wandering into villages and warning the locals not to cooperate with the NATO forces.

For the British, Dadullah's offensive caused them to disperse their large formation into smaller groupings, trying to maintain platoons in several key districts while also providing cover for the outlying areas. Detachments were placed throughout northern Helmand, in Now Zad, Musa Qala, Sangin and Kajaki, where the dam formed a strategic target for the Taliban to attack and the British to defend. The soldiers were placed into platoon houses in district centres, and these became magnets for Taliban attacks. Ferocious fighting took place at many of those spots, involving gun battles, mortars and rockets. The names of the districts where this fighting took place became familiar to everyone embarking on a deployment to Helmand under the operational title Herrick. Unfortunately, the air power that it took to keep the British position from being overrun caused massive destruction to civilian homes, and sometimes to the civilians themselves. The Brits were holding ground, but losing the support of the locals that it belonged to.

To avoid being captured by units like C Squadron, Dadullah would move about regularly, never staying in the same place for more than one night. He would contact his subordinates, issuing orders, and giving reprimands if he didn't think they were fighting ferociously enough. Dealing out a tongue-lashing to one he considered too cautious, he shouted into his satellite phone: "Why aren't you fighting? Are you not a Muslim?" The chastened subordinate immediately responded, and summoned his fighters to the village that he was in. It proved a mistake, as the unusual movement was spotted, and a US airstrike killed seventy Taliban fighters.

The US authorities, in public at least, showed little interest in Mullah Dadullah, denouncing him as no "big deal" with nothing but a "dark vision for the future of Afghanistan". "He's basically a coward, influencing younger Taliban to burn schools and kill civilians," said Brigadier General Anthony Tata of the US Army's 10th Mountain Division. But in practice they were very interested in Dadullah – they just didn't want to alert the Taliban to this.

In the face of a stubborn Allied reaction to the Taliban's offensive, which prevented the insurgents from achieving the objectives they'd been set in taking and holding important regional centres throughout central and northern Helmand, Mullah Dadullah decided to deploy his newest weapon: suicide bombers. When they'd undertake attacks in the cities and towns, Dadullah was unable to gather enough Taliban together to strike at the Allied bases there without those mass formations drawing down the firepower of the US and NATO. However, a single suicide bomber could slip into a marketplace, or move alongside the enemy on a patrol, and detonate their explosive vest. Civilians, as well as NATO troops, started to die in larger numbers as Dadullah realised the effectiveness of this tactic. As ever, he would exaggerate numbers, telling an Al Jazeera interviewer that he had "two hundred" suicide bombers waiting to be unleashed. The actual numbers were smaller, but they could still be markedly more effective for the Taliban than a group of fighters up against the air power and military might of the Allies.

In dealing with the press, Dadullah was no different to his fellow commanders. The Taliban had always been enthusiastic about putting its views into the public domain, not just correcting what it considered incorrect reporting of the facts, but ensuring that their views were seen and heard as widely as possible. Mullah Dadullah was no less enthusiastic about this than any of his fellow commanders, but he added one further element, as much of the propaganda he released was about him personally. The regular Al Jazeera interviews Dadullah gave were but a small part of his efforts to put his views across, and he even spoke to the loathed Western press in the shape of the BBC via their Afghan and Pakistani affiliates.

Dadullah's ego was large, and seemingly grew larger every time he appeared in public. Posters, interviews and DVDs, were all employed in the service of getting Dadullah's name and views out to the world. Bazaars in Helmand, and throughout Quetta and Peshawar in Pakistan, sold DVDs for $4 a pop that showed Dadullah clutching his AK-47 and marching along ridgelines, his eyes looking far into the distance; or sitting behind a heavy machine gun, blasting away at something off camera. Some of the DVDs were worse, showing him blessing young suicide bombers before they set out on their ghastly final steps. And, worse still, there were those where Dadullah ordered his men to slit the throats of the men kneeling down in front of him: Afghans accused of spying for the Americans. After beheading the men, the executioners placed the head on the body so that the dead eyes faced the camera. It was straight out of the playbook of Abu Musab al-Zarqawi, a high-ranking member of Al-Qaeda who was responsible for many atrocities in Iraq.

Most of the Taliban leaders were reluctant to be filmed or photographed, primarily for religious, rather than security, reasons. The representation of people or animals was forbidden in Islamic art, but Dadullah basked in the limelight, and in his notoriety. This prominence was one of the reasons he had become such a figurehead for the rank-and-file Taliban: he was someone that they recognised, and they felt that they had a connection to him. These very same reasons were why he was not trusted by many in the Taliban's shura.

Even interviewers ran a risk in talking to him, with Dadullah declaring that those who printed or broadcast "the enemy's lies" would be killed. He would call journalists on his satellite phone, and threaten them unless they carried his messages.

When Dadullah talked politics, his message was clear: "Our terms for ending the war are that America withdraws from Iraq and Afghanistan, and that it unconditionally stops harming the Muslims. Then we will consider negotiating with them." He dictated that their "puppet President" must also flee the country: "If Karzai has the power to fulfil the first condition of the Islamic Emirate [how the Taliban's leadership styled themselves], then the Islamic Emirate is ready to negotiate on other issues, but Karzai is never in position to fulfil the first condition of the Islamic Emirate. Because he was installed after foreign forces came to Afghanistan... he must leave before the foreign forces leave."

That line – about America's behaviour towards "the Muslims" – was another part of Dadullah's message, frequently voiced in these interviews. He made sure that he praised Al-Qaeda, and frequently would be seen on camera meeting known Al-Qaeda members. He said, "We are not fighting here for Afghanistan, we are fighting for all Muslims everywhere and also the Mujahideen in Iraq. The infidels attacked Muslim lands and it is a must that every Muslim should support his Muslim brothers." This message, more even than the videos of beheadings, caused great irritation within the higher circles of the Quetta shura. They had no interest in a war with America beyond the borders of Afghanistan, and they had little time for the efforts of Dadullah to drag them into a war larger than they were capable of managing.

But Dadullah never let up. He continued to push his version of the war, promoting a global jihad and gloating about his links to Al-Qaeda. For the NATO commanders at HQ, Dadullah increasingly became a sharp thorn in their side. And as he started to make his threats personal, the

British took great interest in the messages he sent out in his speeches.

"The world knows that this is the second time that Britain has brutally attacked the people of Afghanistan," said the Mullah. "We will be executing attacks in Britain and the U.S. to demonstrate our sincerity and make them understand how hard it is to endure under a foreign occupation. To make their women weep as our women are weeping; to make their elders weep, as our elders are weeping. And to destroy their cities as they have destroyed our cities. Then, they will know the true meaning of sincerity and also the consequences of brutality. We and Al-Qaeda are as one. If we are preparing attacks, then it is likewise the work of Al-Qaeda, and if Al-Qaeda does so, then this is also our project, too. We are planning to carry out suicide and rocket attacks on those who are committing aggression on Afghanistan."

Dadullah's speech was the very definition of "terror". Unlike so many other Taliban leaders, he was always looking for ways to take this battle on to a larger stage. For Dadullah, any Westerner became a target. Whether or not his victims were innocent, whether or not they were spying for the Americans, didn't matter to him; he certainly didn't know, and he obviously didn't care. All were pawns for him to use and discard as he needed. Eventually the Quetta shura banned these random beheadings, or at least the filming of them. The numbers of men being killed didn't change, but now they were being shot instead of hacked to death. Dadullah boasted of the massacres he and his men had undertaken in the past, in the Shia villages to the north, and there's no doubt that he expected to be able to do so again – only even more violently – if the Taliban were returned to power.

Dadullah openly stated that the Taliban should not exist in isolation, and that he would work with the remaining elements of Al-Qaeda. He imported into Afghanistan the tactics and methods of the Iraqi insurgents, and he made sure – through his interviews – that his followers thought as he did. "We like the Al-Qaeda organization," he told an interviewer in the summer of 2006. "We have close ties and constant contacts. Our cooperation is ideal."

In 2007, Dadullah was videoed meeting Egyptian Saeed al-Masri, the financial chief of Al-Qaeda. The meeting, and the film of it, were carefully choreographed. Armed men stood in a ring around the pair, who greeted each other warmly. A title – "A Meeting Between Brothers" – flashed onto the screen. The two men sat and talked, spouting meaningless slogans about cooperation, before Dadullah announced that he "thanks God" that bin Laden is still alive.

It was not known how news of this meeting was received by Mullah Omar. Or how Mullah Baradar reacted. But neither of them made any effort to affirm Dadullah's assertions, so it's assumed that they weren't happy with his fairly obvious grab for the extremist end of the Taliban, and the influence and power that might come with it.

Dadullah's hard-line attitude and this ominous alignment with Al-Qaeda increased the sense within the Allied camp that he was out of control when compared to the other leaders in the Taliban's organisation. And why it became essential that he was, in the words of the Americans leading the SF response across the country, taken off the board.

There were clearly lots of reasons why Dadullah's name was bumped up to the top of the HVT list – stopping a man supporting terrorist groups was exactly the reason why the coalition forces had gone into Afghanistan in the first place. To lance a festering boil reduces the infection – and it seemed that might be the case with Dadullah.

Until recently, suicide attacks were unknown in Afghanistan. Not one suicide bomber had been used against the Soviets, or during the civil war that followed. The mujahideen believed in family, in individual bravery, and, if it all possible, living to fight another day. Between 2001 and 2004, there were just eight suicide bombings, all in Kabul. In 2006, there were 141 attacks (the majority in Dadullah's "territory" of Helmand, and the Haqqani territory). The rate in 2007 seemed likely to surpass that.

Elsewhere in the world, suicide bombing became a recognised tactic of radical Islam's resistance, and so when Mullah Dadullah started to promote the concept to his fellow leaders, he produced guidance in the form of speeches, writings and messages from Islamic scholars that ran contrary to the widespread belief in Afghanistan that suicide was prohibited by Islam. Dadullah used these materials, and the use of suicide bombers in Iraq, to suggest this was a legitimate form of attack. In the face of overwhelming military might from the coalition forces, Mullah Omar also backed Dadullah on this point, suggesting that hard action such as this was the only way forward.

Dadullah visited insane asylums and orphanages in Pakistan, radicalising children. Some of the bombers were no more than twelve or thirteen, and many of whom had little hope for their future or no understanding of what they were doing. He encouraged them every step of the way, and was even videoed, in front of a Taliban flag, giving some of them his blessing, handing over slips of paper, one of which identified the recipient as "suicide bomber 116". This approach brought in nearly one hundred "recruits" to his cause. Some of the prospective bombers read out speeches on these videos, which were obviously written out for them, as at least two of those filmed read from the same speech. Others struggled to read the words properly. Those boys who were considered mentally ill were preferred by the organisers. They could be accompanied by a believer inspired by thoughts of revenge, who acted as a mentor. When the two reached their target, the mentor would slip away after a few final words of encouragement. Almost always, the young man would then carry through his suicide attack.

Tributes were paid to these "martyrs" once they had carried out their attacks; the Taliban newspapers were filled with pages extolling them. Their families would be paid thousands of dollars – this at a time when half the population was living on less than a dollar a day. With coalition bombs killing civilians, and accusations of war crimes in places like Iraq, it wasn't hard to convince some young Muslim men that their cause was just, and worth killing and dying for.

A suicide bomber "training school" was uncovered in Razmak, Pakistan, near the Afghan border. The Taliban referred to it as a "Paradise facility" and the walls were painted with visions of the life to come, "channels of milk and honey, fruit trees, green mountains, street lights, and animals like camels and horses". There were paintings of virgin girls, filling jugs of water from crystal-clear ponds, although the faces of the women and the animals were obscured, as was the custom with strict Taliban beliefs about depictions of living things. One wall was covered by the names of previous bombers, with each name in red paint.

Unfortunately for Dadullah, suicide bombings were not an exact science and some of his bombers were not able to reach their intended targets, which meant they exploded their vests in the wrong place, or at the wrong time. A Taliban spokesman at the time said as much: "A lot of people are coming to our suicide bombing centre to volunteer. We have a problem with making sure they attack the right targets, avoiding killing civilians. It takes time to train them properly."

After a suicide bomber killed over forty Afghans in the town Spin Boldak, and another killed dozens, including children, in a bazaar in Panjwai, protestors took to the streets, chanting slogans against Pakistan, against Al-Qaeda, and, most troubling for Mullah Baradar and his fellow leaders, "Death to the Taliban."

With a knack for politics, Dadullah found someone else to blame: "This is not a martyrdom-seeking operation. Several innocent Muslims were killed. The top officials [of the government] sacrificed some of their own people in order to distort the image of the Muslims and of the Taliban. Our operations do not kill civilians."

A proclamation was issued: "The layha [the Taliban's Code of Conduct] advised all fighters to take all precautions not to unnecessarily kill Afghan civilians. A brave son of Islam should not be used for lower and useless targets," it said. "The utmost effort should be made to avoid civilian casualties."

If he could be removed from the Taliban's shura, then perhaps the fighting could be kept to coalition soldier against Taliban fighter, both of whom had volunteered to be in harm's way. It was big boy's rules, then. Warriors against warriors, as war should be.

Jay turned the page. It was getting dark outside – scran would be on – but he'd find himself something to eat later. As a young Commando he had been taught that "my weapon, my kit, myself", was the correct order of priorities, and a knowledge of Dadullah was the weapon he needed to be a part of saving hundreds of lives. Maybe even ending the war. Never in Jay's career had a target this important crossed his sights: the thought of everything else was fading into the background. He read on:

"Although in the past they objected to the use of suicide bombings, they reversed their position, and their newspaper, *Al-Sumud*, ran an editorial:

"'Let the Americans and their allies know that even though we lack equipment, our faith has been unshakable. And with the help of Allah the Almighty, we have created a weapon which you will not be able to face or escape, i.e. martyrdom operations. We will follow you everywhere and we will detonate everything in your face. We will make you terrified, even from vacant lands and silent walls. We know we are inevitably heading towards death, so let it be a glorious death by killing you with us, as we believe in the words of the Prophet (Peace Be Upon Him): "The heretic and his killer will be united in the fires of hell." We have thus prepared many suicide operations that even will involve women, and we will offer you the taste of perdition in the cities, villages, valleys and mountains with Allah's help.'"

The human in Jay resented the tactics, but the soldier in him understood them. SAS and SBS raids in the Second World War did not have a hundred per cent chance of death, but they weren't far from it. The enemy in Afghanistan did not have the air power that ISAF forces did. They had no drones, or jets capable of dropping precision ordnance. America used Hellfire missiles to take out enemy "VIPs", often causing civilian casualties, and while Jay was disgusted at the waste of 23 human lives in February 2007, when a suicide bomber detonated his vest at Bagram Airfield, the logic of the Taliban's tactics was not lost to him. Jay wasn't much of a reader before joining the military, but the "hurry up and wait" life of the military had taught him to always have a book handy. He found a lot of writing about war fluffy and overly poetic, but some of it taught him lessons, and certain lines stuck with him, and one written by Hemingway came to him now: "once we have a war there is only one thing to do. It must be won." For Dadullah, that meant suicide bombings. For Jay, it meant taking Dadullah out. It was as simple as that.

Jay looked down at the paper, and skim-read over what was left on the pages, seeing words like "hostage", and "beheading". Then he went through it line by line, concentrating on every word. Something told him that these final pages would tell him how it was that Dadullah had stopped being a desirable target, and become a probable one. It was two of the Mullah's traits that did it: his brutality, and his lust for fame.

Dadullah was already firmly on the JSOC radar, but he was difficult to find, and harder still to track. ISAF needed the enemy to make a mistake. They needed to catch a break.

In March of 2007, they got it...

Mullah Dadullah kidnapped an Italian journalist, Daniele Mastrogiacomo, who had been born in Pakistan. With Mastrogiacomo were two Afghans: his fellow journalist and translator, Ajmal Naqshbandi, and their driver, Sayed Agha.

The three men had been driving through the countryside outside of Lashkar Gah, on their way to what Mastrogiacomo believed was an interview with the "ruthless" Mullah Dadullah, when they were surrounded by Taliban, bundled into the boot of their car, and driven off.

Initially, Mastrogiacomo shared a cell with Naqshbandi, and his friend and translator told him they had been accused of being spies, working for the British. The translator said that he couldn't understand how journalists had suddenly become an enemy, and that this could only be a misunderstanding.

They were soon proved wrong. They were beaten, whipped and humiliated. The three men were moved from place to place frequently, from farms to houses, all the way to the southern borderlands. Mastrogiacomo learned that they were to be exchanged for five senior Taliban prisoners held by the authorities: Mullah Dadullah's brother, Mansoor Ahmad; Ustad Yasir, a minister during the Taliban's brief spell in government, and head of their cultural wing, who was liked to portray himself as an intellectual; Abdul Latif Hakimi, a Taliban spokesman; and two commanders, identified as Hamdullah, and Abdul Ghaffar.

The Italian government tried hard to find a resolution to end the hell: Mastrogiacomo was forced to witness the murder and decapitation of his driver, Sayed Agha.

Finally, with the reported intervention of Mullah Omar, Mastrogiacomo was driven somewhere in the bed of a pick-up truck. It was night. Mastrogiacomo could hear nothing but the croaking of a few frogs, and the distant sound of voices, before the voices stopped and he could hear someone drawing nearer. The sound of their walk was odd, as if with a limp. The figure came to the back of the truck, shone a torch in Mastrogiacomo's face, and studied him. Mastrogiacomo stared back at Mullah Dadullah.

"In the end, you have obtained much more than an interview," the Mullah said. "You have seen how we live and how we think. Do you think yourself capable of telling the truth about us? You journalists never do."

In that same spirit, Dadullah upped his price for Naqshbandi, Mastrogiacomo's interpreter and fellow journalist. In April, a spokesman for Mullah Dadullah said: "We killed Ajmal today because the government did not respond to our demands."

In some reports, Ajmal had been released alongside Mastrogiacomo, but was then taken to hospital in Lashkar Gah and removed from there by the Taliban, after which he was executed. Officials in the hospital were arrested and questioned. In his press releases, Dadullah told Al-Jazeera that the kidnapping had been designed to embarrass the government of Hamid Karzai.

The events caused huge controversy in Afghanistan. That an Italian journalist was released from captivity when two Afghans had been killed made many Afghans very angry; firstly, because a deal had been struck with the Taliban in the first place, and then that one Italian life seemed to be worth more than two Afghan lives. The Italian Prime Minister, Romano Prodi, said he "learned with anguish" about Ajmal Naqshbandi's death, and that "We strongly condemn this absurd crime." Afghan President Hamid Karzai ruled out any future deals with the Taliban.

However, the death of the two hostages may have saved thousands of others, and in a way no one in the Taliban seemed to have imagined possible. As their five senior members were released from Afghan captivity, they were given gifts, including phones and laptops. Anyone with a rudimentary sense of personnel and operational security would have dropped the electronics into the nearest bin, but the senior leaders had apparently held onto the devices which had – of course – been tampered with by US intelligence agencies. Not only could they track the locations, but Gray Fox had remote access to each device.

Jay sat back and shook his head wondering how the Taliban could possibly fall for this? Would they really? It was like the Nazis turning up in London and Winston Churchill showing them round Bletchley Park.

With the ability to track their locations, US drones and surveillance planes uncovered a network of Taliban safe houses and routes. Intelligence services listened in on every phone call, much of which was given without any attempt at code. After decades of war, the Taliban leaders were serving themselves up on a plate.

Jay felt his pulse quicken as he reached the end of the last page. Through the intercepted messages, they now knew the date, and the place, where Mullah Dadullah would be coming back into Afghanistan. Back into territory where Jay and his men could take him off the board once and for all. The Squadron Sergeant Major wasn't much of a one for show, but as he stood and dropped the papers onto the desk, he couldn't help clenching his fist in triumph.

Jay looked back down at the papers. That was Dadullah's story so far. A life of war, brutality and death. It was a long story, and no doubt one that Dadullah was proud of.

He had no idea that C Squadron were about to write his final chapter.

CHAPTER FIVE

Orders

For the next few days, Jay and the squadron's intelligence section went over every detail they could find on Mullah Dadullah, before reducing his bloodthirsty life to slides on a PowerPoint presentation. "Death by PowerPoint" was usually a good way to send Marines to sleep, but as Jay clicked off the last slide, he could see that he had every man's rapt attention.

"That's what is known about Dadullah, so now you're all up to speed," he told them. The senior NCOs of the squadron were squeezed into the briefing room. Behind them were Scott and Richard, the US intelligence experts.

The OC stood up from his chair, and moved beside his Sergeant Major.

"Bahram Chah is the place, and we've even got the date, thanks to Gray Fox." The Major nodded an acknowledgement to the two Americans.

"Open floor," Jay said to the room. "Any qualms or quezzies?" he asked, inviting the experienced operators to speak their mind. The mission would be planned in the ops room, but there were a lot of talented soldiers in this room, and Jay and the OC would consider every suggestion.

A recce on the target compound was clearly the next step. This wasn't going to be a few drug runners caught with their pants down, but a well defended HVT. There was a degree of uncertainty on any mission, but as they had advance knowledge of where Dadullah would be, C Squadron could take some of that off the table with a thorough reconnaissance: in a raid and battle, the difference between where a fire support team was placed, or what alleyway was used to approach, could be the difference between success and failure, life or death.

"We need to get an OP in ASAP, and plan for them being there a while," Manc said. He was a no-nonsense shit-talker from Manchester, which was what had given him his nickname. In downtime he was full of banter, but when it came to ops he was strictly business. "We need eyes on Dadullah. We don't want to be fucking around, changing teams over or doing resupplies. Every bit of high ground out here's exposed as fuck."

Jay and most of the other men in the room were nodding.

"That stuff's all obvious," Manc went on, "but I reckon the big question is how do we take him? If he's coming in by vehicle could we take them by heli on the road? Or are we going to let him put his feet up, then smash the doors in? We need eyes on that compound to be able to plan and prep."

The sergeant beside Manc, a former rugby player named Gaz, shrugged his thick shoulders. "Sounds like he's going to have a lot of protection around him, Boss," he said, looking at the OC. "Are we trying to lift him, or slot him?"

"The Mullah would have a lot of valuable intelligence," the OC replied.

"Meaning that Gray Fox wants to give him an orange boiler suit and a good old-fashioned waterboarding," Manc said, grinning, and the Americans joined in the laughter.

"We'd like to have a conversation with him, sure," Scott confirmed.

"His protection are going to expect trouble when they're on the move," Paul said. "Yeah, he'll feel secure with them in his compound, but they're not all going to be awake and alert, like they will be if we hit them in the vehicles."

Jay nodded. He'd reached the same conclusion.

"I guess dropping a JDAM on him is out of the question?" Adam asked. As one of the squadron's JTACs, it was his job to call in the awesome array of ISAF air support, from bombs, to strafing runs, to the heroic Medical Emergency Response Teams onboard their Chinooks.

"Dropping a bomb is your solution to everything," Manc said, and Adam smiled.

"It works, doesn't it?"

Jay didn't mind these little moments of diversion. He wanted his men to be excited at what was to come. There were hard days ahead. So long as high spirits didn't descend into anarchy, he was all for it. Cheerfulness in the face of adversity was a key part of the Commando ethos, the code that Royal Marines, and Jay, had been taught to live by.

"We'll have a hard time interrogating Dadullah if he's spread out over the countryside," Scott said. "But hey, this isn't a science. So if it comes to a point where the risk gets too much for the reward, you do whatever it takes to get your guys out alive. If that's a JDAM or five, then so be it."

Jay saw the words instantly sober the men. The smiles were gone, replaced by the grim masks of determined operators. It was time for him to speak:

"With well sighted OPs, and a good recce, we can plan a deliberate attack on this fucker. It won't matter what protection he's got, we'll lift him."

The OC stepped forward: "Fighting season is almost here. As soon as the harvest is over, a lot of men will be leaving the fields and becoming ten-dollar Taliban. If we take out Dadullah, we can make a lot of people think twice before taking a shot at our troops."

Jay turned to a laptop that rested on a podium knocked together by the engineers, and brought more images onto the projector: satellite photos of the target building and surrounding compounds.

"As you can see, they've chosen a location surrounded by civilian habitation. It's safe to assume they know our rules of engagement, and that we can't just flatten the place. Not unless we know those other buildings are clear of local population, and the only way of knowing that is by getting in close for a look."

"What are you thinking in terms of strength, Boss?" Manc asked the OC. While Jay would no doubt have told the OC how many men he thought the job needed, it would be up to the Squadron Commander to balance the books, and spread his assets over the steady stream of jobs that came in from JSOC.

"Two troops for the recce," the OC said, and that raised a few eyebrows: that was half the squadron, which was often scattered to the winds on a nightly basis. The OC explained his reasoning.

"We're going to need four OPs, and I'm not having less than six men in each. The target is about as close as it gets to Pakistan, with a nearby town that is fully under Taliban control. If Dadullah was going into some place like Sangin we could stand to the local battle group for QRF, but down on the border, the patrol will be on its own. I'll not send you down there with your bollocks swinging in the wind."

Everyone in the room knew what had happened during Operation Red Wings in June 2005 when a SEAL team was compromised and ambushed after being discovered by local goat herders. Only one member had made it out alive, and more of their comrades died during the rescue mission. Risk was a part of the job, but there were a few nods of gratitude from the gathered NCOs that the OC wasn't playing fast and loose with the lives of his men.

"The SSM is going to lead the recce phase," Major Wood said then, and Jay felt his men's eyes on him. He met the looks, seeing full confidence in the OC's choice of leader. Usually it would be an officer who would lead such a mission, and though the Troop commanders outranked Jay, there was no one in C Squadron who carried more experience.

"The Troops will likely be working independently of each other," the OC explained. "I want the Troop commanders focussed on their own Troops and task, and Jay will be my eyes, ears and authority on the ground."

It was usual for the OC to direct his squadron from the Ops room. Particularly when he would have other parts of his unit cut away to targets other than the recce.

"How are we going to insert, Jay?" Paul asked.

"We can't do it as a road move. We'd be dicked from the moment we got into the desert, and I don't want to guess how many mines there are between here and Bahram Chah. We'll need to do a heli move, get dropped, then make the rest of the way in by vehicle or foot."

"I've put in a request for the Chinooks," the OC nodded. "The US wants Dadullah badly. If the RAF can't accommodate us, they will."

"I can vouch for that,' Scott said from the back of the room. "You need any strings pulling Jay, just ask."

"We'd also like to involve 373," Richard added, referring to the American Task Force who were carrying out the same missions as the British.

Manc turned to face the Americans. There was a little scowl on his face, and Jay thought he must be worried about a US unit coming in to take the target once the SBS had done the recce: "Just for the helis, yeah?" he asked them.

"Sure," Scott nodded, "we're not gonna fuck with another man's stag."

The Mancunian stared back blankly.

"It's a hunting reference, mate," Jay said with a smile. "About deer."

"Ah," said Manc and turned back to the Americans. "We don't get them in Gorton."

Robbie and Scott smiled a little awkwardly, then looked to Jay: the SSM had a question.

"As the boss said, we're going to start to see an influx of new fighters now that the harvest is over. What sort of numbers are we talking about?" Jay asked. "And will those numbers be increasing all over the province? Do we know whether there's much regional variation? Are you hearing anything about it, and can you tell us anything about that?"

"Yeah," Scott replied, "let me pull that up." He reached behind his seat, and pulled his laptop. An intelligence man through and through, Richard could see that Jay had something on his mind. A look between the two men was enough to ask: what?

"Up at this end of Helmand we've faced only small numbers of Taliban, it's not that big of a problem on a daily basis," Jay explained. "We don't get the same amount of poppy fields growing up here as there are down south. So, I want to know if the big influx of new Taliban is going to be right where we're heading. We can't drop every armed man we see. Are they even fighters? If that's heavy poppy country, then there are going to be drug and war lords with their own fighting forces. Where do they sit on Dadullah? If he calls, do they come running?"

Scott looked up from his screen. "I've got some numbers here. When the civil war ended, over three million refugees came back to one of the poorest countries in the world, and they wanted work. Growing poppies is more labour-intensive than growing wheat – you need about nine times more labourers for it – and so that became the jobs of a lot of people. Looking at the estimates for Helmand, the region has two hundred thousand potential additional Taliban. Not all of them will take up arms, of course, but it's likely you'll get the kids being used as spotters. Some families will be given the job of storing weapons, or providing places for Taliban to stay when they're moving around the province, giving them food and stuff. But, there is the potential that up to two hundred and twenty thousand Afghans could become a part of the Taliban's war effort. Every political movement has a heartland, and this is theirs."

Jay didn't let the numbers phase him. The figures were just a practical problem to overcome. "We need to work out a route that avoids going anywhere near villages and tracks. Four Troop, start using sat phots and maps to come up with potential OP sites lying-up points then work backwards from there on routes in, and possible HLSs for the heli insertion."

Paul nodded: "Keeping the Supacats out of sight will be the biggest drama, if we're using them. Could we just yomp in?" He asked, but Jay shook his head.

"We could, but I want the firepower and extra ammunition that the cats gives us. This could turn into a proper scrap, and we can use them for casevac as well as fire support. I'd rather solve the problem of how to hide the vehicles than how to yomp in with everything we need."

The Major spoke up. "Intelligence tells us that Dadullah's shura will take place in five days' time. We need to get this insertion done ASAP, and take him out before all his guests and their bodyguards turn up."

Richard spoke up from the back. "You tell me where you want to get set down, and I'll get a Predator to pass and get us some up-to-date images so you can see exactly what the area's like, and who's nearby."

"Thanks, Richard," the OC replied. "Jay, have a word with your opposite number in the SFSG, please. They're due back today from an op with the Afghans. Find out what the deep desert's like in terms of terrain, what to watch out for, that kind of thing."

"Roger, Boss. Anything else?"

"Not for now." The officer turned and looked at his gathered SNCOs. There was no need for a big speech. Everyone knew what was at stake.

"Let's get to work," was all he had to say.

• • •

After speaking to a few of his NCOs privately, ensuring that everyone was happy with the big picture and their role in it, Jay walked over to the part of the camp that was home to the SFSG.

Sure enough, suntanned soldiers with stubble beards and wild hair were unloading and reservicing their vehicles, ready for their next op.

MOGs (Manoeuvre Operations Groups) had been utilised to try and get some momentum into Operation Herrick, the British deployment to Afghanistan, rather than units being pinned down in platoon houses. It was an idea rooted in the concept of Special Forces warfare as envisioned by David Stirling, the father of the SAS and modern day SF operations.

The SFSG patrol only just returned from a desert MOG to the south of the "Fish Hook", where the Helmand River turned west to head into Nimroz province. Jay found their senior NCO in his office, and gave a happy greeting:

"Alright Tommy?"

"Jay. How's it going, mate?" Sergeant Major Bryce asked. They shook hands, and Jay slipped into an offered seat.

"Fancy a wet?" Bryce offered.

"Love one. Ta."

Bryce set to boiling a kettle. His hair and sideburns were thick with dust.

"You been driving across the desert or swimming in it?" Jay asked.

"Mate, I rather this dust to the mud in winter. We got a few wagons stuck as usual, but it's a lot easier to get them out of soft dry sand than soft wet sand. Anyway, what can I help you with?"

"You're already doing it," Jay explained. "We've got an op coming up that's going to need a vehicle move. We don't have much experience out here with that, and you do."

"Gotcha." He handed the tea over to Jay, and knew better than to ask the Tier 1 guys about an upcoming op. "Right then mate, here's everything you need to know about driving in this shithole…"

When Jay had finished his brew and got his notes, he went to see how Paul was getting on with the vehicles, which would need to survive a punishing trip in the desert.

"We'll be pushing the weight limits," Paul said, "but I'm getting as much ammunition and water on as I can."

Jay approved of that. "If we can't find a spring, or another source, we'll just have to ration what we bring. Replen's out of the question. Too likely to compromise us."

He put his hand against the hot metal of the Supacat. They'd had little chance to use them on the tour, but Jay was a fan. He didn't doubt their ability to overcome adverse terrain, or their use as a heavy weapons platform.

"Are you sure you just want to take one out?" Paul asked. "If we take two, we can tow one if there's a breakdown. Plus, we'd be able to take more ammo in if it comes to a fastball or even launching straight into a Deliberate Action."

Jay shook his head. "We'll take the chance. Only OP North has the terrain that looks like we can hide it for a couple of days, and twice the vehicles could mean twice the potential fuck ups. We'll just go with the one Supacat, and two bikes as scouts."

"Let's go over the ammo and weapons," Jay said to Paul, and as they talked about thousands of rounds, and dozens of rockets, Jay couldn't help but acknowledge the feeling of excitement and anticipation. He was looking forward to this mission. Really looking forward to it. What wasn't to like about taking helicopters into the desert, sneaking into positions to recce an enemy, and then coming in the night to take them out? It was an SF operator's dream come true.

Jay thought of the rest of the squadron, and then of the lads back at base in Poole, all of whom would envy him for being in this position.

You haven't done anything yet, he chided himself, *there's a lot of ways you can fuck this up. Stay focused on the job.*

"I'm going to check in with Manc and the snipers," he said to Paul.

Jay had left the job of planning routes in their hands: they'd done a great job, plotting potential sites for OPs, LUPs, Fire Support Groups, several routes in and out, and multiple choices of HLS. Richard had really come through for them, with detailed, up-to-the-minute intel about wind, temperatures, sun-up and sun-down times, contoured maps and the positions of settlements of all kinds: goatherd huts as well as smaller homesteads, and then little villages.

Jay would have to make a full and proper briefing to the OC about their planning, after which he would have to present plans up the chain to JSOC, which would eventually end up in Northwood, north-west London, where Joint Operations Command had their HQ. Once Northwood had approved the plans, they'd issue the name for the operation, and Jay and his men would have the green light.

"Show me your best bet," Jay asked his recce experts. As well as Manc, two of C Squadron's best snipers were working on the plans: Robbie, a dark-haired Scot in his late twenties, and John Bush, known to all as JB, lived and breathed their trade, and they had been gagging for a mission like this.

Robbie picked up a sharpened pencil, and used the fine end to point to a map: "We reckon this is the spot to set down here, to the north-west of Bahram Chah. This is a flat bit of highland between the mountains of Kuh-e-Samuli to the south, and Boti Narunki to the north. It's open enough for the Chinooks to get down easily and because it's high up we don't believe there'll be dickers hanging about."

That made sense to Jay. Up around Sangin, there were certain parts of the valley that would be constantly under watch from enemy spotters. Further south, it was unlikely the enemy would keep a watch over every patch of ground that could accommodate a Chinook: especially when pilots had shown they could fly so skilfully that they could place a tail ramp on a mountain goat's arse.

"There's one large farm building close to the HLS," JB went on. He was an Australian who'd joined the Royal Marines after getting bored of working in London pubs. "But Richard's had some assets fly over at different intervals, and there's no sign of life. Maybe it's used in the winter, for housing goats or something, but it seems to be empty now.

We could put a clearance patrol down before the Chinooks carrying the vehicles come in, and check it?"

"Maybe," Jay said, stroking his chin. "Let's look at everything you've got so far and we'll come back to that."

Robbie picked up the route. "There's a dry riverbed that runs down the eastern slope of the mountain into the valley. About two-thirds of the way down there's another small collection of houses but these are damaged and are definitely empty."

"The valley floor's at about 1,500 metres above sea level," JB said, using his pencil to point at the map, "and this big one here, Kuh-e-Samuli, is about 2,100 metres. We figured that its height would give cover to the drop-off and maybe the Chinooks could fly off to the south-east after they've put us down, so anyone who was really interested might think they're heading that way and that they just lost sight of them for a few minutes when they were behind this big one."

"Nice," Jay said, nodding. "Good work. And from there?"

"We'd follow the trail from the drop-off point down to the riverbed, which the reconnaissance photos show is dry," JB went on. "We cross that, heading east, and move up the slope to this wide, flat space by the edge of the river. It isn't that high but it's concealed from the villages below and to the south, so we can regroup at this point if we need to. From here, the teams will take different routes to set up their OPs. North and Eastern OP teams could follow the riverbed east, along the edge of the valley, and carry on up into the low hills behind here, before setting up OPs here and here."

He finished by pointing out two ringed points up in the hills, back from the nearest collection of houses. "You'd have a great view over the whole range of buildings and fields, where Dadullah's due to hold his shura, to the south of you. You should be able to set up there and be able to identify him when he arrives."

Manc leaned forward and pointed out other positions to the west and south: "My troop will split between these two, and I'll take this one here, close to Pakistan."

"Good spot," Jay said. "You'll be the first to get eyes on Dadullah when he crosses over."

"His convoy at least," Manc said. "I don't see a Little Chef around there that he'll be getting out at," he added, looking down at the map for a moment. "There's no way either Paul's or my lads can go in vehicles, though, it's too risky, the noise would be a giveaway. Those three teams will need to go in on foot. We'll need to go down the hill towards the road that runs from this part of Bahram Chah to the village out at the western end, and up the other side to the hills overlooking the frontier. There are houses at the top of this slope but again they're empty – we figured they're seasonal like this one back here. Maybe the OP could be set up in one of them. The lads would have to get up this steep slope and will also have to take greater care crossing the riverbed here, as we can see from the vegetation that it's clearly wet, but on the plus side that means they could carry less and pick up water as they passed."

"Yeah," Jay said, then he was silent for a long moment. It looked as if the Southern OP was going to be the most challenging one to get to, and to stay in. But, once the team was in place, they wouldn't need to move from there. Trying to work out what to do when things went wrong was part of Jay's job, and problems were a lot easier to solve with mobility.

"As for where you're going," Manc said, "Richard's getting us more detail on the gradients, but you can see tracks going up here and here, so vehicles can get up it OK – it's not too bad."

"You see any ways up without using tracks?" Jay asked, and Manc guessed what the SSM was worried about: mines.

"Good news on that. The area was never held by the Soviets, so we don't need to worry about legacy mines that they planted to defend positions."

"That doesn't mean Terry hasn't put any up there..."

"It's a possibility," Manc conceded, "but considering they've been uncontested around this village I think we can say it's about mine-free as it gets in Afghan."

Jay nodded. There would always be risk on a mission. "Great job, gents. I'll give you a couple of hours to try and find any holes in it, or think of a better way, then I'll bring the OC over for you to put it to him."

Jay could see in the men's eyes that they appreciated that. Jay wasn't taking their work, and passing it on as his own. He wanted the men responsible for the plan to be the ones to deliver it to their Squadron Commander.

"Reference the lone building by the HLS," Jay said, "I'll speak to Gray Fox. If we can keep eyes on it from the air, and there's no signs of life, we can move forward without putting a clearance patrol on it. It's tempting, but we're strapped for time, helis, and load carrying as it is."

"It's not cutting a corner," Manc agreed. "So long as we can get eyes on one way or another."

Jay looked at the map. It was the border with Pakistan that was drawing his eye. "Did Richard and Scott give you anything from south of the border?"

"Rog," Manc confirmed. "He showed us some drone footage of the area and it's as quiet as on the Afghan side. It's all just the same, walled-off homesteads. There's no sign of any large-scale logistics base for vehicles or anything of that sort. Further south, there's more. There's the old refugee camp, Gerdi Jangal. But there's nothing there that could react quickly to a response from the Afghan side of the border, other than a few pickups, if somehow we were spotted. Richard will keep eyes on while we're there, he said, so that if there's sudden movement we'll know about it."

Jay rubbed a hand over his beard. "I'll go and speak with the OC," he said at last.

Only a few hours later, the recce plan was approved.

• • •

The next morning, after demolishing a massive breakfast, Jay gathered together all the men who would take part in the recce task. They looked hungry for it.

"You've been taking on hard jobs all tour," the OC told the assembled operators, "but we haven't done anything like this. Not only are the logistics of the mission different, but so is the prize. Mullah Dadullah is about as high as high value targets go. He's a unique player, and taking him out changes the face of the war, and ISAF's chances of success. We all know that, tactically, our troops can outfight the Taliban, but that doesn't matter if we lose the support of the locals. For this mission, the less contact we have with them, the better. Assume that any movement will be reported to the enemy. Assume that every shot fired, and every Afghan killed, will be looked at and reported on by the press. I know, and you know, that we are not fucking cowboys, but like it or not, perception, not reality, is often what determines the outcome of a war. It's not enough for us to just be good. We must be flawless."

Jay looked over the faces of his men. None of them had joined the Special Forces to be anything other than the best.

"Jay," the OC said, "take us through it, please."

The two Troops that would conduct the mission listened to the Orders Group with their full attention. Some of the men had questions, but nothing came up that required a change to the plan. Jay knew that it was important that his men not only believed in what they were doing, but how they were doing it, and there was no dissent over how the recce would go down. Jay had heard stories of wars gone by when men had argued over how best to carry out a mission, and even of people refusing to go along with the plan, but these two Troops of C Squadron were solid, and eager. When there were no further questions, Jay looked over his men. They were dark from the sun, and as fit as professional athletes. Many were bearded, and others had hair that would give an RSM a heart attack. In a mixture of civilian clothing and military kit, they looked like a motley crew of bandits. They were, in Jay's eyes, the perfect men for this mission.

"Alright then gents. Square your kit, get fluids down you, and get some rest if you can. We've got an early scran at 1630, and the Chinooks will be here just after last light. We'll load after last light, and wheels up at 2030."

He scanned the faces of his men one final time, looking for any niggles of doubt, and questions unasked. He found none.

"Let's crack on."

• • •

That evening, although weighed down by his weapon and equipment, Jay walked to the HLS with a steady, almost unde- tectable smile on his face. Since the Orders Group there had been a buzz throughout the camp. Every mission came with adrenaline, that was part of what made their job so addictive, but tonight was different. A person can get used to anything – even door kicking – and this task just felt different. From the method of insertion, to the target, this felt *big*.

Jay wasn't surprised to find the patrols already at the HLS. Some were standing around chatting, while others were sitting on their Bergens. One or two were even flat on their backs with their eyes closed, resting their heads on their webbing. Some of the men wore baseball caps, one or two cut-down bush hats. A few had bandanas to keep sweat and long hair out of their eyes. All had the "operator look" that was the envy of all military personnel in the war on terror.

Jay didn't insult his troops by doing kit checks. He trusted his men and NCOs to have everything squared away. Instead, Jay checked in with the Supacat's driver, asking if he was happy that they had everything they needed. Sometimes, even in the world of Special Forces, it took a sergeant major's word to get certain stores released.

The weaponry on the Supacat was fearsome. Jay had opted for the mounted .50 cal machine gun over the Grenade Machine Gun. The vehicle was also fitted with a

General Purpose Machine Gun (GPMG) that could easily be dismounted if they wanted to split the firepower. Stored on the Supacat was also a Javelin missile system, a shoulder-fired disposable light anti-armour weapon and light mortars. C Squadron were not messing about.

Like most of the men, Jay carried a spray-painted carbine, and a holstered pistol. Some of the men had light machine guns. The snipers had brought their rifles of choice, as well as carbines. The thirty men would be bristling with weapons.

Of course, a weapon was little use if the man holding it was a heat casualty. Water had to be prioritised. So did spare parts for the vehicles, ammunition, smoke grenades, med kit and rations. They needed camouflage netting, equipment for digging in, OP kit and the vital communications equipment: there was no point in putting in a recce if they couldn't tell the headshed what they'd seen.

Jay knew that if they found Dadullah they would have to go in fast, so whatever they needed for an assault, they needed to take now. He hoped they would also get reinforcements, but there was no guarantee of that. Jay had to get in his mind that – once they went wheels-up – they had everything he needed to fight their way to Mullah Dadullah.

As the sun dropped beyond the horizon, and the Afghan sky turned a hundred shades of red and purple, the thumping sound of helicopter blades became audible in the distance.

The unmistakable *whock-whock-whock* of the Chinooks' rotors grew louder, and then Jay saw their silhouettes, black against a sky now turning the colour of blue ink. He turned his back as they came in to land, the hot air of rotor wash beating over him.

Jay turned and looked to his men. There was no going back now.

"Mount up!"

CHAPTER SIX

Recce

The Chinook's ramp touched the Afghan dirt. Jay was off first, nothing to see through his night vision except the dust cloud kicked up by the heavy rotors. When the massive machines had lifted into the air, and the dust finally settled, Jay found the Supacat ready for action with its engine off. The RAF, and the people who had designed the Supacat to fit inside a Chinook, had really done an amazing job, and now the patrol were quickly mounting the .50 cal.

The moments during and straight after landing were always vulnerable, but with an old soldier's sixth sense, Jay knew in his gut that this was a clean infiltration. The silence of the desert was absolute. Out here, away from the vegetation of the green zone, there wasn't even the buzz of insects to disturb the night. In the distance, the sound of the Chinooks was fading away. The rest of Jay's men were on board the second heli: foot patrols who would be dropped closer to the site of their OPs. Slowly but surely, the noose was being placed around Dadullah's neck.

Jay and his men scanned the area around them through night vision, and thermal sights. They saw nothing, and after a soak period, Jay was fully convinced they had come out undetected.

"Mount up, lads."

Rusks – real name Farley – was the vehicle's driver, and started the engine once the other seven men were aboard. It was a heavy load for the Supacat, but not impossible. Beside the driver was the usual commander's spot, but Jay had told one of his men to take it. In the event of a contact, Jay would be more use on the radio than behind the pintle-mounted GPMG.

Almost in the centre of the wagon was the .50 cal, and Tricky was taking the first stag on that. Jay was just behind him, where he could duck into cover to check maps, or stand to see the terrain. Robbie and JB were on the dirt bikes to act as scouts and outriders, and the final two men made themselves as comfortable as they could on the piles of ammunition and stores at the back of the Supacat. It wasn't the most comfortable way to ride into a fight, but it was a long way to walk.

Rusks drove steadily, listening to instructions or warnings from the other men on the vehicle, or the snipers on the dirt bikes. The desert was mostly flat, but there was always the chance of an unexpected rock, or wadi. Thanks to the star-lit Afghan night, the visibility through the NVGs was good, and a look through a thermal sight was even better. They made good time, and Jay listened in to the radio net: all of the insertions had been successful. No hot HLS, no contact, and no one dropped in the wrong position.

Jay allowed himself a little smile. *This was it*. About as "operator" as it gets. Him and seven of his men, alone, cutting through the Afghan night to put an OP on an absolutely vile creature who needed taking out of the game. If Jay didn't love what he was doing right now, then he was in the wrong fucking job.

Of course, they weren't alone, not really. Somewhere in the sky would be a drone or surveillance aircraft tracking their movements, and covering them on all sides. If they were being followed, they should know. If someone was setting up ahead of them, they would say. A perk of being a Tier 1 asset was having the best of NATO's weapons and gadgets at your disposal. Richard and Scott would be watching live feeds of the mission. In the Global War On Terror, bad guys got whacked on TV screens. Imminent danger to Jay and his men would be an exciting video for generals and politicians, but Jay was alright with that: let them see how good his patrols are.

Jay adjusted the rag around his face. They weren't eating the dust kicked up by a convoy, but the Afghan dirt had a way of finding its way into mouths, eyes, ears and nostrils no matter what you did to keep it out. By the time that Jay's men reached their target, their clothes would be stiff with dust.

It was a bumpy ride, but nothing the Supacat couldn't handle. Jay had seen the stories in the papers about British troops being dealt a shit hand with kit. He'd been in a few Snatch Land Rovers in his time, and knew that they would still be digging those out of the HLS, or struggling to get them started, but the Supacat was a brilliant machine, a six-wheel all-terrain vehicle that did exactly what it said on the tin. He had no complaints.

At times the vehicle came to a stop: there were wadis ahead, or dodgy looking pieces of ground that needed to be checked out. Better to be safe than sorry, and let the outriders do a recce. In times like this, Jay wasn't worried about IEDs or mines. They were in the middle of the desert, away from tracks, and coming from a direction where no British forces were located. Any IEDs out here were far more likely to take out a Taliban truck than ISAF.

After a few hours had ticked by, Jay decided it was time for the Supacat to actively seek out one of the wadis that dissected the desert. Robbie, the furthest ahead, spotted what looked like a scar in the ground: one of several wadis that had been identified from aerial photos as a potential LUP. They drove closer to it, and after dismounting and walking along its length, Rusks found a suitable point where the Supacat could enter. In trials, the vehicles had got in and out of some impossible obstacles, but in trials they hadn't been deep into the enemy's heartland, and Jay wanted to make things as easy for his driver and wagon as he could.

Wary of soft sand causing a roll-over, the other men dismounted before Rusks drove down into the wadi. Sometimes men would take turns at the wheel, but Rusks was born with diesel in his veins, and so Jay had been happy for him to shoulder the drive: he'd make sure that Rusks got a long rest now, and before they moved off again at last light.

It was time to lie up. The OP site was too far to reach in one night without being reckless, and so they would wait out the light of day in the wadi. Their most powerful weapon wasn't what was mounted on their vehicle: it was concealment. Nature had done a great job of providing cover, but they gave it a helping hand with camouflage netting. Though there wasn't an Afghan in sight for miles, the men kept their voices low out of habit. First thing was putting two of the patrol on stag while the rest refuelled the vehicles from jerrycans. The vehicles were their weapon platforms and must be always ready to move and fully serviceable, in the same way that their weapons needed the dust cleaned off before the patrol could rest.

"Robbie, you and me will take the first stag," Jay said. "The rest of you, get your heads down."

On a small patrol, commanders need to take their turn on watch the same as the rest of the patrol, and Jay knew he wouldn't be able to sleep until he heard from the rest of the OP teams. Once they'd all checked in, and Jay knew they were lying up, some of the weight came off his mind, but not all: he still had exposed teams in one of the most hostile places on earth.

With a shemagh wrapped around his head to break up the shape, and to protect himself from the sun that would soon be rising, Jay raised his head over the lip of the wadi to look south as Robbie watched north. There were scorpions and other beasties in the desert, but Jay wasn't worried about them. He'd been bitten once before, and while it hurt like a bastard, it wasn't something that would require him to be casevaced. He kept his mind on things that could really hurt him, like Taliban picking up their tracks from the HLS, or stumbling across one of C Squadron's LUPs.

Stag can be a boring time, but it passed quickly for Jay as he ran over an endless list of what ifs? *What if the Supacat won't start? What if OP South gets compromised? What if OP West can't get good eyes on? What if Dadullah is late? What if he's early? What if the Americans decide they want this op and we are left in our OPs just watching it happen? What if we take contact in the OP? What if we hit a mine? What if Dadullah hits a mine?* On and on it went, but it was not paranoia, or over thinking. It was simply the due diligence of a leader who needs to consider every possibility: Jay owed that to his men.

As black night became grey first light, the shape of mountains began to appear out of the gloom. To Jay's left, the horizon turned golden, and then a shimmering red sun rose into the sky. Sunset and sunrise had always been Jay's favourite times of day. First as a young surfer, and then as a Commando. He'd travelled the world as a Royal Marine, and then with the SBS, and Afghanistan was one of the most beautiful places he'd seen: at least, when he wasn't treading in human shit, or wading through an irrigation ditch that reeked of it.

Jay had to answer his own call of nature. He moved further down the wadi, and took a piss. Once they were in the OP every bodily function would need to be deposited into bottles and bags, the reason being that human waste would attract wildlife and domestic animals and so the possibility of compromise. What was more, the patrol might have to return to their OP positions if the operation was cancelled and then reinstated, and so there must be no sign left that could also compromise their location.

As Jay looked back over the lip of the wadi he heard something that sounded like thunder. Dawn was a favourite time of the Taliban's to fire RPGs and small arms at ISAF positions, but the "thunder" was the sound of fast jets dropping down from their station to try and ID, then engage, the enemy before they could slip away. Jay thought about the young Royal Marines and British infantry soldiers at the end of those Taliban attacks, many of them just 18 and 19 years old. They didn't have the training that Jay did, but he still thought that Britain had the best trained soldiers in the world, and some of the toughest. There were no conscripts in the British ranks. Every man and woman who was here was here because they had volunteered to leave the comfort of Britain behind for something difficult, and dangerous. He knew that the young Royal Marine he once was would have absolutely loved to have been out here, clearing compounds and going toe to toe with the Taliban, but he was almost twenty years older than the young bootnecks, and *this* was Jay's war: small teams of the world's most highly trained fighters.

Jay heard a noise beside him, and turned. It was his relief, JB, and he was early.

"Couldn't sleep," the sniper said, smilling, and he didn't need to say why. The excitement was clear in his eyes.

"Two hours of staring at an empty desert should sort that out. Wet?"

"Love one."

Jay moved quietly to the vehicle, more worried about waking his sleeping men than alerting an enemy beyond the horizon. He took a Jetboil from the kit, and added coffee and sugar to the bubbling water.

"Here you go, mate." He handed it to the Australian-born operator, and settled in alongside him. Jay wasn't ready for sleep either. "Mind if I take a look through that?" he asked, gesturing to JB's sniper rifle.

JB shuffled aside so that Jay could move in behind it, and look through the scope. Suddenly the empty desert took on more features, and the high ground behind them came into sharp focus. At the base of the high ground was a small hamlet.

"There's been a bit of movement there," JB said, "but looks like normal pattern of life."

Jay took the map from his pocket, and laid it on the ground next to the butt of the sniper rifle.

"What do you think next for the route?" he asked his recce expert. "Still happy with what was planned?"

JB took a stem of weed that had fought its way through the sand and began to lightly trace a route on the map with it.

"There's a good, wide riverbed that the sat phots showed is dry this time of year. It would keep us further from any compounds, but the drama is that any clear entries and exits into it could be IED'd or mined."

"Good thing we've got the Supacat then," Jay said. "We can break track out of the wadi somewhere they wouldn't expect it."

Jay went back into his map pouch and pulled out satellite photos that corresponded with the map.

"Tracks in the wide wadi," JB said, referring to the dry riverbed. "The locals must use it, so it can't be toppers with mines."

Jay didn't want to think about what a mine strike would do to the mission. If it was anti-personnel, the Supacat might be able to shrug it off, but if it was an anti-tank mine the wagon would be fucked, and the best that the patrol could hope for would be to get launched into the air like Superman, and hopefully land without too many broken bones. Worst case, some of the team would be mangled flesh within the twisted wreckage.

It was thoughts like that which made Jay look over their route again, and again, and again. He weighed up the risks of rewards of each one, and then he weighed them up again, and again. When he finally made his decision, he would be decisive, but he had the time to think, and so he used it.

"Make sure whoever is on stag keeps a good eye on the direction of that wadi," he told JB, "and I'll ask ISTAR to get on it too. If there's normal pattern of life using it in the day, I'll feel good about using it at night. If there's any VPs that the locals are clearly avoiding, that should let us know where any nasty surprises arc waiting."

"No dramas," JB said. He'd come to the same conclusion himself.

"Alright," Jay said, "I'm gonna get some head down."

• • •

Sleeping in uncomfortable terrain was an art form that Jay had mastered over the years. The first priority was to be dry, and that was pretty easily done in the desert. The next thing was a good pillow, and Jay's webbing did for that. Finally, a cut down roll-mat was enough to keep the stones from embedding themselves in your back. After Jay pulled his cap down over his eyes, he was out.

The sun was high and hot by the time Jay opened his lids, but the cam netting did a good job of keeping some of it out, and the wadi was drawing a breeze off the desert. As far as LUPs went, it was far from the most uncomfortable place where Jay had spent a day.

He went to the sentry positions and checked the notes each had passed on to the other: nothing to suggest enemy, and not much to suggest anything out of the ordinary in the civilian pattern of life, no combat indicators like civilians leaving an area en masse, as they often did before a fight.

Jay got on the net to the headshed to send SITREPs, and also to pick up anything from Gray Fox and ISTAR: there was no change in Dadullah's expected arrival, and nothing to suggest that any of the teams on the ground had been compromised, or were in danger of being so.

The day passed in naps and stag duties. By the time that night fell, every man had had his fill of sleep, and was ready to get moving.

Jay sent his outriders out first. Once Robbie and JB were happy with the route into the big wadi, the rest of the team followed in the Supacat.

The moon and stars turned the shingle of the river-bed silver. It would be full of water in the winter, but now there was no more than a trickle. There was the chance they might come across smugglers, or other people who wanted to avoid the Taliban or ISAF in the night, but such people were not looking for confrontation. If Jay saw any, he reckoned giving them a wide berth would be all it took to avoid compromise, but in the end it felt like they had all of Afghanistan to themselves: the desert and wadi were almost totally devoid of life. Only a fox, seen through a thermal sight, let them know that they weren't the only predators on the prowl in the night.

High ground ahead of them began to grow sharper in their sights, then steeper under the wheels. They were close, and Jay allowed himself to smile:

He fucking loved his job.

• • •

Later the next day, beneath a high and hot sun, Jay lay flat and still on his stomach in a natural hollow carved out by billions of years of rain and wind. Above him was a sheet of material to keep the worst of the summer sun off, and over that was camouflage netting. Scrub had also been added to the outside of the hide, but not too much of it. Camouflage needed to match the surrounding area, and the mountain was almost bare.

Tricky, a wry-faced and lanky Northerner, laid beside Jay in the OP. He held a small pair of binoculars to his eyes.

Jay looked away from the landscape and down at a large notepad. Since he had been a young Royal Marine on his first OP, Jay had been filling in logs and tracking any occurrences that they witnessed from the OP. Jay read over the notes, seeing nothing that would be considered out of the ordinary in this part of the world: a kid collecting wood from a store; a man looking out from a doorway for five minutes, then going back inside. No sign of weapons. No sign of an obvious leader. No combat indicators as an early warning that the patrol had been compromised.

Though they were trying to take the entire jumble of compounds into account – what would pass as a very small village in the west – there was one compound that had higher walls and a larger footprint than the others, and it was on this structure that Tricky was focussing his binoculars. Despite their height on the mountain, the compound walls created dead ground that Jay's OP could not see, but that was no bother: he had other teams out to cover every angle, and what they couldn't see from a distance, they would get a look at close up. Before any attack on this target, they would conduct a Close Target Reconnaissance (CTR) on the compounds, which was the military's way of saying that they would stick their head into danger as quietly as possible, looking for obstacles, enemies, routes and anything else that would be useful in building the intelligence picture, and preparing for a possible assault.

Content that there was no immediate danger to his men – at least, by Helmand standards – Jay turned his head and whispered to Tricky: "Take a break and get some scran in you, mate." Tricky didn't need to be told twice, and uncoiled himself from his position before moving into the back of the OP. Jay lifted the binoculars he had left behind him, and as Tricky began to quietly dig into his kit for a ration meal, Jay scanned across the hostile landscape.

There was a high wall laid around a scattering of buildings of different sizes and heights, some obviously just storerooms of various sorts, and a second, large walled-in area, with more buildings and enclosures for animals. He moved his view slowly, left to right, scanning the area to the edge of the collection of buildings, and then to the right, where the track led to the nearby town of Bahram Chah, beyond which lay the border with Pakistan. In the mountains beyond the border, a no-man's land for Pakistan's police, lay a network of labs that processed Helmand's poppies into opium, which would then then be turned into heroin. It was from this direction that C Squadron's target would come, and if their intelligence was good, then *he* would be here soon.

Tricky reappeared beside Jay. He had a mouthful of chicken and pasta and looked a lot happier than he had done a few minutes ago. When Jay had joined the Commandos the ration packs had been the subject of a lot of jokes, but since the war in Afghanistan had begun they had come on in leaps and bounds. Jay gave Tricky a moment to enjoy the last mouthful, then got back to business. Noise discipline was important in an OP, but that didn't mean that the men never talked. Jay was confident with their position in the mountain, and just like he had been brought along by his senior NCOs in the past, he wanted to test his men's knowledge, and instruct where necessary.

"What have you been able to work out so far?" he asked in a whisper.

Tricky was one of the squadron's explosive experts, and he understood what Jay was really asking: "Where do we breach the walls, and assault the compound?"

Using reference points, Tricky guided Jay onto where he had been looking: "These compound walls are solidly built. See how the wooden poles stick out at the side, near the top of the main building? That means the whole thing is structured on a wooden frame. Once that's up they've layered straw and mud and other shit all over it. It's an old way of doing things, but very effective; it'll be tougher than concrete up to about two metres high. After that, between that level and the roof, you can see the mud bricks they've used to run between the poles. I guess they've left those without the top layer because they didn't need to make it thicker there. That base is probably a metre thick in places around the main poles."

Jay knew from experience that such a structure helped keep the heat in during winter, and out in the summer. He looked through his binos at what appeared to be a lean-to structure on the wall.

"Wood store?" he asked Tricky. There was no gas or oil heating here. If the locals wanted heat to cook, then they got it from wood fires.

"There may be animals there, too." Tricky said. "We've not been able to work it out from here."

Jay carried on searching the buildings. "There aren't many windows. Any other entry or exit points?"

"None that I can see, just that one to the left of the doorway. If you follow round that next wall you'll see a window space that's bricked in. Seen?"

"Seen."

"My bet is that's a firing point. A thin layer of bricks they can push out in case of attack," Tricky said, impressing Jay with his attention to detail. It was what was expected of Special Forces soldiers, but that didn't mean that Jay wasn't proud of his men.

"It's the building wall that's bothering me, though," the dems man explained. "It looks almost as thick as the fucking compound wall. You can bet it'll be just as difficult to break down."

They both knew the truth of that. Against compound walls, even the chain guns of Apache helicopters struggled, let alone firearms. There was a reason that so many bombs were being dropped in Helmand: often, the 500 and 1000lbs of high explosive were the only things that could put an end to an enemy firing point.

As was the way with life in OPs, the two men fell into silence. After a few minutes of peering through the lenses and thinking, Jay had come to his conclusion.

"We're either going to have to scale the wall, or smash the gate." The first would silhouette them without cover. The second would channel them into an area that was surely covered by enemy fire, a killing ground. By their very nature, breaching and assaulting were a dangerous business, but it was possible to cut down on that risk by coming from a place that provided cover, and using the element of surprise. At least, if they did scale the walls, they should have that; the village was a warren of ditches and walls – perfect for a concealed approach.

Jay looked again at the wider area: it was a flat, feature-less plain, made of gravel, sand and rock, sprinkled with tufts of scrub grass, dotted with single-level homesteads, some as large as small farms, clustered together near a shallow river-bed. Straight lines of flat buildings rose up from the ground, the stone and mud cut through with doorways, leaving gaps like an old man's grin. Twisted bits of metal protruded from the tip in front of one of the dwellings; perhaps there were old pylons, as the few cable-carrying pylons remaining sagged wonkily.

A young boy appeared from behind a wall, head down, leading a few goats. He crossed the open space at a slow pace, while the six or seven goats stumbled about. A man appeared at the rear, pushing them ahead. They disappeared behind another wall and Jay lost them. He moved his binoculars about, scanning further afield: there were a few trees around one or two of the homes and some brownish scrub bushes near the riverbank. In the near distance were empty flat fields, with piles of rubble collected together; and then another branch of the river, with thicker vegetation running along the bank. Beyond that, there was more level plain, with more rubble strewn across it. In the further distance, there were more buildings – a larger gathering of houses, many of two or more storeys – and, beyond that, a couple of small hills. Rising up behind, so far off that they were only shadows, was a large chain of mountains, and Pakistan. The roads were tracks, beaten earth and no more. Everything was grey, or brown, with a few splashes of green. There was movement visible in the far-off part of Bahram Chah – a few pickups and motorbikes – but close to the target compound, it was as still as a fucking morgue. Jay had been taught a long time ago that the absence of the normal was a combat indicator: if there was movement and normal pattern of life in Bahram Chah, then why wasn't there here? Was it what was missing that was a cause to be suspicious, rather than what *could* be seen?

A light, welcome wind swept through the mountainside, and cleared the hot air out of the OP. Jay could hear it rustle the scrub before silence fell again. He put the binoculars down, made some notes in the log book, and then looked out over the seemingly endless expanse of Afghanistan. Jay had been born more than 3,000 miles from this place, but he was as comfortable here as he was in his own garden back in Poole. This wasn't the place for large units, and conventional armies, but it was perfect for the SBS. Far into Taliban territory, there were taking the fight to them in exactly the way Terry fought, skirmishing, attacking in small numbers rather than in an overwhelming force, hiding out in the hills and striking when it was their moment, and not before. If the British were meant to feel vulnerable here – strangers in this land – then Jay and his lads were going to turn the tables on the complacent enemy.

A few seconds later, one of Jay's other callsigns raised him on the net. It was Manc in OP South, and as he spoke, Jay's pulse began to quicken:

"Three vehicles, mobile," Manc said. "Crossing in from Pakistan. Wait out."

Jay clenched his fist. The intelligence had been correct, and one of the most wanted men in the war was on his way into a trap.

CHAPTER SEVEN

Target Confirmed

After Jay acknowledged his message, Manc lifted the binoculars back to his eyes and looked towards the north: there was a smudge against the desert. A dust cloud, that meant that vehicles were making best speed along the shoddy roads. It wasn't long before Manc could make out the details of the convoy: three vehicles were heading for the outskirts of Bahram Chah. It would be an uncomfortable, bumpy ride for whoever was in them, but being on the end of an American Hellfire missile would feel a lot worse.

With a seasoned soldier's instincts, Manc knew this was the target they had been sent to recce. There were a lot of reasons for people to move fast in this part of the world, but the time and the place linked up with the intelligence, and Manc was certain that in one of these vehicles was the man they'd come to identify: Mullah Dadullah, whose orders were leading to the gruesome deaths of hundreds of people in Helmand Province, including both Afghan civilians and coalition soldiers.

Through the dust rising around the convoy, Manc could make out a couple of dark Land Cruisers at the front, and a battered Hilux at the rear, its flatbed bristling with armed men in their black Taliban turbans. They were an intimidating lot, at least to the locals, who gave them a wide berth. Personally, Manc couldn't wait to get closer to the unsuspecting enemy.

Manc lifted the radio's handset back to his ear, and relayed what he was seeing to Jay, and OP North.

• • •

Jay wrote down Manc's message, then turned to look at Tricky. Time living in each other's pockets leads to soldiers being able to communicate with little more than a look, and Tricky understood the eye contact and nod that Jay gave him: "Keep eyes on."

Jay slowly crawled back out of the OP, moving tactically down the slope. Here, out of sight of friend and enemy alike, the Supacat was hidden by boulders and scrub. Two men were missing, on stag a little further out. Of the other four, two were asleep while Robbie and JB sat silently around a Jetboil: it was never too hot to get the wets on. Now, they looked at Jay expectantly. They could feel something in his body language, and when Jay smiled, they smiled back: the hunt was on.

"They're coming in," he said quietly. "Robbie, JB, go and join Tricky. We need enemy numbers, their positions, and we need to confirm the target ID."

The two snipers moved quickly and silently. All of the squadron had spent time studying pictures of the target, but for Robbie and JB, it had been taken to another level. They'd watched hours of videos, even bringing the DVDs into the field with them, just to be sure that they could confirm the target at a distance when the time came.

Tricky came onto the radio, confirming that the three vehicles were coming out of Bahram Chah and heading towards the large compound that he had been assessing with Jay. This was the house that intelligence assets had indicated, and Jay reckoned the source must have been very close to the Mullah, or that the Mullah's men were incredibly lax on their countersurveillance and operational security drills. So far, the int had been right at every step of the way. It was the green slime and Gray Fox who had provided this information, and Jay smiled to himself: when it came to handing out nicknames, the Brits were definitely less generous than their American allies.

It was from these agencies that Robbie and JB had received their videos, and studied it like pro athletes study their opponents. They noted Dadullah's height compared to the others around him, his most obvious visual distinguishing mark, and how he walked – badly, as he only had one leg. They recognised how his followers behaved around him: how much space they gave him, how far behind him they followed when he walked, and so on. They memorised the colour of his turban, and the way he wore it. Other Visual Distinguishing Marks were just as important as his gait. They'd watched interviews with him, carefully copying his hand movements until they could mimic the Taliban commander. They watched to see how the Mullah lifted his head at the end of a sentence, whether he stared left or right when thinking of an answer, and a hundred other details that would help identify the man they had been sent to hunt.

Jay, ever curious as to the nature of his enemy, had sat in with the two snipers during their film study, and one speech, which he was already familiar with, kept playing in his mind:

"We are planning to carry out suicide and rocket attacks on those who are committing aggression on Afghanistan," the Mullah decreed in a tone of steel. *"To make their women weep as our women are weeping; to make their elders weep, as our elders are weeping."*

Jay didn't take the words personally: this was war, and he didn't expect his enemy to try and do anything else but kill him. He, for his part, would be trying to do exactly the same, and not for glory, or religion, but because it was his job, and he was fucking good at his job. He had no choice but to be, because failure meant the death of British soldiers.

Perhaps unsurprisingly, other parts of that speech stuck with him too: *"We will be executing attacks in Britain and the U.S. to demonstrate our sincerity and make them understand how hard it is to endure under a foreign occupation. To destroy their cities as they have destroyed our cities. Then, they will know the true meaning of sincerity and also the consequences of brutality."*

Hearing this again, Jay felt a different kind of sensation. This wasn't talk of soldier fighting soldier, but a deliberate targeting of civilians. Jay had learned a long time ago that letting anger control you would not lead to success, but he had felt it bubbling beneath the surface.

"I can't wait to meet this dickhead," Robbie had said. The words had been delivered coolly and calmly, and with all the confidence of a man who can kill you from over a mile away.

Back on the hillside, Jay watched the two men disappear up into the OP, then spoke quietly to the men still waiting below. Now that the target was in the location, they could afford to drink extra water, and though Jay knew he could trust his men to admin themselves, it was up to him to OK the extra use of their supplies. A quiet buzz of excitement was passing from man to man. They had the smell of prey in their nostrils, and Jay could feel how happy this made them. His operators came from every background and corner of Britain, but here they were, putting everything on the line for a common cause. Jay did not consider himself a chest-thumping patriot, or a bloodthirsty maniac, and he didn't see such traits in his men, either. They were warriors, but they weren't berserkers. Once Jay had given a few quiet orders, he slipped back up the mountainside.

"No change, Tricky?" he whispered in the now cramped OP, the men packed in shoulder to shoulder. Tricky shook his head, and Jay sighted his binoculars on the approaching convoy. They were out of Bahram Chah, and had to slow their pace as the state of the dirt tracks worsened. Instead of their rifles, Robbie and JB had long-lense cameras mounted on tripods pointing at the vehicles.

Finally, the convoy drew to a halt beside a tangle of compounds. The men in the Hilux swarmed out, and formed lines around the Land Cruisers. As the doors on the Toyotas opened, the men around it drew in closer, forming a loose scrum by the doors, making it impossible to be sure exactly who, and even how many, were exiting the big vehicles.

These were not run-of-the-mill Taliban fighters; before leaving their base, Jay and his patrol had all been briefed that Mullah Dadullah would be guarded by Tier 1, the most capable Taliban soldiers, mostly foreign fighters with extensive combat experience. These fighters knew how to operate, and would always be aware of possible threats, even in an area the Taliban thought of as their own. Though they could not be considered the grade of soldier that Jay's men were, they were battle-worn, loyal, and had likely received training from members of Pakistan's Inter-Services Intelligence.

Jay swore, and gave some grudging respect to the enemy. "Good drills. I can't see Dadullah in that. Anyone seen?"

Robbie and JB stayed silent, still watching intently.

"I count twenty-one pax," Tricky said. "Maybe twenty-two."

"Twenty-two," Robbie said firmly, his eyes still glued to the viewfinder of his camera.

A group of men now appeared from around the edge of the target compound that Jay and Tricky had been watching, bowing low as they greeted the new arrival.

"There's the welcome party," Tricky said. "That guy at the front is the one who I saw at the door earlier." The locals started to mingle with the new arrivals, and the group around the convoy began to shift. Gaps appeared amongst them, and Jay felt Robbie and JB tense as the spaces opened, hoping they could catch a glimpse of figures behind the wall of Taliban guards.

For a brief moment, a slight figure with a bushy beard and wearing a black turban could be glimpsed within the group moving towards the locals. "Is that him?" Jay asked, even as the target was swallowed up by men moving alongside him.

"Not sure," said Robbie.

"Fucking nothing yet," JB added.

Jay strained his eyes, but he couldn't get a clear view of the target amongst the group of men, and he kept silent: JB and Robbie knew what was at stake with their ID. The lives of many hung in the balance.

Trusting his men to do their job, Jay put his commander's hat on and thought forward to what would happen next if it wasn't the Mullah, and what would happen if it *was*. If they had the wrong man, and the int was wrong, then they'd most likely extract tonight back to the Forward Operating Base. If it was correct, then they had their target and a chance to lift him. No doubt commanders in the RAF would want the honour of killing Dadullah, and petition to level the place with the biggest bomb in their arsenal, but Jay wasn't having that. It had been his men lying amongst the hot dirt and scorpions. It would be them who got to capture or kill the bastard.

The group of Taliban moved towards the gateway that Jay had considered as a poor form of entry for his team. It was open wide, and needed to be for the large group that started to filter through it. With such a scrum of men, Jay accepted the fact that making the ID from the OP was impossible. Like any good commander, he didn't let his disappointment show.

"It's not a drama," he said as he heard JB sigh. "We'll just get down there on a CTR tonight."

That cheered them up. There was nothing the snipers loved more than stalking around in the enemy's backyard, and Jay issued a few orders for what was to come.

A positive identification was vital; Mullah Dadullah was listed HVT – a High Value Target – but without that ID Jay couldn't risk proceeding with the mission. The Squadron Commander had drummed this into him before he'd been sent out on this recce, not that Jay needed the reminder. Any mistake and the Mullah would disappear into hiding in Pakistan, and they'd never get another chance to attack him like this, but that was fine by Jay and his men: they hadn't come all this way to fail.

• • •

For someone who had grown up in British towns, the Afghan nights were a surprise. There was no light pollution in Helmand Province, and as a result the sky was blanketed by billions of pinpricks of light, the stars enough to take anyone's breath away.

But Jay wasn't looking up tonight. He was carefully placing one foot in front of the other as he followed Robbie and JB through a ditch between the fields: their mission, to conduct a close target recce on the target compound, and confirm the presence of Mullah Dadullah.

Time was of the essence. The high-ranking member of the Taliban hadn't come across the border for fun, but for a meeting with other commanders in his organisation, known as a shura. Each one of the attendees would come with their own guards, and if Jay and his men didn't confirm the target, and move on it soon, then the number of fighters they were facing would keep growing and growing.

Before last light, Jay had stayed in the OP, hoping for a look at the elusive target, but there was little movement in the cluster of compounds. The whole area seemed to have been emptied out in anticipation of the bigwig's visit, which made Jay feel confident that their HVT was somewhere inside the compounds.

As he had lain in the OP, Jay had thought over what would be discussed at the Dadullah's war council, and what C Squadron could prevent by taking him down: plans to transport suicide bombers, and execute attacks; money for weapons and explosives; intelligence on Afghans in Helmand who supported the government in Kabul.

Every bit of the shura was deadly, and needed to be stopped.

Jay and his men were taking a risk by slipping into the village, but he felt it was a calculated one. They could watch and wait on the mountain, but never get a chance to see their target. And, if the guards were well trained, they were certain to send guards to sweep the high ground at some point. Such men could be dealt with, but it wouldn't matter: the alert would be raised, and the Mullah might escape their grasp, and slip back to Pakistan.

Jay and JB went prone and watched rooftops and alleyways as Robbie crawled ahead. They were on the edge of the dwellings now, and he was going forward on his belt buckle to listen and watch for any sign of enemy listening posts and sentries. Finally happy, Robbie called Jay and JB forward over the radio. Jay had no concerns about pushing on into the buildings, his flank covered by a four-man team who had pushed in from OP West, and ISTAR assets covering from high in the sky. Back on the high ground to the north, a Javelin-missile operator watched through his thermal sights.

If things did go noisy, then there would be plenty of covering fire to support their extraction.

Before leaving the OP, Jay and the snipers had agreed on a vantage point in the village which would give them a good view of the target compound. Even though the entire place looked empty of civilians, they couldn't overlook the possibility that the locals were just staying inside and out of the Taliban's way, and so they had chosen a domed building that appeared to be a store of sorts.

Robbie led the way, sticking to the deep, dark shadows cast by compound walls. The starlight above was perfect for night vision goggles, enabling Jay to see the world in shades of light green. Human eyesight wasn't made for operating at night, but his sense of smell was up to the job. There were a few unpleasant ones in the village – no flushing toilets here – and then, as they drew closer to the compound, there was the unmistakable smell of a wood fire. The sense of sound seemed to sharpen at night, and a diesel generator was chugging away in the direction of the target compound. Noise like that could be a double-edged weapon: it would be a lot louder in the target compound and would do a lot to cover any noise that Jay's team made, but if there were Taliban patrols and outposts...

It was Robbie who spotted them. Jay could tell it in his body language as soon as he stopped. He was like a bloodhound with a scent in his nostrils, pointed and ready to go.

Jay followed the direction of Robbie's carbine barrel. His angle wasn't as good as his point man's, but he could see it now, and smell it: in the darkness of the village, light was being thrown up onto a wall. There must be a fire hidden beneath the lower walls. Jay waited, listened, and in the end he heard the voices.

Robbie turned back and looked at his Sergeant Major. In Jay's night vision, his scout looked like a green ninja covered in weapons and armour. He knew why Robbie was looking at him, and Jay gave a single, pronounced nod. A second later, Robbie was moving like a ghost towards the Taliban position.

JB gave cover for the two operators so Jay could keep eyes on Robbie. He was one of his best recce operators and snipers, and could sneak across Salisbury Plain like a rat up a drain pipe. Jay wasn't worried about Robbie's safety – he had the drop on the sentries, who had ruined their night vision by having a fire, probably to keep the insects away – but dropping them now would alert the target building. Even if no one came out to relieve the guards and found the bodies, the gunfire would kick everything off. Their carbines weren't silenced but suppressed. It was a bit like putting a muffler on a sports car's exhaust: you're still going to hear some weapon report.

Robbie was within ten metres of the enemy now. Jay saw him lean, and guessed that he had an angle to see through an entrance into the space. Robbie didn't hang around, no more than five seconds, and then he was creeping back to the ditch where Jay waited and prepared to drop anyone who came out on Robbie's heels. The Taliban weren't usually equipped with night vision, but it wasn't hard to buy them on the open market, let alone on the black, and there was no way in hell that some sympathetic Pakistani officers hadn't been filtering gear to their mates fighting the infidels.

Robbie silently lowered himself into the ditch, and even this close to the enemy, Jay couldn't help a flash of pride at how good his patrol was. Robbie looked at Jay, and showed three fingers, then pointed at his own carbine: the sentries were armed.

They could be Taliban. They could be smugglers. They could be men protecting their village. There was no way to tell, so the CTR had to get eyes on the target.

Jay nodded once to Robbie – "good work" – then gave a hand signal for his point man to continue. They were inside the enemy's perimeter now, exactly like every Special Forces soldier dreams of.

One careful step after the other. Scanning. Listening. Even smelling. The radios were silent, every man keeping the net clear. Only if there was imminent danger would they break it. This was the CTR's show, and everyone in support watched and waited.

Jay's small team reached the domed building without incident. They hadn't brought a ladder with them – even the telescopic ones were too cumbersome and noisy for such a CTR – but there was a reason why his instructors had put such an emphasis on obstacle courses when Jay was an aspiring young Commando. He was the heaviest of the three, and so he would go up first. Robbie and JB put their backs against the wall, and cupped their hands. Using a hand on Robbie's head to steady himself, Jay put a boot into each pair of gloved hands, and then the lads boosted him up onto the roof. Jay scanned the rooftop, and then, happy that no Afghans were sleeping up there to escape the heat, he signalled for the others to join him. Robbie came next.

That left JB, the lightest, and he used one foot to push off against the wall while Jay and Robbie took a hand each, and lifted him up. It wasn't quite Cirque Du Soleil, but for three armed men it was about as silent and graceful as it got.

Jay wanted to get eyes on the Mullah, but that wasn't his job. As the SSM, he was already pushing things by being on the CTR himself, which would usually just be done by the sniper pair, but he justified it because this was such a big mission for the squadron. It wasn't that he didn't trust the others to do the job, but as a leader the buck stopped with him. If they were going to put a raid in, or if they weren't, Jay believed that he needed to shoulder the responsibility for what went into making the decision. Still, it was Robbie and JB who had spent weeks memorising everything about the man's appearance and mannerisms, and so it would be them who would look through their thermal sights and long lenses while Jay provided the protection.

As he did so, Jay didn't just scan the village for threats: he looked for the cover that could save his men's lives. *Would that building do as a forming up point? Would that ditch work as concealment to the breach? Would that rooftop give good arcs for fire support? What was the best route to evacuate a casualty back?* Robbie and Jay would both be sketching and noting, and Jay committed as much as he could to his mind.

The Afghan night is a still place and sound carried easily. That was why Jay and his team kept chat to minimum, only talking if it was essential, but the Taliban guards must have missed the lessons on noise and light discipline given by their rogue ISI allies. The sound of a door opening on the target building was the first thing that drew the

CTR's attention, and then two men emerged, backlit by a fire inside. For a split-second Jay wondered if the enemy had been alerted to their presence, and were sending out a clearance patrol, but the two men stopped in the weak light of the interior. Jay could still hear the chugging generator, and decided it must be powering electric lights inside the building. Maybe charging phones and radios, too. There wasn't a grid to speak of in this part of the country: heat came from wood fires or bottled gas, and electricity from diesel motors.

The two men continued to chat as they pissed into the courtyard. Jay waited to see if they would spark up a cigarette when they were done, and when they didn't, but stood chatting, he added one more mental note that built the case that these men were Taliban: the population of Helmand were heavy smokers, but the stricter members of the Taliban forbade it. Maybe the men were just waiting until they got inside, but every little piece of intelligence and pattern of life builds the picture...

The two men went back inside, closing the door behind them. Jay was almost surprised when Robbie appeared beside him. The sniper squeezed his shoulder, and whispered directly into his ear:

"Got him."

CHAPTER EIGHT

The Plan

In their positions, and with their different angles, Robbie and JB had been able to see through the open doorway and into the lit interior of the building: Mullah Dadullah, one of the biggest chess pieces in the war, was here in C Squadron's reach.

Now it was time to take him off the board.

Jay and the CTR got back to the hide not long before first light, just before the sky turned from black to blue. In the growing light, Jay could see the smiles on Robbie and JB, and why not? The lads had done a good job. They'd ID'd Dadullah, and now Jay would fire those photos up to the headshed to get them double- and triple-checked by Gray Fox. Everything on the recce so far had been a success, but that counted for fuck all if they made an arse of the next stages.

Jay didn't need to tell his patrol that. They knew that everything they had done would count for nothing if the Taliban were alerted to their presence now. Perhaps an air asset would be able to smash him as he tried to flee to Pakistan, but no one wanted to take that chance. This had become personal to C Squadron. Jay remembered how people had talked – still talked – about how bin Laden had escaped from Tora Bora. He didn't want anything like that hanging over his lads.

The pressure was still on, but Jay wouldn't have been human if he didn't get a little buzz from what they had just done, sneaking past enemy sentries to steal a look at the person they were supposed to protect. Some armchair general back in the UK might ask why Robbie and JB hadn't taken shots with their weapons instead of their cameras, but the answer was pretty fucking simple: it wasn't a suicide mission. A CTR was great for getting intelligence from under the enemy's nose. It wasn't so good for breaking contact when Dadullah's guards would have come pouring out into the night. If that had been the *only* way to get him, then so be it, but Jay and his men enjoyed life, and the British taxpayer had poured millions into their training. It made no sense for them to go on one-way missions like Dadullah's suicide bombers. Besides, there was the bigger picture to consider: the Americans wanted him alive for interrogation that might save even more lives than if he was dead.

Back down by the Supacat, there was a hot wet waiting for Jay and the others.

"Get sippers on that," Tricky said, handing it over to Robbie, who passed it onto JB, and then finally onto Jay. The tea kept making the rounds as the two snipers selected their best photos. Jay crouched over their shoulder as they worked, and he smiled behind them.

"That's definitely Dadullah. Great fucking work, gents."

When the final photo selection was made, Jay uploaded them to a laptop-like device that had been suitably soldier-proofed for work in the field. Once a satellite signal had been established, he bounced the files over to the headshed.

"What next, Jay?" Tricky asked. "They'll let us get a crack at him, won't they?" he said, anxious to take down one of the highest of high value targets.

"First priority, keeping eyes on, then scran and sleep." Jay replied. "Nothing's going to happen in daylight from the rest of the squadron, so we just need to keep building up the intelligence picture from the OPs. Now that Dadullah's men have had a night to get their heads down, they might start sending out clearance patrols. If that happens, we've got to avoid contact at all costs. We can't spook this fucker."

Tricky nodded and said nothing else. In the dawn light Jay could see that Tricky's eyes were red from the long night. He doubted that he looked any better himself, and suddenly felt exhausted. There was nothing he wanted to do more than get his head down and sleep, but there were other things to be taken care of first: his weapon needed cleaning, and it wasn't a good idea to try and operate on an empty stomach.

"Pass us your gat," Tricky said, "I'll clean it for you while you get some scran. Robbie, JB, you too, lads."

No one objected. Although the weapons were personal, they belonged to a team. There had been days where they had cleaned Tricky's. What went around came around. As Tricky cleaned the carbines one after the other, Robbie and JB went over their sniper rifles, and Jay got scran on for the lot of them. The weapons weren't stripped and cleaned as if they had finished a day on the the range. What they needed was tactical cleaning, making sure the working parts can go back and forth to do their job: get rounds down on the enemy. If the patrol was compromised, they'd need them in mega seconds.

By sharing the work it was done quickly, and the patrol were able to eat a hot ration before the sun was up. Even the May nights were warm in Afghan, but eating hot meals had been drilled into Jay so rigorously as a young Commando that to do anything less than that felt like nod behaviour, and falling below the expected standard.

"Need a dump," JB said, taking one of the shitter bags from the Supacat, and crouching down beside one of the wheels. The rest of them didn't pay him any notice: they'd shit in front of each other so many times that it had stopped being funny a long time ago.

Jay checked his radio settings out of habit. The sentry would also be keeping a radio stag, as would the OP, but Jay liked to sleep with his headset on when he could, and he was happy that they had enough batteries to see out the op, and then some.

There were two men up in the OP, two others on stag, and Jay, Tricky and the two snipers in the admin area. It wasn't the biggest force, but it would have no trouble dealing with any Taliban patrol that came across it. It wasn't danger that worried Jay as he closed his eyes, but failure. If they were compromised, the best that they could hope for was a Hellfire missile into Dadullah's chest. He would be dead, but Jay's – and C Squadron's – tour would end on a note that was less than perfect. He didn't want that, and neither did his men.

Jay rested his head on his webbing, and pulled his shemagh over his eyes. The Afghan dawn was heating up, but nothing could stop him from falling asleep. The last thing that he pictured was the face of Mullah Dadullah on Robbie's camera, and then he was out.

• • •

Jay was woken by Rusks a couple of hours later. He and another of the operators had come down from the OP, and would now go on stag, while the two lads who had been on sentry duty would now sleep. The two waking men would go up into the OP, with the idea that the freshest eyes would be watching the target compound and the area around it. Some units would choose to change one man at a time to overlap, but that required double the amount of movement, and Jay had decided to keep that down to a minimum.

Of course, "fresh" was a relative term in the military world. Jay had just spent two hours sleeping on hard dirt, and he felt every day of his 18 years in uniform. He wasn't a young nod anymore, and his knees creaked and his back ached. Still, he was a soldier, and an operator to boot – there wasn't time to grumble about aches and pains, just a job to do.

Jay crawled into the OP and relieved the operator. Once there was space, Tricky crawled in beside him. The sun was high now, the temperature well into the 30s – not comfortable, but not horrible, either. Whoever was fighting out here in the high summer could look forward to temperatures around 50C. Jay spared a thought for the men and women who spent their entire tours in that kind of heat: he knew the best way he could help them was by taking Dadullah and his suicide bombing operation out of the game.

"How you feeling?" he asked Tricky.

"Like a microwaved shit." The reply was meant to get a smile out of Jay, and succeeded. Tricky looked back out over the barren lands of south Helmand, and Jay looked down at his watch. Any moment now, the other OPs should be checking in.

He breathed an inward sigh of relief as they came in, one after the other, clockwise in their relation to compass points: north, east, south, west.

Once the other three OPs had checked in with "all OK, nothing to report, over," Jay got on the net with a message for all callsigns:

"Primary is confirmed at the target location. OP South, stand by to hold your position. Roger so far, over?"

"OP South, roger." It was Manc's voice, and Jay thought he could hear the disappointment in it: Manc understood that his small team wasn't going to be a part of Dadullah's surprise.

Usually, Jay would keep the comms to a minimum, but he was confident in their secure, encrypted radios, and British radio traffic in Helmand was not uncommon. He quickly weighed the decision, then added: "OP South, if the target squirts then they'll be coming straight for you. We'll need you to call in CAG and stop him getting over the border, over."

"OP South, roger, understood, out," Manc replied. If Dadullah made a run for it, it would be Manc and his team who would have to call in the airstrike to stop him. It wouldn't be as satisfying as taking him out in person, but there was a lot to like about putting warheads on foreheads.

Jay got back onto the net: "OP West, OP South, be prepared to move on my location immediately after last light, over."

The two OPs confirmed Jay's order, and he didn't need to spell out why: C Squadron was concentrating its force for a deliberate action. Almost two Troops would be at Jay's location, and he expected the OC to come in with the rest of the men that night. If Jay had to, he would go in with what he had, but that would put their numbers and the enemy at roughly equal, and only a fool wants a fair fight in war. Fair fights can mean dead comrades, and Jay intended to count every one of his men off the Chinooks, and back into camp.

Once he was happy that the OPs understood their orders Jay gave an "out" and the net went silent. He picked up the binoculars, and began to scan over the small hamlet that housed the target building. Now that Jay had been inside the twisting warren of compound walls, his mind could fill in the spaces that he couldn't see through the telescopic lenses. What was the ground giving him? Should it be a straightforward assault, or was a little trickery needed? Could they leave Dadullah a gap to escape, tempting him from behind his walls, but instead into an ambush? It would be a lot easier to kill him if he wasn't behind the massive ramparts of mud bricks, but would Dadullah run, even if he got the chance?

Jay thought back to the intelligence dossier. As much as he despised Dadullah, there was no way to think that the man wasn't courageous, and although Dadullah had paid his way out of a Northern Alliance encirclement, he would know that wasn't an option against a JSOC assault. Jay believed the Mullah would stand and fight, and that was OK with him. His mission was to kill or capture the man, and if Dadullah didn't want to come quietly, then C Squadron could oblige.

Jay didn't worry too much about his own death. It wasn't that he didn't fear it – he wouldn't be so careful if he didn't care about dying – but that he just accepted it for a possible part of the job, and an inevitable part of life. There was no escaping it, so don't stress over it, but that wasn't the same as not fearing it. The thought of never seeing his family again left Jay's stomach feeling hollow and his mouth dry.

He'd heard people say they weren't scared in war, and he reckoned they were either full of shit, or psychos who didn't have the normal wiring of most people. Besides, if soldiers weren't scared, and if they didn't fear death, then why would people make such an effort to recognise heroes? If the person charging a machine gun position wasn't afraid of death, then the act didn't require courage. Jay was proud of his people not because they didn't have fear, but because they overcame it on a daily basis. They did not let it control them, they did not let it stop them, but every man dealt with it in their own way: some pushed it down, some made jokes, some lifted weights, some meditated, some thought about Corps tradition and those who had gone before them. There were a lot of different ways to deal with fear, but it was there in all of them: Jay didn't believe he had any psychopaths in his squadron, just courageous men who had mastered their emotions.

Every one of those men wanted to go home alive at the end of the tour, but that wasn't true of the people they would be fighting. At least some of the enemy would be seeking martyrdom, and that made Jay's job harder in some ways, and easier in others. It meant that they wouldn't surrender, even when it was clear they could not win, and those could be the hardest fighters to dig out of a position: the threat of a suicide vest or grenade was fucking high. On the other hand, the belief of martyrdom often meant that jihadi fighters did not bother with such basics as fire positions. This exposed them to Jay's men, and the lack of stable firing platforms also meant that the enemy's fire was often wildly inaccurate. Of course, the bullet that wasn't meant for you could be just as deadly as the one that was. The further apart the two sides, the greater this issue of accuracy became for the Taliban, but up close, "spray and pray" could be highly effective.

From the numbers that they had seen disembarking the convoy yesterday, Jay knew that they would be up against at least a platoon strength of the enemy – about 20 to 30 fighters – and that, given the proximity of Bahram Chah, and its support of the Taliban, it was very likely that a protracted gunfight would draw an enemy Quick Reaction Force from that area. How quick that would be, Jay didn't know, but he had seen plenty of occasions of jihadis mobilising quickly, utilising motorbikes and pickups to get into a fight. If they thought that their Mullah was in trouble – and given his legendary following in the Taliban's rank and file – it was easy to believe that many inside the town would be willing to lay their lives down for Dadullah.

The quality of these men was anyone's guess, but Jay was certain that the Taliban guarding Dadullah were as good as the Taliban got. This assumption came from the way the guards had moved and secured Dadullah during his arrival, and something that Jay had picked up in the photos from Robbie and JB.

When Al-Qaeda had supported the Taliban – which bin Laden had done by providing financial support, and by carrying out actions that Mullah Omar hadn't been able to achieve, like assassinating the Lion of Panjshir, Ahmad Shah Massoud – they had also offered several hundred men to stiffen the Taliban's resistance. This unit, the 055 Brigade, was incorporated into the Taliban but remained a separate force within it. These were the battle-hardened veterans of global jihad, from Bosnia to Baghdad, and although the Americans had killed many during the battles at Tora Bora, hundreds of the 055 Brigade had survived and travelled south to Pakistan with bin Laden and the Taliban leadership. There they had formed a paramilitary organisation that handled, among other things, the security of the key leaders. This group then called themselves Lashkar al-Zil, or the Shadow Army. Made up primarily of Pakistanis, Afghans and Iraqis, there were also a number of Libyans and Egyptians amongst them. They wore military equipment draped over the traditional garb of the region, the *shalwar kameez*, loose trousers, and shemagh round their necks, and, the tell-tale sign of the Shadow Army, they would travel with black hoods completely covering their faces.

Almost all of the men who'd stepped out of the vehicles, and who had surrounded Dadullah, had been wearing such hoods.

Of course, much like British line infantry liked to get away with as much civvi and "Gucci" kit as they could to look "operator as fuck", it was possible that other Afghan fighters modelled their style on their highest tier of their own forces. It was a possibility that this was what Jay had seen, but not a likelihood. Who better for 055 to be guarding than Mullah Dadullah, the darling of the most diehard of jihadis, and Al-Qaeda in particular?

"See anything moving out there, Tricky? Any signs we disturbed anyone last night?" Jay asked.

"They look oblivious mate. Seen a few pax milling around, but nothing that resembles a patrol. An unarmed fighting age male and a young lad left earlier, both carrying bedrolls. Looks like they fucked off in the direction of the town. Probably good news for the kid."

Jay knew what Tricky was referring to: some of the habits in the region disgusted Jay, to say the least. Jay knew that they couldn't right every wrong in the province, but the abuse of children sat on the top of Jay's list of unforgivable sins. Jay asked himself if emotions were in any way clouding the plan he was forming to take down Dadullah: after all, C Squadron had lost two men on this tour, quite likely to men who answered to the Taliban leader. There was no use saying it wasn't personal, because it fucking was, but Jay needed to make sure it remained professional too.

"We've got a few options," he said to Tricky, "now that it looks like the civilian and his kid have left, I think we can confidently say that whoever is in the target building now is a combatant."

Tricky nodded. "Definitely."

"So, we could just paint the target with lasers and put a few thousand pounders on Dadullah's head. I don't think we'd have any trouble getting a Spectre on station, and anyone who somehow survived could get the good news on the end of that."

Tricky nodded again.

"There's a few problems with bombing or strafing this place," Jay said, "and the first is that it will be hard work to ID Dadullah if whoever is in that building is vapour. And, like Gray Fox said, it will be even harder to interrogate him."

"You reckon we can take him alive?" Tricky asked, and Jay shook his head.

"I'm not gonna lie, Tricky, I think there's fuck all chance this guy comes in alive. He might be a total sack of shit in the personality department but there's no doubt he's a fighter, and I think he'll go down swinging. If he had a smaller body-guard and we could catch him in bed in his pyjamas, fair one, we might have a good chance of capturing him, but in that compound, with those guards, I don't see how this doesn't go noisy."

"Is it even worth trying to get him then?" Tricky asked, and not from fear, but because it was the right thing to question the methods from all angles.

Jay nodded. "If we have a shot at lifting him, we should take it. Let's be honest, Gray Fox and friends aren't shy when it comes to getting information out of HVTs. Dadullah could spill a lot of beans, mate, and I think that's worth the risk of trying to take him alive."

Tricky turned and grinned at Jay: "Who knows, maybe he's ready for a change of scenery. I know I'd be ready to defect if I lived out here."

"There's another consideration," Jay said, still thinking through their options, "Dadullah might not come in alive, but who knows what intelligence they have on them? If we drop him and his guards before they can destroy it, then that could be big."

"Even if they do smash up hard drives and stuff, I'm sure those Gray Fox dweebs could pull it off."

This time, Jay did smile. "I'm not sure those lads are as nerdy as you think, mate. They've probably signed off on more dark shit than we can think of."

"Yeah, but do they do it themselves though? It's not that I don't respect them, I'm sure they're great at their jobs," Tricky pointed towards the compounds, "*this* is proof of that, but I don't know, mate. It's never sat right with me that people who pass death sentences don't go in the firing line themselves."

"That's twenty-first-century war, Tricky. Not everyone can kick the door in."

"I suppose. Is that what we're doing then, yeah?"

Jay turned and looked at his teammate. "We didn't come all this way to watch pilots do our jobs for us, did we?"

Tricky grinned. He knew what Jay meant. They had come a long way in their lives, through Commando training, then Selection. They had earned their place in the SBS, the squadron, and on this tour. They were far from home on this baking hot mountainside, and with the enemy in their sites.

"Nope," Tricky smiled back. "No fucking way."

Dadullah belonged to them.

Jay got onto the net to the headshed and told the OC what he had planned.

CHAPTER NINE

Battle Prep.

Major Wood looked around the ops room. As well as the usual Squadron HQ staff, he was joined by two of his Troop commanders, as well as Sergeant Major Bryce and a Major of the SFSG: their men would be providing a heliborne Quick Reaction Force (QRF), as well as putting in an outer cordon with the ANA. It was imperative that SFSG were on the same page as the SBS.

The OC looked to Staff Sergeant Jenkins. The stocky Welshman was usually employed in an admin role, but he was an experienced operator, and was wearing some of Jay's hats while the Squadron Sergeant Major was out on the ground. "What do you think, Jenks?"

"I think what Jay sent us is solid, Boss. He's on the ground, so if that's his call, then it'll be the right one."

The OC looked to his two Troop commanders next. They were almost mirror images of each other, handsome, fair and built like Olympic rowers. The operators in the squadron had nicknamed them "the essence twins".

"Are your guys recocked after last night's op?" the OC asked them. Far from being idle while the CTR was going in, the rest of C Squadron had taken down an MVT outside of Musa Qala. Some of the men had voiced their concern about going on an op while Jay and the recce were in a precarious position, but the OC had full faith in the SFSG, and a QRF had waited armed and ready beside the HLS, the men sleeping in the open next to the helicopters: in the case of a compromised recce patrol, seconds could be the difference between life and death.

Both of the younger officers confirmed that their men were good to go back out on the ground. They had been within a half hour of landing from last night's op. The OC knew as much, but asking was a formality. Just like normal safety precautions on a weapon, there was a mental checklist for the Squadron Commander to check off in his mind.

"Myself and the ops room staff will liaise with the air wing, ISTAR, Gray Fox, and JSOC," he said. "We'll have to get this approved but I don't see Northwood getting cold feet at this stage. The fact that there's no local population in the village, and a HVT possibly surrounded by Al-Qaeda is about as good as it gets for JSOC, and us. SFSG will continue with the QRF so that our two Troops here can get their heads down after last night. There will be no move before last light, ready to move and brief at 1630."

"I'll have a word with the galley, Boss," Jenks said, "and get the briefing room squared away. It'll be a squeeze, but we'll get everyone in."

The OC nodded his thanks, then looked around the room. "Northwood haven't signed off on this yet, but they have given us a name for our planning: the mission to capture or kill Mullah Dadullah will be known as Operation Tetris."

Staff Jenks couldn't help a laugh. The two Troop commanders looked at each other in amusement.

"No chance of a Phantom Fury?" one of them asked the OC, referring to the name of an American operation in Iraq.

"Sorry, gents, Operation Tetris it is. Don't ask me how they come up with the names, but it is what it is. Oh, and one more thing, Jenks. The Americans obviously know about this op, and there's a few who want to come out on it. Given that we're going in squadron strength, Poole are happy for them to join our HQ Group. Do you mind picking them up from Scott and Richard? They should have landed by now."

"On it, Boss."

• • •

There was no missing the three American operators. Sitting on top of their packs, weapons by their side, they wore sunglasses, baseball caps, beards and a mix of different desert fatigues. It wasn't unusual for SF to wear the desert patterns of other countries, and none of the men had any insignia. What stood them out as Americans was that two of the men were pinching tobacco from a tin, and putting it between their gum and cheek. "Dipping" was popular in the US military forces, and used to suppress hunger and raise alertness. Combined with energy drinks, "rippin' and dippin'" was to these operators what brews and chocolate were to the Brits.

There was no sign of Richard and Scott, but the three Americans recognised a fellow operator and stood to greet Staff Jenkins.

"What's up, brother?" one of them said, "Richard and Scott are in there." He jabbed a thumb over his shoulder at the secure CONEX. "Dip?" he said, offering the tin of tobacco to the Welshman.

"I'm good thanks, mate. I'm Jenks. I'm standing in for our Sergeant Major, who's already out on the recce." He shook hands with each of the men in turn. They introduced themselves as Corey, Bam and Jimmy. Jenks knew that the men had come from Task Force 373, which was made up of a number of Special Forces units, and from the men's laid back style, he guessed that they were Green Berets rather than SEALS. As the old joke went:

"How do you know if someone's a Navy SEAL?"

"They'll tell you."

Like many in C Squadron, Jenks had spent training and working alongside different American Special Operations Forces units. SOCOM itself was massive, almost the size of the entire British Army. While DEVGRU and CAG were on par to the SAS and SBS, there were a lot of other SOF units that were considered a lower tier, though that in no way diminished the difficulty of obtaining a place in one of them. They all had their own rigorous selection process and training, and each had their own identity and ethos. Some men in C Squadron loved the SEALS, and fought over the liaison jobs to America, while other men, like Jenks, preferred the less glamorous image of the Green Berets.

"You guys 7th Group?" he asked.

"Yessir," Corey said. He was evidently the leader of the trio, and saw no danger sharing that knowledge with the SBS SNCO. After all, they would soon be riding into the fight together.

Jenks dropped the names of a few 7th Group members he'd met over the years. The top end of Special Forces was a small world, and a mutual acquaintance helped build bonds quickly.

The 7th Group's primary responsibility was for Latin America, where the United States supported many friendly governments, and those in opposition to the not-so-friendly governments. Since the start of the Global War On Terror their men were needed all over the world, including Afghanistan. Green Berets were some of the first Americans on the ground after 9/11, and the early days of the war had been textbook Green Beret tactics: embed a 12-man Operational Detachment Alpha (ODA) with indigenous forces, and fight alongside them. These "A Teams" had been developed during the Vietnam War, fighting beside the Montagnard tribes in isolated outposts. After the Northern Alliance's success, and when the new government was established in Kabul, the ODAs worked alongside their new Afghan Army counterparts. Others were pulled away into Task Forces like 373, which was working its way through the JPEL (Capture-or-Kill list) just like C Squadron.

Bam turned and spat brown tobacco juice onto the dirt behind him. "Thanks for having us along on this," he said to Jenks, and something in his tone made Jenks think that this mission was personal. Perhaps they had lost a comrade to one of the Dadullah's suicide bombers.

"Our ODA was working with the Northern Alliance when the motherfucker got away," Corey said, reading the question that Jenks had in his eyes. "We were with a different group than the one Dadullah bribed, but you know how these things go."

Jenks nodded. He knew well. All four of them were standing here, far from home, because they were fierce competitors. Jenks had been a promising rugby player, but not quite good enough to think about going pro. If they'd lost a game because someone else had missed a tackle, and not him, it didn't change the fact that it was still a loss for him. On a team, everyone's mistakes were your mistakes.

"I know how that goes," he told them.

"Where's your accent from?" Jimmy said. "Are you Irish?"

"Welsh."

"Is that in England?"

After educating the three of them on the difference between the countries in the United Kingdom, Jenks saw the CONEX door open, and Scott emerged squinting into the sun.

"Sorry about that, guys, we had to make some calls."

"Alright, Scott?" Jenks asked.

He got a thumbs up. "Everything's looking good. Briefing's at 1630, right?"

"Rog."

"OK, cool," Scott said, then looked at the three American operators' kit. Jenks got the message.

"If you don't need them, these gents are welcome in our lines."

"Ah, thank you, Jenks. Gets a bit tight in here."

"No room to swing a cat, eh?"

Scott looked puzzled for a second, then ducked back inside.

"Y'all are swinging cats?" Corey asked, bemused.

"Old saying, mate. Back in the good old days of the Royal Navy, they used to punish sailors, and Royal Marines, by whipping them with something called a cat o' nine tails. You need good space to properly draw it back and whip, see, so if there was no room below deck to do it, they'd say there's "no room to swing a cat".

"So we better not fuck up tonight, huh?" Bam joked. "I'm not lookin' to get a whippin', chief."

"Don't worry, we left the cat back in the UK," Jenks smiled. "Come on, I'll show you to our lines."

As they walked through the camp, Jenks pointed out the basics. "The galley's there," he said, before correcting himself, "sorry, that's where we eat. What do you guys call it again? The DFAC?"

"That's right," Corey said. "Dining Facility. That's what Army and Air Force call it, but our Marines call it a chow hall."

"There's Marine Corps units out here now, isn't there?"

"Yeah, has been since the beginning, and more on the way. Rumour is there's going to be a lot of them coming into Helmand, and I mean *a lot* lot."

Jenks was pleased about that. As a Royal Marine he'd worked alongside the USMC, and he put their Recon units on a par with the British Commandos.

"That's the Afghan part of camp," he said then, pointing down a road that ran through the FOB. "How have you found working with them?"

"They've got balls," Jimmy said. He was the quieter of the three, and the tallest, with an intensity to his blue eyes.

"Yeah, they do," Corey agreed. "We've found that the more we get them involved, the happier the locals are. They see it as us supporting the government, rather than the government supporting us, right? They've got to see this is Afghanistan against the Taliban, and once they do that, we can go home."

Jenks believed him, and made a guess. "You join up because of 9/11?"

Corey nodded. "Yessir. I didn't ever plan on being in the military. I had a nice career going, but when I saw the towers come down I knew I had to do something. I went down the recruiting station the next day. The recruiter said, what do you want to do, and I said 'I don't know, kill fucking bad guys', so he put me down for the 18 X-Ray program."

Jenks had heard about that. To undergo Special Forces Selection in the British military, a person had to already be serving, but the 18 X-Ray program allowed for civilians to go straight into the SF pipeline. After basic training they went straight to the Q Course, where they mixed with soldiers who had volunteered for the selection from across the army. The Q Course culminated in an exercise known as Robin Sage, which was similar to the British SF's escape and evasion. If a candidate had made the grade, they would then be awarded their Green Beret.

"Sounds like a good program," Jenks said. "You probably draw some people in who are a bit older and wiser?"

Corey nodded. "I think it's been good. I don't know about the wiser bit, but we definitely pull in a wide range of life experiences, and when you're working in small teams, the wider the experience the better. Someone might come with solutions or a way of looking at things that you never would have got if you'd all served six years in an

Airborne infantry unit. The army's an institution, and the longer you spend in an institution, the more institution-alised you get."

Jenks nodded. Part of the reason they cross-trained with other nationalities' forces so often was to look for new and better ways of doing things. "You said you had a good career before 9/11," he said to Corey, "doing what?"

"I was a software engineer."

Jenks couldn't hold his laugh in. "Fuck off," he said, looking at the bearded operator with arms like corded metal rope.

"Bro, I swear. I was a software engineer. I'm a fucking nerd, bro. I played Dungeons & Dragons as a kid and I geek out on coding. I'm just here because some fuck faces flew the planes into the towers. Once we can hand this mission over to the Afghans, I'm done, bro. Turns out I love this job, sure, but I fucking miss America and I miss my family. I'm not staying here a day longer than I need to."

Jenks heard the truth in every word. He looked at Bam and Jimmy.

"I'm just here to fuck shit up," Bam laughed. "Best job in the world."

Jimmy kept his reasons to himself.

Jenks led them into an unoccupied tent with cot beds. "Not Buckingham Palace, boys, but you're welcome to it. There's a crate of waters at the end of the tent, help your-selves. Did you guys eat? There's scran – food – at 1530."

"Thanks," Corey said, shrugging off his pack. "Yeah, we ate pretty good before we flew."

"You heard about the British food then?"

Corey laughed. It was well known that the Brits lagged behind the Americans when it came to food, and creature comforts for the troops.

"You really think the Afghans will be able to take over our ops?" Jenks said then, still thinking about what the Green Beret had said. "I've heard mixed reports from the SFSG guys, who are working with them here. They all speak highly of their courage, but there seems to be a cultural issue with getting them to drop the one-man macho-style, and work as slick parts of the same machine."

"The ones who can do it right now are few and far between," Corey admitted, "but think about it. We've been here going on six years now. The new soldiers coming up, they've experienced life without the Taliban. We see it in Iraq too. These are the guys we can really mould into our ways of doing things."

Jenks thought about that, and agreed. "Not going to be a short war, is it?"

Corey shook his head. "It takes as long as it takes." He reached into his pocket then, and handed something to Jenks.

"Usually we would give these out after a mission, but I can't take this on the ground with us, and hey, we might be dead," he laughed. "Sounds like we're going to get a real fight, tonight."

Jenks looked at what Corey had handed him: it was a specially minted coin emblazoned with the 7th Group insignia. USSF were big fans of challenge coins, and there was a growing collection in the ops room.

"Thanks, gents. And please, make yourselves at home. I've got a few admin tasks to do, then I'll come find you for the briefing."

Corey took out his tin of tobacco, and put another pinch into his mouth. "Can't wait."

• • •

Bahram Chah

As Jenks was meeting the Americans, Jay, Robbie, JB and Tricky were clearing an area of ground beside the Supacat. Everyone had had a chance to get a couple of hours' gonk, and that small amount of sleep would have to be enough. With two men in the OP, and another two on stag, everyone in Jay's part of the recce force was now awake, and would probably remain so until they were back in their pits at Juno.

Once the dirt had been cleared, Robbie retrieved a canvas bag from inside the vehicle. First he withdrew tent poles, which he handed to JB, but rather than use them to erect a structure, the poles were being laid flat to frame the 2 x 2m piece of ground which had been cleared. Inside the canvas bag were also a couple of old tobacco tins. Robbie held onto one, and passed another to Jay.

Jay opened his. Inside were different-coloured ribbons, small pegs and houses from a Monopoly set. Once Tricky and JB used their entrenching tools to carve out lines representing wadis, and build up areas of high ground, Jay and Robbie began placing buildings and tracks down. Model making was a skill taught to the most junior of soldiers, and was an important part of the Orders process. Once they were happy with the lay of the land, they then pulled taut pieces of string over it from each side, forming grid squares that correspond exactly with what they'd see on the map.

Later, when the men from the other OPs joined him, Jay would use this model to brief them on the plan, but right now he would use it – and the experience of his men – to "war game". And that involved asking questions like, *What would happen if we did this? What would happen if Terry did that?*

"We already know there's Terry in this building," Jay said, using an antenna as a pointer. "But that doesn't mean they'll be in the same one tonight."

"I'll put money on it they are," Robbie said. It had been him who'd got close to them. "They were sitting around a fire at night, which killed their natural night vision. If they're daft enough to do that, I don't think they're switched on to move their stag position."

"Agreed," Tricky said, and Jay nodded: he'd come to the same conclusion himself.

"They might have just been dossing it yesterday," JB said, "they'd come in off a drive from Pakistan. Maybe they had a long day and they were feeling sorry for themselves. Tonight might be different."

"Yeah," Jay agreed, then pointed towards the target building. "Safe bet is that most of them are out here, but JB is right, and they might be a bit more switched on now that they've had a rest."

"Or they get even more complacent," Tricky said.

"Possible, but let's plan on them doing a better job. If we see anything that looks like an uptick in activity, we're going to need to put a second CTR in, agreed?"

They nodded. "Definitely," Robbie said.

"JB, if that happens I'll take Tricky and Robbie tonight. I want you to find a vantage point for the night. See anywhere you like?"

The sniper pointed towards a low rise. "That'll give me good arcs."

It was the same position that fire support had been placed the night before, about 300 metres outside of the hamlet: spitting distance for a sniper as skilled as JB who had taken down a moving target with a standing head shot at 200 metres.

"That's not fair," Robbie said with a smile, and Jay knew what he was referring to: the two men were almost neck and neck on their confirmed kills, and now JB was in prime position to add more.

"I just need you for the CTR if it goes ahead," Jay said. "If there's no need for it you can go on the FSG."

"Mega."

"So fire support in the same spot as last night?" Tricky asked.

"Yeah, that same slight rise as JB. We can fit a whole Troop on there, and we can drive the Supacat in once things go noisy. From there, using the bank as cover, they'll be able to fire the fifty cal without exposing the vehicle. There's unobstructed ground between the bank and the edge of the village, so if we need it, they'll be in a good place to do a dirty dash for casevac."

"Can we get the other squadrons to bring another fifty cal out?" Tricky asked. A .50 cal was technically man-portable, but it required a lot of carrying.

Jay shook his head. "Unless they're going to bring an ATV stacked with fifty ammo, then it probably won't be worth it. In any case, we'll have plenty of GPMGs on that ridge, and we'll have Apaches up. As far as tonight goes, one of the Troops will basically be acting as a machine-gun platoon. They'll be able to cover the target compound from here, plus have a good arc of fire down towards the town. If any Taliban reinforcements come from Bahram Chah, they'll change their mind about joining in when they see a solid line of tracer right in front of them, and if they don't, they'll be driving almost flank-on to the guns. We'll have the Javelin there too."

"So basically," Robbie smiled, "anything coming from Bahram Chah is going to get royally fucked up."

"When the rest of the squadron comes in we're looking at about two to one, maybe three at best," Jay said. He was referring to the ratio of attackers to defenders. Conventional wisdom said that the ratio should be 3:1 at least, and although his unit was far from conventional, tonight's tactics would have more in common with Royal Marine battles in Normandy than they did with modern insertions from submarines.

Thinking about the fight ahead brought memories of other battles, and skirmishes. There had been a lot, most of them in the last four months. Many had blurred together, but one remained as a very clear memory: the Spīn Ghar mountains, and the two Taliban that Jay's patrol had killed at their DShK heavy machine gun. Those two enemy fighters had battled on to the end, and it had taken grenades to finally silence their position: Dadullah had at least ten times that many men with him, and they would be at least as fanatical as the two men who had died on that mountainside in the first months of the war.

Jay took one more long look at the model: *what was he missing? What advantage was there to gain that would seal the end of the enemy's lives, and protect his own men?*

"Lads, keep working on this, see if there's anything we're missing," he said, recognising that the best way to ensure his men survived was to allow them to apply *their* talent to the plan. They were all here because they were good – *great* – at what they did for a living.

"I'll be up in the OP," Jay told them. "Tricky, relieve the stags one at a time so Robbie and JB can fully familiarise everyone up on the model. I want us to know this village as well as our homes."

Then, Jay quietly creeped up to the OP and slipped through the back.

"SITREP, mate?" he asked Rusks beside him.

"Nothing to indicate they know they've been rumbled, Jay. There's been some comings and going," he handed the logbook across to Jay, "but not fighters. Some old came out to unload off the back of pickups. Crates of pop, sacks of potatoes, that kind of thing, and those big yellow drums of oil that they use for cooking."

Those empty drums were often filled with home-made explosives to make IEDs, but Jay didn't think that was what was going on here. Bomb factories, by their very nature, were dangerous places. They wouldn't turn the location of an upcoming shura into a keg of explosives.

"Any sign of Dadullah?"

"Neggers. He's been keeping inside. Probably worried about ISTAR seeing him."

Jay looked down over the notes in the logbook. Other than the deliveries, there was nothing to report. "No sign of them scoping out this high ground, or putting out patrols?"

"A couple of them went wandering around the village but they had their AKs slung on their backs. Looked like they were on the nose for something to loot, rather than looking for us."

The sun was high in the sky and baking the dirt of the desert. No doubt it was keeping the Taliban in the shade, where the thick mud-brick walls offered some kind of defence against the heat. There was nothing like that in the OP, and beads of sweat ran down Jay's face.

"Harry von Redders, isn't it?" Rusks smiled, using boot-neck slang for "very, very hot".

"Sweating my balls off," Jay confirmed. "I prefer it to winter in the mountains here though."

"How long ago was that?"

"Going on six years."

Rusks smiled. "I was at Lympstone then," he said, meaning that he was in the earliest stages of his military career. "How long do you reckon this war will go on for? Another six?"

"I have no idea," Jay said honestly. When he'd first deployed in 2001, he was confident that Al-Qaeda could be smashed in months, but then the war had become about the Taliban, and now it seemed to be about upholding the government in Kabul long enough that they could fend for themselves: how long would that take? "I don't know how long the war will go on, but I know we bring the end on a bit faster by taking out Dadullah."

Jay stayed in the OP for another half hour, praying that Dadullah and his men would not come out, mount up and drive away. He looked at his watch, and saw it was 1455. Jay needed to check in with the headshed, let them know if there were any changes to the plan, and give the OC time to finalise his Orders. In a perfect world, all of the squadron would brief together for a deliberate op involving all Troops, but war was far from perfect. The OC would brief the two Troops at Juno, and once last light had passed, 16 more men would make their way to Jay's position from OP East and West. Jay would deliver the Orders to them, and then they would move to the start line.

Jay looked at his watch again: 1500. He lifted the handset to his ear, and called into squadron HQ.

• • •

FOB Juno

Major Jeremy Wood stood in front of the packed briefing room and took stock of the men: as well as two full Troops of his squadron, there were also the familiar faces of his HQ element, as well as elements from ISTAR, the RAF, Gray Fox and the three American operators. It was, quite frankly, a rather formidable looking group, and the Major felt very proud that he was about to lead them into the fight. He had earned his place here the same as the operators had – first through the Commando course, and then through SF selection – and from that small group of selected officers he had been kept on and given command of a squadron at war. To lead this squadron was his dream, and to fail these men was his nightmare.

"Before we start the Orders, I just want to introduce a few new faces. We have three members of TS373 joining us," he said, and at this, Corey and his two partners put up their hands. "We're happy to have you along for this. According to our recce, we're in for a good fight."

As the OC had intended, that ratcheted the attention up another notch.

"These are your Orders for Operation Tetris.

"Situation enemy forces. The intent of Dadullah's men is to protect his life at the cost of their own. We know that there is a three-man sentry position here." He pointed at the map. "With the rest of them concentrated in the target building here, and possibly these outbuildings here. Some may also be resting inside the vehicles in the courtyard. The enemy had two Land Cruisers and a Toyota pickup, all currently parked outside of the target building.

"It is considered highly probable that the enemy are Tier 1 Taliban, and made up of the seasoned Jihadis from Al-Qaeda's 055 Brigade. They are equipped with small arms, RPGs and possible suicide vests. It is possible they also have night vision capability. This town here, Bahram Chah, is also under Taliban control. We don't know the number of fighters there for certain, but it's at least in the hundreds if the drug lords who really run the show throw their weight behind the Talibs.

"The enemy's key vulnerability is that they don't expect us. Dadullah would never be waiting here if he had the slightest suspicion, and there has been no indication that they are aware of our OPs, or the CTR that went in last night.

"That being said, their morale is incredibly high. They know that they are gaining momentum in this war, and Dadullah is beloved by his rank and file. Any questions so far?" he asked, but there were none.

"OK." Major Wood brought up a series of satellite images that had been overlaid with traces to pick out compounds: numbers were attached to each building. "This is the small village where Dadullah has gone to ground. This target building will be known as 'Casino'.

"Now, the strength of the enemy is that they have received training from Pakistani agents, and they have experienced fighters. Their weakness is that most of this fighting came against Soviet conscripts and poorly trained Afghans. Pound for pound, they simply aren't a match for us, but they do have the advantage of being willing to die, and in a very secure position.

"So, the likely course of enemy action. They realise they are cut off from reinforcements, and will fight us to the death and try and take as many of us with them as they can."

The OC let those words sink in before he continued.

"Worst course of enemy action. Dadullah's men hold us off long enough for reinforcements to come from Bahram Chah, and possibly Pakistan, and we have to break contact and return here without having our target."

Just the thought of that soured a few faces.

"Situation, friendly forces. Intent: the purpose of this mission is to kill or capture Mullah Dadullah to stop the increase in the use of suicide bombers by the enemy, to disrupt the command and control of the Taliban's coming offensive, and to remove a member of the Taliban's shura who is responsible for the kidnapping and murders of Afghans, and foreign nationals.

"Two Chinooks will fly us in along with two Apaches, which will stay on station. We also have our pick of the air cover in Afghanistan, depending on what we need. Anything from AC-130s, to Predators, to A-10s, to B-1s. If it flies, it's on call for us tonight, right, Adam?" he asked his JTAC.

"Yes, Boss," he said, grinning like a kid in a sweet shop.

The OC went on to describe the Squadron's disposition, as well as the SFSG and ANA. After asking if there were any questions, he outlined how they would deceive the enemy, and surprise him to the best of their ability. This information had come from Jay, and Major Wood hoped it would give them something of an advantage over an enemy who were well trained and willing to die.

"Our mission: to capture or kill Mullah Dadullah." He read that a second time. It was clear, and concise, but to execute it would require blood, sweat and tears.

"Concept of operations. It is my intent that the remainder of C Squadron will launch from FOB Juno to form up with the recce element already on the ground, and launch a deliberate action against Target Casino.

"Scheme of manoeuvre." At this point, Major Wood brought a map onto the projector, and talked through the plan that he had decided on with Jay. "Our main effort is to assault Casino and capture of kill Dadullah."

After giving some key timings, the OC began to give mission statements for each element, including those who weren't at the briefing: it was important that each Troop knew what the other was doing.

"One Troop, you will conduct the assault," he said, pointing out the map, and talking through the plan that Jay had recommended.

"Two Troop, you will be the reserve. Be prepared to join One Troop in the assault on Casino, or to take down secondary enemy positions.

"Three Troop and half of Four Troop will form a Fire Support Group on this piece of high ground outside the village," he said, pointing to the map. "The other half of Four Troop, under Manc, will hold their position in OP South.

"The Supacat team will be part of the FSG, but will be prepared to aid in casevac."

The OC then went into a long list of coordinating instructions: anything from what time they needed to be at the HLS, to how they would re-org after the assault. Even the media were mentioned:

"Be aware that the media from Pakistan are very likely to come and cover the scene that we leave behind us. Anticipate that every shot you take and person you drop will be scrutinised."

Major Wood could see a few of the younger operators scowl at this. The older men in the room had accepted that the media look over your shoulder, and knew that second-guessing every action from the comfort of a desk, was part and parcel of Special Forces operations.

"Any questions?"

A hand went up. "Boss, is it not possible to land to the north of that high ground that the recce used as an OP? It would put us in cover and allow us to have a proper forming up point and line of departure, rather than coming in close to the village."

"It would," the OC agreed, "but it's not so far away that they won't hear the Chinooks come in, and if they spook, they'll run. We can't risk losing Dadullah. We considered landing further away, but it all just adds complications. The best option is to set down just outside the village. They'll hear us coming, but we should have enough buildings between us and them that their fire won't be effective. By the time they're alert, we'll have our toehold in the village."

"And the fire support will be in position already," Jenks added. "Minus the Supacat, which will close in once the Chinooks are audible. By the time that you land, there'll be a lot of fire going down."

"Any other questions at this stage?" the OC asked, but none were forthcoming. "Jenks?"

Jenkins continued with the Orders Group.

"Alright gents, CSS," he said, "ammunition." He went on to say what every Troop needed to be carrying. "I'll leave it to you to decide how to break it up, but that's what you need to have. This could turn into a long fight, so no three-mag wonders on this job.

"Casevac. Medics will be a tactical bound behind the assaulting Troop. If you're injured and you can move yourself, get yourself back to them. If you're down, try to control the trauma yourself. If you can't, the man next to them is to take control until the reserve Troop arrive, then you are to get back into the fight. Any Cat As that we need to get out fast will be picked up by the Supacat and driven to an emergency HLS here," he said, pointing to the map on a screen, "and an area behind the FSG."

Cat A were critically injured casualties who would die without urgent care in a hospital. Any Cat B or Cat C non-critical stretcher cases and walking wounded would wait until the fight was over.

The OC stepped forward. "Once the compound is secure, and Dadullah is captured or killed–"

"He'll be dead a hundred times over by this point, Boss," someone chipped in, and the room laughed.

"The *or* is important," the OC said, smiling, "but at that point, we will gather intelligence, search the bodies, and photograph the enemy dead. Any injured enemy will be controlled and given medical attention.

"While that's happening, the RV and the HLS will be secured by the FSG.

"One Troop will collapse back first, followed by HQ, followed by Two Troop. First onto the Chinooks will be the Supacat and any remaining Cat A or B casualties. Then One Troop with any captives, followed by Two, followed by Three, and then Recce. Any questions?"

"What's the prize for nailing Dadullah, Boss?" one of the lads asked.

"The thanks of a grateful nation who will never know what you did," the OC replied wryly. Neither he nor the other men in the room had joined the service, or undergone Selection, for recognition by anyone other than themselves. They would know what they'd done tonight – how they had performed – and that was all that mattered to them. That, and the respect of their brothers and peers. Having a few

Americans along for the show certainly cranked up the regimental pride.

"Mullah Dadullah has been at war for longer than a lot of people in this room have been alive, so don't take him or his men lightly. We've been in a lot of scraps on this tour, but nothing like this. When we come off the back of the Chinooks, gents, it will be full on."

• • •

Jay stopped his own briefing and looked over the twenty men. Their faces were hidden by the night, but their outlines were visible beneath the moon and starlight. When the sun had gone down, OP West and OP East had collapsed and yomped quickly to his position, both reaching him within three hours of last light. It was hard work moving like that in the dark, especially over terrain like southern Afghanistan.

"Everyone happy then?" Jay asked quietly, noise and light being kept to an absolute minimum. Jay had taken the Troop commanders and SNCOs up to the OP so that they could get eyes on the hamlet, taking them through each building in turn so they knew exactly which was which. Jay also identified important terrain features, such as dead ground like wadis, and gave distances from the fire support point. Ideally, he would have liked one of the incoming Troops to have been fire support for the op so that they could bring in several GPMGs in sustained fire role but, with so many Taliban on target, Jay knew that they needed their FSG to be in position to get rounds down before the Chinooks' wheels hit the dirt. That meant that it had to be the Troop that had just come from OP East and West, supported by some of the recce lads in the Supacat, and Robbie and JB on their sniper rifles. That left Jay and Tricky to act as guides for the incoming Troops. Jay would be there to meet the helis as they debussed the rest of C Squadron, and then he would lead them into the village, and let them off the leash. After that, he would need to drop back a tactical bound, oversee "combat service support", like ammo and casualties, and doing what sergeant majors are expected to do: solve problems. What those would be, time would tell.

Jay checked his watch: there were still a couple of hours until they needed to form up, then depart for the start line. They needed to be in position early, but the longer they were there, the higher the chance that they might be compromised by some local farmer deciding that around midnight was a great time to take his favourite donkey on a date. Jay wished that was a joke, but he'd seen too many things through thermal sights during his time in Afghanistan.

There was time to kill, and so Jay made his way up the slope into the OP. He was impressed to find the 3 Troop's commander still up there, his eyes glued to a pair of thermal binoculars.

"How are we looking?" Jay asked.

"Not very lively," the younger officer replied, "although I did see a chicken cross the road."

For a moment Jay wondered if he was being set up for a bad joke, but no: that was the only activity in the village.

"Do you reckon they've got bomb shelters in the target building?" the officer asked.

"It's possible. The Afghans like digging in," Jay said, thinking back to the caves in the mountains during his first time here. In Sangin, the enemy had tunnel networks going from compound to compound, enabling them to materialise seemingly from nowhere. There was a tradition of digging into the Afghan dirt: without it, they would never have the wells and irrigation that they needed to turn barren land into fields. The wells themselves – often surrounded by little more than a low wall – were a real hazard for ISAF soldiers. What looked like a safe firing position to escape enemy rounds could turn into a twenty-foot drop. "I'll pass the word around," Jay said, chiding himself for not thinking of it before the briefing: if there were tunnels out of the target compound, Dadullah might be able to pop up some-where behind them and make a break for it.

Jay smiled: *Thank God the twat only has one leg.*

"Have you ever done an op like this before?" 3 Troop's commander asked him.

"No, Boss. I don't think the Corps has done anything like this since the Second World War. I could be wrong, but I believe the ops in Korea were launched from submarines and involved recces and intelligence gathering. It could just be that we haven't heard about it, but yeah, I think we're about to do something that hasn't been done in over sixty years."

"Nice to be a part of history," the officer said calmly, but Jay could hear the true excitement behind the words. Their tour was already one of firsts for the SBS, and now this? What more could an operator ask for?

"I'm going to call into HQ," Jay told him. "If there's been fuck all movement, we won't risk a second CTR."

"I think that's the right call," the Troop commander agreed. "Things look very different if all of a sudden we have a three-man team trapped in the middle of the enemy. There's a chance that they may have moved some sentries out without us seeing it, but it's the smaller chance to take."

"Agreed," Jay said, and then he spoke into his radio, "Zero Alpha, Three Three Alpha."

The OC's voice replied a second later. "Zero Alpha, send, over."

"Three Three Alpha, Gibraltar. I say again, Gibraltar, over."

"Zero Alpha, roger, Gibraltar. Out."

• • •

Gibraltar: it was a battle so famous to the Royal Marines that the word was inscribed on their cap badge. It was three hundred and three years since the Royal Marines had won that battle honour, and since then the history had been a long and a proud one. Like most men in C Squadron, Major Wood had earned his green beret, and he was proud of his history as a Royal Marine. The SBS was, in many ways, the elite of an elite, and tonight they would add another victory onto the long list of Corps successes. Tonight, "Gibraltar" was the code word that meant that the recce phase was over, and that Operation Tetris could go ahead.

Major Wood lowered the radio handset and looked at Jenks. The Welshman gave a nod.

"Everyone's at the HLS ready to go, Boss."

The OC's kit was beside him, prepped, bombed up, and ready to go: a full fighting order, a radio, rifle, plate carrier and helmet. He hadn't been able to wear the rig as often as he would like on this tour, having to coordinate different DA's from the ops room, but tonight he would get the chance to lead his men into the fight. He knew that tonight was one that was unlikely to ever be repeated, at least not by him. This was a World Cup final. It would be the moment that Jeremy Wood would look back to as an old man and say: "Operation Tetris. *That* was the pinnacle of my life."

The OC pulled his gear on, and clipped his helmet to his plate carrier. With his weapon held in his left hand, he shook hands with the men who would be remaining in the ops room. Among them, Staff Jenkins. The old hand was too much of a professional to let his disappointment show, but the OC knew he would be gutted not to be flying into the fight.

"We'll be relying on you and the Squadron 2 I/C here," the OC said, and that was partially true. If things went well on the ground, there would be little need of the ops room. If things *didn't* go well, then they would need the coordination of casevacs, air assets and potentially reinforcements: if Jay or the OC went down, that might include Jenks and the 2 I/C as replacements. The chances of that happening in a night action were slim, but Major Wood had read too much military history to expect that things would go C Squadron's way forever.

"Smash the fuck out of them, Boss," Jenks said with a firm handshake. At least he had Sergeant Major Bryce for company, and the SFSG added his own crushing handshake.

"Tell Jay he's a lucky bastard," he said, grinning, full of envy that he was missing a fight, and full of pride that his friend wasn't.

The OC left the OPs room with his signaller and JTAC in tow. The two Troops, the trio of Americans, and the squadron medics were waiting in lines at the HLS with their kit on the ground behind the idle Chinooks. At any moment the pilots would begin spinning them up and doing pre-flight checks. If one of the two couldn't take off for any reason, then a third was on standby at Bastion to act as replacement. It would mean pushing H-Hour to the right, but better that than risking a downed helicopter due to a malfunction.

Wood knew that they were taking a risk in flying the Chinooks close to a target. Two years ago, during Operation Red Wings II – the mission to find and extract the SEAL team ambushed on the mission Operation Red Wings – a Taliban RPG had hit a Chinook belonging to the 160th SOAR, killing the eight SEALS onboard, as well as the eight aircrew. With the amount of Special Forces missions being flown, Major Wood knew that it was only a matter of time before such a disaster struck again, and that was no slight on the incredible aircrews – it was just a matter of odds. Put your head in the jaws of death, and sooner or later you'll get bitten.

Wood looked at his men, lit by the lights of the HLS. The massive amount of kit and weapons were a giveaway that they were about to go into something heavy, but the manner of the men was easy. Some were smiling and joking. A few were even napping. He didn't see anything that could be considered stress, or jitters. It was something special to see his men like this, their faces dark with camouflage cream. This was what they had all volunteered for: true Commando work.

He looked down at his watch. It was just coming up to 0015. A few seconds later there was a whining sound as the

Chinook's engines came to life, and then slowly, very slowly, the rotors began to turn.

Major Jeremy Wood had never been more happy.

• • •

Bahram Chah

Jay checked his G-Shock: 0015.

The OP and LUP had been broken down. All OP kit was now strapped down in the Supacat. All the men had on them was what they needed to fight.

"Robbie, JB. Lead off."

Jay counted the men out as they filed past him. Only four would remain with the Supacat, onto which the two dirt bikes had been manhandled. Their orders were to wait until they could hear the Chinooks coming in on their approach. Only then were they to turn on the engine and make their way to the FSG: anything earlier could tip the Taliban's hand, and that could be disastrous to a landing Chinook full of men. It was a shame they wouldn't have the .50 cal from the outset, but the Supacat's Gimpys (GPMGs) had been dismounted and were being carried by 3 Troop. A lot of the disposable LASMs were also being carried: one operator had four under the top flap of his Bergen. "You sure you've got enough?" Jay had asked him.

Now, as he counted the last man out, Jay followed on at the back of the formation. Usually, he liked to patrol towards the front, but he had full faith in his two recce lads leading the way, and Jay had heard about a Special Forces raid in the Falklands War where one Troop – who were supposed to be the assault group – had lost a man on the insertion. By the time that they'd made it to the start line they were too late for H-Hour, and they had to wait in reserve as another Troop were pushed into the assault. Jay didn't expect any of his men to wander off the path chosen by Robbie and JB, but better to be safe than sorry, and so he followed on at the rear, watching the winding snake of men in front of him through the cool green tones of his night vision.

To say their equipment had improved since that special forces raid in the Falklands was a massive understatement. Every one of Jay's men had outstanding night vision, and many had thermal vision. With their SOPMOD units on their carbines – all fitted with the longer barrel as they were in fire support – the men in the FSG would be able to paint targets as they saw them. In Jay's first contact in the White Mountains they had used tracer to bring attention on to a target, but now it could be done without firing a round. Any Taliban outside of cover would be lit up and in their sights before they even knew the FSG were there.

Robbie and JB set a slow and methodical pace to the chosen FSG position. Snipers know how to be patient, and these two were as good as it got. They read terrain as easily as most people read text messages, and the route they chose hid them from view without being hard work on the men's ankles: a non-combat injury could be just as debilitating as a gunshot wound, and no one wanted to go over now. It was always a risk when traversing adverse terrain with heavy kit, and skilled as they were, they were still men, not mountain goats. But Robbie and JB knew their stuff, and they led the FSG to their position without any man piling in.

As Jay had asked them to, his two snipers had stopped just short of the position he had chosen for the FSG. Now, starting with the machine gunners, Jay placed the men down, giving each their arcs, and confirming both the target building and where the assault would go in. Jay didn't have to repeat himself once, every man switched on for the fight ahead.

Once the FSG was in place, Jay let the snipers choose their own positions. There was no enemy visible yet, but there were a few very likely firing points that the enemy would rush to once things went noisy, and the snipers dialled in their sights on those positions: as soon as a Taliban fighter put his head up, it would be coming off his shoulders.

Jay made one final check of the FSG's positions, then checked in with the Troop commander who would be commanding it. Because it was Jay who had done the recce, there were no hard feelings that he had made the decision on where to sight the guns: ego had no place in the battlespace. At least, not when it came to dealing with your own side.

"We're good to go here," the Troop commander said quietly, "cheers, Jay."

"No worries. I'll take Tricky and get over to the HLS."

"Rog, good luck, mate."

Jay patted the officer on the arm. "Smash 'em."

He checked Tricky was on his shoulder, then led him out to the open space where the Chinooks would be coming in. They found a slight ditch on the southern side, and lay down in the dirt.

Now on his belt buckle, and with his head empty of immediate needs, Jay found himself thinking about their target: would he see Mullah Dadullah? What if he got the chance to talk to the man? What would he say? Jay had never met him, and yet, since the OC had told him he was a target, Jay had tried to learn all he could about him. Truth be told, he knew more about Dadullah's life and background than some of the men in the squadron. How would it feel to lay eyes on? How would it feel to capture him? How would it feel to see his body?

Like a mission completed, Jay told himself.

And then he looked to the skies to the west, and waited.

• • •

Major Wood turned and looked down the length of the RAF Chinook. The aircraft was stuffed to the gills with men, not an inch of space on the canvas benches, operators bunched shoulder to shoulder. Wood had been the last man onto the ramp, and he would be the first one to go down it. If he was leading his men into enemy fire, then it was only right that he should face it first. There would be some who would argue his place was at the back, and when the Troops went into the assault he *would* be behind them, but a leader had to take his share of the risks if he expected to hold the respect of his warriors.

After the Chinooks had lifted off from the HLS, they had banked and headed in the direction of Bastion. To any Taliban dickers, it would look like any other resupply, but over the desert they changed course, and changed course again. Then, they were joined by their escort of two Apache gunships, armed to the teeth with cannon, rockets and Hellfire missiles.

The Chinooks had their own weapons: a minigun in the side door, and an M60 machine gun on the tail ramp. Given that there was a high chance the HLS would be hot, the crew had informed Major Wood that they would be test firing their weapons when they were over the empty desert.

The M60 fired with the traditional *dun-dun-dun-dun-dun* sound of a machine gun. The minigun sounded more like a massive power drill, its rate of fire so quick that the noise of each round firing blurred into the next. It was a fearsome weapon, perfect for keeping enemy heads down long enough for the Chinooks to lumber up and away from a HLS.

Wood looked at his own weapon, a carbine. It was between his knees with the muzzle pointing downwards, his gloved hands resting on the butt. As they disembarked he would cock the weapon, and chamber the first round. Unlike his men, Major Wood hadn't fired a single round on this tour, and he was OK with that. It hadn't been necessary. Tonight, it may be. If he pulled the trigger, it would be because the mission demanded it, and not him. He knew that there were some officers who wanted to "get rounds down" so that they'd have a good story for the mess, but Wood had always measured himself on his accomplishments, not his actions. The only story he wanted to tell was how his men executed their mission, and he took them all back to Juno, alive.

The OC felt a tapping on his left shoulder, and turned: it was the loadmaster, and through his night vision Wood saw them hold up five fingers: "Five minutes!" they shouted, barely audible against the sound of the Chinook's turbines and beating rotors. It was like flying in a bus, but being seated inside the engine compartment. Conversation was impossible, so Wood held up five fingers for the next man, and shouted right down his ear. That way, the message got passed along.

Wood looked down at his watch: 0055. As they had been all tour, the pilots were bang on schedule.

He watched the aircrew lean out over their weapons. They were scanning the ground around them for the tell-tale launch of missiles, or incoming tracer. The Apache escorts would be doing the same. They could be firing now, Wood thought to himself, and he wouldn't even know until he ran down the ramp and saw the rockets streaking through the air. In the cramped, noisy confines of the Chinook, the world and war was reduced to a few metres. Most of the tightly packed men wouldn't be able to see anything expect the man in front of them, but Wood had the option of turning his head and looking out of the open space where the ramp was down: he saw mountainous terrain, green for the open sides, dark for the sheltered ravines. It was good territory for OPs: little wonder the Taliban hadn't found his men, who were experts at exploiting such ground.

Wood's mind rested on the thought of those men. This plan was largely the brainchild of the recce team, and the Sergeant Major in particular. A lot was resting on Jay's broad shoulders. Wood wasn't sure if he had ever worked with a more dependable man. He would trust the safety of his own wife and child in the hands of Jay.

He looked at his watch: sixty seconds. As if on cue, the helicopter lurched and lurched again, throwing the men around in the back: only the fact that they were packed so tightly stopped them from falling out off the benches, and the centrifugal force grew stronger as the turns got tighter. The evasive manoeuvres were to throw off anyone trying to draw an aim on the descending helis.

Suddenly there was a *BANG-BANG-BANG* and flashes of brightness. Wood had been on enough flights to know that it was the Chinook's pilot dispensing flares to throw off the guidance system of missiles. Doing so would alert anyone to the helicopter's presence who was unaware of it from its sound – the light would carry far further than noise – and so, if the pilot had decided the flares were needed, then Major Wood felt it safe to assume that they were currently under fire.

He could feel excitement rushing through his body, but he kept his mind clear and focussed. He knew how to control adrenaline, even this much of it, but he did not know if he'd ever been so alert: so aware of everything around him.

Looking out over the open tail ramp was the looming shape of high ground. A quick glimpse of compounds. The ground was coming close now. Closer. Faster.

BANG!

The wheels touched down. The dirt kicked up.

Major Wood was already running down the ramp.

And the last thing he saw was the tracer streaming towards him.

CHAPTER TEN

Contact

Jay heard the Chinooks before he saw them. The *whock-whock-whock* of the heavy blades, and then, against that backdrop, his expert ear could pick out the higher pitched drone of its Apache escorts. Jay was glad to have those guys along for the op. The arsenal of an Apache was fierce, but it was the quality of its sensors and the skill of its crew which really made it formidable. In Afghanistan, the British crews had really proved themselves, placing accurate fire onto enemy positions that the troops on the ground just couldn't hit. A thick wall was only good for cover so long as an Apache didn't appear above.

Jay was certain that they would need them tonight. As much as he would have liked to have believed that they could take the enemy unawares, it just wasn't going to happen. Jay could hear the helis, and there were at least twenty enemy fighters with Dadullah. One of them would raise the alarm. Perhaps they had already done so: Jay's hearing had been pretty battered from twenty years of gunfire and explosions, and some of the enemy 055 Brigade were probably half his age.

Jay picked out something in the sky: the first of the helis. It was an Apache, making a direct run in front of the Chinooks. In the cockpit, the gunner would be calmly scanning for targets. They would be able to see Jay and Tricky in the field that would act as the HLS, and the line of men on the FSG position. Every man would show up as a thermal signature, and every member of the raid was wearing a flashing IR marker, invisible to the naked eye, to help distinguish between friend and foe.

Jay went into his pouch and pulled out something similar in shape and design to a torch. The Firefly was an Infrared strobe which Jay would use to guide the pilots down onto the HLS, the bright flickering light easily visible to them through their night vision. Jay tried not to think about what it would mean if the 055 Brigade fighters had one pair of night vision goggles between them: he would basically be standing in a field with a flickering sign over his head which said "shoot me".

The Apache was so close now that Jay could make out its features. It banked right just as it got to the HLS, keeping its altitude, but Jay could see the cannon beneath the cockpit continuing to look left. Wherever the Apache's gunner looked, the gun tracked to that position, meaning that it could quickly take shots that other close air support might miss: a fast jet would have to line up and come in straight for a gun run. An Apache could hit you even when it had passed over and was turning away.

Now Jay could see the Chinooks, big lumbering beasts that came over the high ground in a wall of sound. Knowing they were crammed with his men sent shocks of fear and pride through Jay: fear, because they were so vulnerable in this moment: pride, because they knew that, and came anyway.

The Chinooks were about 60 metres off the ground when the first enemy tracer started to fly up towards them.

• • •

It all happened in a few seconds.

First there was green tracer flying so close to the first Chinook that it didn't look like it could miss. Then Jay turned his head, instinctively looking for the firing point. From between two compounds he saw enemy muzzle bursts from the assault weapons, and then the point where Jay was looking at seemed to burst into bright white light. A split second after that, he heard the *BOOM-BOOM-BOOM* of High Explosive cannon shells landing. Only then did he hear the report of the circling Apache's cannon.

No more fire came from that enemy position. By the time that Jay turned his head back to the HLS, the Chinooks were almost on the deck, and brown dust was already whipping into a cloud around them. He saw them touch down, the airframes rocking on the wheels, and then the Chinooks were swallowed by the storm that they had created.

Jay's head snapped towards the FSG position: a gimpy [GPMG] had opened fire. Then there was the crack of a sniper's rifle. His men had seen something, and were opening up: more Taliban had rushed into the fight, and suddenly, as though a ref had blown the whistle for kick off, red and green tracer began flying in all directions.

It came from the compounds towards the HLS. It came from the FSG towards the compounds. And then, as the Chinooks lifted off empty back into the sky, it came from the miniguns of the door gunners as the big girls lifted, the pilots pushing the noses down as they fought for speed to climb out of the killing area. The night was alive with streams of red and green. What had been a still, silent night in the desert had been transformed into an absolute riot of noise and colour.

"Fucking hell," Tricky, said, laughing with adrenaline. "What a way to start."

Jay couldn't look away from the Chinooks. If one of them went down, everything would change, and rescuing the crew would become a priority. Automatically, he started running through the plans they had made before the attack, and given in the Orders: actions on downed aircraft.

"Fucking hell, don't let it come to that," he thought to himself.

Jay's stomach tightened as he saw one burst of fire pass under the rear Chinook, and another over it, at the same moment. Then the blinding light from the Chinook's door as the gunner depressed the trigger and sprayed hundreds of rounds back at the firing point.

And then the Chinooks were up. They were away, and clear, and Jay had no time to breathe a sigh of relief, because there were men running towards him in the darkness.

• • •

Major Wood ran to Jay's position and took a knee. The last thing he had seen before the dust cloud enveloped him was green tracer whipping in. He didn't think he had ever been so close to death, certain that the enemy fire would cut him down, and every man that followed, but the FSG and the Apache gunners had saved their bacon.

"We've got a man down," he told Jay, giving the downed man's details, "gunshot wound as he came off the ramp."

"How bad?"

"Don't know," the OC answered honestly. "The lads threw him into the back and the aircrew took over."

That was the right decision. They could quickly get him back to Bastion and in front of a surgeon. God knows how long it would be until a MERT [Medical Emergency Response Team] could be flown into this: there was tracer everywhere that Jay looked.

"We need to get into the top end of the village," Jay said. So far, the enemy fire was coming from the far end, around Casino. Now that the Chinooks had peeled away and vanished beyond the high ground, the enemy were concentrating on shooting back at the FSG. "Tricky, put an IR illum up."

Tricky fired an Infrared parachute flare, but unlike the Schermulys that lit up the battlespace for both sides, this flare only gave an advantage to those with night vision. It uncovered some of the shadows in their path, and Jay was happy that no Taliban had snuck onto their route in the chaos of the landing.

"Uglies say there's no sign of anyone in the compounds ahead of us," the JTAC said, referring to the Apache by their callsigns, "nothing from ISTAR, either."

"Let's get going then," Jay said to Wood. "Alright, Boss, me and Tricky will lead."

"I'll be right behind you," Major Wood said before giving his commands. "One Troop! Two Troop! On me!"

Jay stood up and started running. The last time he had visited the village had been on the CTR, when they had moved with painstaking slowness, but the time for that had gone. As the guns of the FSG kept on hammering away at the enemy's flank, and then a LASM boomed across the open ground to smash against a compound wall, Jay led the rest of the force at a run through a ditch, across a track, and then to the first compound wall. Even with the assurances from their eyes in the sky that the nearest compounds were clear, Jay had still been running with his heart in his mouth. If a machine gun opened up through a murder hole in the wall he would be the first to get it, but it wasn't that that worried him: it was the thought of who caught it after him.

It was a long compound wall, and the thirty men spread out along its length. Jay looked down the line of operators, seeing them bristling with weapons and equipment. "Boss, let's get some lads from the reserve up on this rooftop. They can watch over our heads as I take the assault Troop forward."

Major Wood understood what wasn't said: his place was now command and control, and that required being further back, with the reserve.

"I think I'll get up on this rooftop myself," he said, grasping the opportunity that Jay had given him. A ladder had already gone up, and a team from 2 Troop were clearing the compound, and the building inside it. They moved quickly, knowing that they needed to get men up onto the roof of the compound's building.

"Clear!" they shouted, the message relayed by the man on the top of the ladder. The JTAC went up, then three tough-looking operators that Jay guessed must be the Americans. Finally the OC squeezed Jay's arm, and leaned close.

"Great fucking work on this, Jay," and then he was gone up the ladder himself. It wasn't the first compliment Major Wood had ever given Jay, but usually they would come during the debrief after an op or an exercise, or when the two men had a hot wet, or something stronger, and were talking in private. The fact that the OC had spoken now, in the middle of a fight, was different, and Jay knew why: there might not be another chance to say it.

Tracer flew and bounced into the sky. There was the boom of an RPG launch, then the blast of its detonation. Apaches roared overhead, a chain gun firing. This was not the door-kicking raids where C Squadron had surprised the enemy in their sleep. This was a dog fight. A heavyweight slugfest with two sides going toe to toe.

Jay got the message in his headset that the overwatch was in position. It wasn't usual for a sergeant major to do what he was about to do, but he knew the village better than anyone except Robbie and JB, and their rifles were cracking away to the flank. Jay could have sent Tricky ahead as the guide, but Jay had never been someone to pass a dangerous or undesirable job onto others.

He turned and looked at the men behind him: fifteen operators looked back.

"On me!" Jay said, and then he led them deeper into the village.

• • •

Major Wood kneeled up and looked over the lip of the small wall that surrounded the roof of the building. To his front was the small hamlet. Between him and the target compound were several other buildings, but none fully obscured his vision. He couldn't see inside the target compound, but he knew from the CTR that there was only one building in the small village that could, and that it was so close to the target that it wasn't viable as a Command Post (CP). Wood needed somewhere where he could see the FSG, the target, the HLS, and as much of the village as possible.

"This is as good as it's going to get," he said to his JTAC. "Work for you?"

"Yeah, all good, Boss," Adam replied quickly, and then he was back to talking to the Apaches, "Ugly callsigns, this is Widow. Friendly callsigns now occupy compound eight. More friendly callsigns are pushing into the middle of the village in the direction of compound four, over."

"Ugly Three Five, compound eight, roger, out."

"Ugly Three Six, yeah, roger, out."

Major Wood could see the Apaches circling like hungry vultures. They'd fired their cannons, but the Afghan compounds, and their thick mud walls, could be a great defence against the 30mm shells. What the Apache pilots really wanted was a clear target that they could put a Hellfire missile onto.

"Their firing's died down a bit," one of the Americans said to the OC. Corey was the apparent leader of the trio, and Major Wood could smell the chewing tobacco on his breath. Apparently, being in the middle of a scrap was not a time to kick the habit. "Your fire support group did a great job," Corey went on. "Kept their heads down and shut them up."

That was true. For a couple of minutes, the sound in the village had been monstrous, an unending clatter of gunfire and the bang of rockets, but neither side had the ammunition to keep that up forever, and suddenly the fight had fallen into a slower tempo, a tit-for-tat of machine gun burst for machine gun burst, punctuated by the crack of sniper rifles.

Wood knew that Jay needed all of his attention on leading the assaulting Troop closer to the compound, and now wasn't the time to disturb him. Instead he turned back to Corey. "Do you or your guys know how to operate a GPMG?"

"Sure," Corey said. "It's basically a two-forty like we have."

Wood called over to the team that had cleared the compound, and who had now placed a machine gun to cover the village.

"Leave the gun and your spare link here," he told them, "and re-join your Troop. Tell the Troop commander he's to follow on behind One Troop, and keep a tactical bound behind them."

"Roger, Boss."

No one objected to leaving the gimpy and its belts of ammo behind. Sometimes a Troop will deploy in a conventional role with dedicated machine gunners, but for this mission, Jay and Major Wood had foreseen that there might be the need for a higher level of flexibility, and the machine gunner had his M4 carbine strapped to his pack. A few extra kilos of weight for the advantage of being able to switch from machine gunner to assaulter.

"Bam, Jimmy, man that gun," Corey said, and the two operators did so gratefully: their night was suddenly looking a lot more fun.

Now that the Squadron Commander had reformed 2 Troop, and sent them to follow on behind the assaulting Troop, Major Wood checked in with the other parts of his force. He considered calling in to OP South to see if there was any movement on the border, but decided that no news was good news. Instead, the first callsign he raised was the Supacat, who assured him they were a few minutes out from joining the FSG. Good news, as that vehicle would be vital if they took more casualties. Next, Major Wood raised the Troop commander controlling the FSG :

"Four Zero, Zero Alpha. SITREP, over."

In contact, a commander must keep his radio traffic short and sharp. His troops need to clearly understand what is being said while in the confusion and noise of the fight.

"Zero Alpha, Four Zero, snipers have taken two down around compound four. Guns have a possible, two or three down. Out."

Wood understood. Through their thermal scopes, his snipers would have seen masses of brain splatter out the back of their target's head. The machine gunners would have someone spotting for them, but it was still harder work to confirm hits than through a sniper's optic. Two down at the very least, though. Maybe more.

"How many do the Apaches think they got?" he asked his JTAC.

"One for sure. They said he's spread out along an alley."

"Two Zero, Zero Alpha. Can you confirm an EKIA in the alleyway between compound three and four, over."

EKIA meant Enemy Killed In Action.

"Zero Alpha, Two Zero. Yeah, roger. There's one EKIA here, over," the Troop commander replied, leaving out that bits of the man were now in the tread of his boots, and that the alleyway was full of the stink of blood and torn guts.

The SSM came on the net then, Jay confirming that he was one tactical bound away from the compound: "Before we hit it, we need HE into the three vehicles inside?" he asked the OC, who agreed and passed the message onto the JTAC.

"On it, Boss."

As the JTAC sent the word out to the Apaches, the OC let his squadron know what was coming. It would have been nice to let the pilots hit the Taliban vehicles with Hellfires, but he had men in the village, and so he would use the smallest munitions to get the job done. A few rounds of HE would tear up tyres, and mash machinery.

A few moments later, an Apache's cannon boomed in the sky. There was the sound of exploding rounds, and then a *BANG* and a *WHOOSH* as a fuel tank went up.

The Americans ripped off a burst on the machine gun.

"Saw a dirty fucker with an RPG come onto the rooftop, target compound." Bam said. "Must have come up to take a shot at the Apaches."

"You get him?" Corey asked.

"I don't know," Bam replied, "definitely made him shit his pants though."

"Adam," the OC spoke up, "get the Apaches to check out Casino's rooftop." In the wake of the exploding fuel tank, the village was falling quiet. While the JTAC did that, the OC radioed back to Juno and asked if they had an update on the casualty: Jenks informed the boss that the Marine was a Cat B, with a gunshot wound to the leg, but it looked like a clean through and through. His tour was over, but he would live.

The JTAC signed off to the Apaches and turned back to Wood: "There's a dead guy with an RPG on top of Casino."

"Fuck, yeah" Bam said quietly.

"… other than that, they can't see any of them. Looks like they've gone to ground, Boss."

Fuck. That was bad news, and Wood reckoned he knew what it meant: the enemy fighters had given up on exposing themselves to keep the raiders at a distance. Now, they were inviting them in for close quarter battle. Mindful of possible casualties, Wood called into the Supacat's crew: it had just reached the FSG's location. His final check in was with the SFSG callsigns that had set blocking positions with the ANA to the south: everything was quiet on their end. Not a shot fired.

"All callsigns, this is Zero Alpha. The enemy has pulled back into Casino, over. No sign of any moment from the Uglies, or ISTAR. One Zero, advise when you are ready to breach the target compound. Two Zero, stand by to support one Zero. Three Zero, hold your position. Be prepared to provide cover for casevacs, or extraction. Three Three Charlie," this was the Supacat crew, "if we take any casualties on the assault, you are to make your way immediately to my position to deal with casualties, acknowledge? Over."

"Three Three Charlie, yep, acknowledged. Out."

"Zero Alpha, out." There was nothing else to say. Wood needed the plan simple, and he would leave the details to his commanders to work out.

It took him a moment to realise that there was no gunfire, now. Not even a single shot. The enemy had fallen silent, retreating no doubt to positions where they could engage the raiders up close. They would have that chance, soon, and for a second, Wood considered pulling all of his men back, and simply ordering the compound obliterated by the air assets.

But that wouldn't do. There was too much information in Dadullah's head to not try and take him alive, and if he was to be killed here, then let them have a body to show to the world. If Dadullah was vapour, then the legend would go on that he had slipped away, and was still in the fight. ISAF needed to show that they had got their man. Only that would take the spirit out of Dadullah's spring offensive.

There was no other option. C Squadron's men would have to do what warriors had done for thousands of years, and storm the breach.

• • •

Four enemy dead confirmed, hopefully more, but Jay couldn't count maybes. He had to assume that there were still around twenty of the Taliban left fighting, and now that they had gone to ground in the buildings, they would be a lot harder to kill. The silver lining was that he was able to approach the wall of the target compound without fear of an AK or grenade coming over the top: every asset in the sky was looking, and no one could see the heat signatures of the enemy, except for the dead.

Jay made a quick estimate of how things had gone so far: all things considered, it was so far, so good. The Chinooks had been able to get in and out, and taken one Cat B casualty with them; the assaulting Troops were at the walls of the target compound; the Supacat had joined the FSG without incident; and none of the enemy had attempted to flee in their vehicles. The exploding fuel tank had been a bit close for comfort, but Jay had full faith not only in the Apache crews, but also in the people who had built the thick Afghan walls. The HE rounds had landed no more than sixty metres away, but thanks to the layers and layers of mud brick and wattle, Jay and his guys had been perfectly protected. Unfortunately, the same would now be true for the Taliban that they would have to assault.

After a quick confirmation to make sure that the Apaches were holding their fire, Jay had led the assault Troop forwards, and shown them the breaching positions: the thin part of the wall identified by Tricky, a thicker section of wall to the east, and the gate: Jay knew that this would be covered by fire – a killing ground – but he planned to breach it anyway, and when they'd been told why by Major Wood in the O-group, no one had objected.

"Let's get those dems set," Jay said, then he spoke into his radio, asking his snipers if they had eyes on any of the enemy: he got a "negative" from both of them.

Fuck's sake… the Taliban inside the compound weren't going to do them any more favours.

Jay had no time to think of anything else. The three assault teams reported over their PRRs [Personal Role Radios] that they were all in position.

Jay looked at his watch. "Standby ten seconds," he said on the chat net, then repeated it on the Squadron net.

He watched the seconds tick by:

3... "Standby"

2... "Standby"

"Breach."

CHAPTER ELEVEN

Into the Breach

Three explosions roared simultaneously: the first was at the weak point in the wall that Tricky had spotted. The demolition charge tore through it, throwing chunks of mud across the courtyard, and a thick cloud of dust into the air. Within a second of the detonation, Assault Team 1, led by Sam, were pushing through the breach and into the left-hand corner of the courtyard.

On the other side of the compound, the second detonation chewed a piece out of the wall, but no more. There was no breach.

At the compound's gates, the charge blew the metal into scrap, ripping the gates off their hinges. Within a second of the detonation, fire from at a least a half dozen enemy weapons was pouring into where the gate had been.

And they hit nothing.

"Up," Jay told Assault Teams 2 and 3 as soon as he heard the enemy firing at the diversion. Only the first breach into the weak part of the wall had been intended to provide a breach for a team. The thicker part of the wall and the gate had just been diversions to draw the enemy's attention, and fire. With the Apaches and ISTAR confirming that the roof was clear, Jay was now able to lead his men up a series of ladders: floor to wall, wall to rooftop. It was a precarious route, but there was a reason aspiring Commandos must complete the Tarzan assault course, testing their agility and confidence high above the ground. By seizing the rooftop of the target building they would be able to fight top down, while Assault Team 1 would apply pressure from below.

By tasking the Apaches to destroy the Taliban vehicles, Jay had created cover from fire and view for Sam's team, and they used it to close up to the burning vehicles, one of which was still spewing thick black fumes. None of Assault Team 1 were under the illusion that it was a good idea to inhale the smoke, but it was preferable to catching a round, and so they took cover around the vehicles, sighting through the wrecks and firing through cover rather than exposing themselves over it.

More bursts of enemy fire were going in the direction of the gate, which the Taliban must have expected would be the main thrust of the attack. Assault Team 1 had to use their advantage before the dust cleared, and exposed the feint. Red flashes were coming from the building where the Taliban were shooting through pre-prepared murder holes. As Tricky had noticed from the OP, bricks had been pushed out to reveal firing points. Two of Assault Team 1 extended and armed LASMs, placing them on their shoulders, and sighting in on the enemy muzzle flash.

BO-BOOM! They fired within a split second of each other, the launches overlapping, rockets smashing into the enemy positions almost instantly, high explosive and masonry blowing inwards into the building. Almost instantly there was a long, agonised screaming from within. One of the enemy was hurt. Badly hurt. Others were shouting. Others were firing blindly.

Jay dropped down onto the rooftop behind the first two men across the ladders. He was looking for hatchways, ready to double tap an enemy face that appeared, and to follow it up with grenades for the fighters inside.

Fuck, he said to himself, seeing nothing. There were no rat runs or ladders leading inside, just the wide exterior steps that led down into the courtyard.

No matter. If there wasn't a hole, they could make one, and Jay was turning to shout the order when things started to go wrong.

• • •

The OC watched from the CP as his men clambered up onto the enemy rooftop. The Sergeant Major's plan of using three breaches, two of them as decoys, seemed to have worked perfectly. The enemy had been focussed on the gate, giving one team time to breach the wall, and another two teams the chance to start getting on to the roof, from where they could either find a way in – or blow a way in – to the second storey of the building. The Taliban fighters would either be killed from above, or they could try and run and be cut down by Assault Team 1, or the reserve Troop that were covering the alleyways around the compound.

Major Wood was tempted to call the FSG forwards so that he could push more men closer to the target compound, but decided against it. Jay had the reserve if they needed them, and the FSG were in a good position to deal with contingencies.

"What's ISTAR seeing in Bahram Chah?" the OC asked his JTAC. Surely they would send a recce patrol, if only to find out what all the shooting was about.

"There's movement, Boss, but no sign of any convoys leaving."

"Roger." The OC kept eyes on the target compound rooftop. There was the sound of two explosions, and Assault Team 1's commander reported that they had put two rockets straight down the enemy's throat. The fire suddenly slackened for a moment. The OC could see Jay waving back down to his men for something, and then there was another explosion, and from the rising cloud of black dust and debris, the OC knew that it wasn't on an enemy position…

A few seconds later, the call came over the radio:

"Man down, man down."

• • •

The suicide bomber had one job to do, and he did it well. Knowing that they were going to be assaulted, Dadullah's men had left a boobytrap waiting for "the infidels". Jay had his deception plan, and the Taliban had theirs. The RPG gunner that the American gun team had shot had been clipped in the shoulder with one round, and a second had grazed along the side of his head. He was hurt badly, but not dead, and when he heard the "infidels" talking on the rooftop, he detonated his vest.

Not putting rounds into the "body" was the first mistake that Jay had made on the mission, and it was almost his last in life. Only the angle that the fighter was lying in saved Jay, and the two other operators on the rooftop. From a bed of plastic explosives, hundreds of ball bearings exploded outwards. Most flew harmlessly into the sky, but a few did not, and that was enough.

The two men on the roof with Jay suddenly dropped and cried out with pain. Jay felt something strike his carbine. He knew at once that it was shrapnel. He'd been saved by luck, and nothing more.

"Man down! Man down!"

Fuck! Everything had changed in an instant. *Fuck! Fuck! Fuck!*

Jay moved quickly and knelt between the two men, both of them gritting their teeth and groaning to hold back the pain. Jay didn't need to be a surgeon to know that one man was badly hurt: through his night vision, he could see blood pumping out into the air. The high pressure meant that an artery had been cut, and now the injured man's life was measured in minutes.

Jay dropped down onto him and drove his knee into the point where his leg met the groin. He needed to apply pressure, and he used his bodyweight to do it as he went into the pocket on the man's upper sleeve, and withdrew a tourniquet.

The operator's name was "Biscuits" Brown, and he groaned in agony, but Jay could see he was fighting to be as still as he could to allow Jay to work on him.

"Fight it, mate, fight it," he said, and then he was slipping the tourniquet around the leg, feeling hot blood pump out onto his gloves. Biscuits' right thigh had been chewed to mush by the ball bearings, and Jay swore as his first attempt to apply the tourniquet failed. It was too low, on damaged tissue, and so he slipped it higher, then pulled up to tighten it. This time it found purchase. Jay tightened the strap off and began to crank on the windlass that would draw a metal wire tight inside the fabric. He felt Biscuits convulse underneath him as the flow of blood to the leg was cut off. He must have been in agony – total fucking agony – but Biscuits refused to scream out in pain.

Movement to Jay's left made him turn. It was the second injured man.

"I'm OK," he said, but then buckled as he tried to stand.

Already more operators had crossed the "bridge" and were on the rooftop. Some covered the stairway while others came to the casualties' aid. Jay had to make a decision, and quickly. Biscuits needed to be in a hospital and he needed to be there now, but what was the fastest way to get him there? Could they clear the compound, and extract him from the field just on the other side of the wall?

The sound of continuous gunfire below him gave him the answer to that. Not even Assault Team 1's rockets had done anything but stem the flow of Taliban fire for more than ten seconds. More men had come into the fight. They were too well dug in, too numerous, and now Jay had two casualties. How many more of the enemy had S-Vests? All of them? That wasn't a stretch of the imagination. Jay knew what he had to do.

There was no time to fuck around. No time for anything except the most basic plan. Jay knew his soldiers well, and picked out the two best men for this job.

"Bannon. Gregor. Get these two onto your shoulders and get them across that fucking ladder. Now!"

They were two of the strongest and fittest men in a squadron of strong fit men, and they were full of adrenaline. In seconds, they'd hoisted the casualties onto their shoulders. Now they had to walk across the rungs of a ladder suspended six metres above the ground. It was an impossible task for a man, but these were not ordinary men. They were amongst the most confident and well-trained operators that a military had ever produced, and first one man crossed the chasm with his load, and then the others. Years and years of training and drills all for a moment like this, and it did not fail them.

"Listen in!" Jay shouted to the remaining men on the rooftop. "We're pulling back. Drop smoke down the sides of the walls." Assault Team 1 would need all the help they could get before pulling back.

"Assault Team 1, have you got total cover from fire if you fall back now?"

"Not total, no," Sam came back.

"Then hold where you are. Let us get off the roof and then I'll call the Apaches in to hit the building as you pull back."

"That's danger-close, Jay."

"It'll be danger fucking close mate, but it's the best way to break contact."

"Yeah, fuck it, you're right. Out."

"Go!" Jay said to the last man on the roof, and then he followed on across the ladder, trying not to think what would happen if the enemy uncovered another murder hole.

Jay reached the top of the wall. He dropped onto the next ladder down to the alleyway. He pulled the ladder back and dropped it down beside him, then took the rungs quickly until his feet were on the dirt. As soon as he was down, he was on the radio:

"JTAC, we need HE into Casino."

"Confirm HE into Casino. We have Troops in the compound."

"Confirmed. HE into Casino. Make sure they're aware."

"Roger that. Wait out."

Although the Apache didn't need to be straight on to do a strafing run, it was the safest way of doing it. If it attacked over the heads of Assault Team 1, a round aimed too short would hit them. If it attacked in the direction of Assault Team 1, a round aimed too long would hit them. The Apache needed to come in so that the Assault Team was to the flank: even then, it was a dangerous fire mission, but having them break contact without it would be even more dangerous.

"Sam, as soon as that HE hits," Jay told them over comms, "get moving."

"Roger!"

For a few moments there was the back and forth of small arms fire between the Assault Team and the Taliban, and then the sound of the Apache grew louder as it turned towards them and started its attack run. Perhaps the enemy knew what was coming, because all but two of their guns fell silent.

Cannon rounds started smashing into the roof of the target compound. What was left of the RPG gunner was sent flying in all directions as the Apache turned and banked after drilling its target. Assault Team 1, who had crouched against the hot metal of the cars, sprang up and ran back towards the breach. They were pelted with dirt falling from the sky, but better that than rounds. Within five seconds of the strafing run, all of Assault Team 1 had gone through the breach, and were back outside the target compound.

"Assault Team 1," Jay heard on his radio, "clear."

Then there was another voice in Jay's ear. It was the OC, and he asking for a SITREP.

Jay didn't need to think about it twice: "Task Spectre."

• • •

"When in doubt, use an AC-130 to fuck shit up," Corey said to himself.

If it wasn't for the fact that they'd just taken two casualties, Adam the JTAC would be smiling. In his job, aside from maybe an A-10, there was nothing that air controllers wanted to call in more than a Spectre Gunship. It was the ultimate tick in their air controller wish list.

There was no part of Major Wood that was excited about the prospect. He didn't second guess Jay's decision to withdraw at all, but the fact was that they were back outside the target compound with two casualties, one of them serious. Wood was still waiting to find out just how bad, but Jay wouldn't have pulled his men off the roof unless he had to. He must have decided that – not only did the enemy positions need softening up – but that the casualty needed an evacuation, and he needed one now.

The OC turned and looked in the direction of the FSG: the life-saving Supacat was already making its way towards the CP to take delivery off the casualty. A MERT helicopter was already scrambling, having been warned off that the squadron had taken casualties. Once the OC had more information, they would send a casevac report to give the crew and its medical team all the information that they needed.

Wood could hear his men somewhere in the village. There was nothing stealthy about this casevac. He couldn't make out the words but there was shouting. He knew it would be commands, not panic. Every part of Jeremy Wood wanted to get on the radio and ask questions, but that would achieve nothing. He just had to wait. Less than a minute and the casualties would be at his compound, and he could revise the plan with his sergeant major.

"There they are," Corey said, pointing down.

Through his night vision, the OC saw two casualties being carried on two lightweight stretchers. That was the problem with working in 16-man Troops. Two stretcher cases required eight men to carry them. Until the casualties were handed over, One Troop were out of action. Wood ran through what would happen if the Taliban decided to counterattack and break out: could they overrun Two Troop? Or at least overwhelm a point of their cordon?

"Two Zero, Zero Alpha. Concentrate on the flank inside the village. Leave the desert flank open. If we have runners, the FSG and Apaches will have that area covered, over."

"Two Zero, roger. None of my guys are between the compound and the FSG, over."

"Zero Alpha, roger, out."

Wood almost allowed himself a proud smile – his Troop commander had already come to the same conclusion, and acted quickly – but the thought of his injured men was foremost in his mind. 1 Troop were bringing them into the CP compound now, and setting them down.

"I'll be back in five," Wood said to his JTAC, and then he was running down the stairs into the courtyard.

• • •

Jay had never had to try so hard to control his anger. He'd fucked up. He should have double-tapped the "body" on the roof, and now two of his men were down, and he didn't know if Biscuits would keep his leg. The wound was horrible, a part of his thigh like bloody mincemeat, but at least the tourniquet had held. Had it not, Biscuits would have already bled to death.

After running across to Two Troop's commander to tell them to cover the breaches, including the wide-open compound gate, Jay had told Assault Team 1 to stay by their breach. Then, with the rest of One Troop, Jay had picked up a toggle on the lightweight poncho-sytle stretchers that had been rolled out, and the casualties placed onto them. The weight of the casualties meant that they sank in the middle, and there was no such thing as a good or comfortable way to bear the weight: every muscle and sinew in Jay's shoulder was straining, but Jay would carry their casualty across the whole fucking desert to Bastion if he had to.

They entered the compound that Major Wood was using as the CP, and set the casualties down. The squadron medics were on them a split second later, going to work by head torches, the brightness revealing wet and glistening wounds. Jay couldn't bring himself to look away. His failure had caused this...

There was a hand on his shoulder. It was the OC.

"Sergeant Major," Major Wood said quietly. It was the first time that he had called Jay by his rank for as long as he could remember, and the words had the intended effect. They reminded Jay that he was not Jay, the man. He was Jay the Sergeant fucking Major, and there was no time to question himself, or feel guilty now. He could do that later. Right now he needed to be a leader for his men.

"Boss, we've got one Cat A, one Cat B," Jay said. "I know what we need to do to get these fuckers. Use the gunship to grip the inside of Casino and make a breach. Then we make entry and end it."

"Alright, follow me up to the roof, Jay. We'll put the Nine-Liner in then go over the plan."

Before Jay followed, he knelt beside the casualties. "I'm going to order your taxi, you mincers," he said. The black humour and bravado was an act for Jay, but one that he needed to put on for the men. Then, as Jay ran up to the rooftop, he heard the JTAC speaking into the radio: "Standby for Nine-Liner, over." He handed Jay the handset.

"Tricky Seven Three, Vader Three Three Alpha.

"Line one. Grid, 5466 7563.

"Line two..." Jay went on, providing the details for the Supacat commander's callsign and frequency.

"Line three, we have one times Cat A, and one times Cat B casualty.

"Line four, Alpha," he said, meaning that no specialist equipment – such as cutting gear or hoists – would be needed for the casevac.

"Line five, litter, two," Jay continued, meaning that both casualties were unable to walk themselves.

"Line six, X Ray," he said, communicating that enemy troops were in the area.

"Line seven, Echo, Firefly," Jay said, meaning that the HLS would be marked out by the use of a handheld flickering IR beacon. He fired off the last two lines quickly, then listened as the person at the end of the radio calmly read back every piece of the report. There had been no mistakes, on either end.

"Roger, all correct, over," Jay replied.

"Tricky Seven Three, roger, stand by, out."

Armed with the information they needed, the crew of the MERT would now be thundering across the desert towards them, joined by its Apache escort.

"Adam," the OC said to his JTAC, "the two Apaches we came in with have been out for a while, now. Can we send them back as the MERTs escorts and keep the two that are coming out?"

"On it, Boss," he said, and started talking to the crews.

"Jay," the OC said then, "you alright?"

"I'm good, Boss. I know how we need to get in," he said. He pulled a notepad from his pocket, and quickly sketched the compound and the target building. "We need the Spectre to put rounds through every door and window they can see. It won't bring the building down but it will be a fucking blood bath in there, and it will blow away any boobytraps they'd got waiting for us at the breaching point. I want us to go through this wall here, this wall here, and this door here," he said pointing to his sketch. "We'll work end to end." That would put the enemy between the assault teams, which would be a non-starter for most units in the world, but C Squadron and the SBS were not most units. They had trained and trained to take down buildings from multiple directions at once, and they had executed that way for months on the tour.

"Tricky is fifteen minutes out," the JTAC told the OC and Jay, meaning that their casualties were fifteen minutes away from being collected.

"I'm going to run down and check on the casualties," Jay said, and then he was moving quickly off the rooftop and down the steps. One of the medics saw him coming, and stood so that he could meet Jay out of earshot of the casualty.

"How are we looking on the MERT, Jay?"

"Fifteen out. They ready to move to the HLS?"

"Yeah, give the word and we can load them up on the Supacat."

"Alright. How are they doing?"

"I've given Biscuits a sedative and plugged plasma into him. He should be stable until they get to Bastion."

"Will he keep the leg?"

"Honestly, I don't know, Jay. There's a lot of damage but they might be able to repair the hamstring. If it's all gone though, they'll probably decide to amputate."

Jay took the feelings that flooded into him and pressed them down deep inside of himself. They would need to be dealt with one day, but it wouldn't be now.

"Alright, let's get them on the Supacat."

It took little time to load the two casualties, helped by the vehicle crew.

"Rusks, drive slow, yeah. You've got ten until the MERT arrives," Jay said. He'd heard of cases where casualties had been evacuated over rough terrain, and dressings and tourniquets had come loose. He knew his medics would be on top of such things, but he couldn't help himself. Handing over the casualty into the care of another man was like handing your child to a stranger. He knew he could trust the MERT's crew, and it was just his protective instincts talking.

"Rusks, throw me down the ammo," Jay said. Then as soon as Jay saw that the crew and the medics were on the Supacat with the casualties, he told them to move off. That left the rest of 1 Troop – minus Assault Team 1 – standing weary and bloodied. Adrenaline and purpose will keep a man focussed during a casevac, but Jay knew that it was crucial not to give the teams too much time to be idle, and have their adrenaline wear off quickly, causing a slump, or to give them too much time to worry about their wounded comrades.

"Right lads, that's the cas done. Ammo states?" he asked, and the replies were quick. Neither Assault Team 2 or 3 had fired much ammunition at all.

Jay started issuing Orders: "Assault Team Three, relieve Team 1. Send them back here to rebomb," he said, indicating the ammo that Rusks had offloaded. "We'll leave it at the bottom of the stairs of the CP building. Assault Team One, you stay here with me. I need your help working out what to get the gunship to hit."

The truth was that Jay knew exactly where to hit, and it had already been decided with the JTAC and OC, but he had two reasons for going over it with Assault Team 2: the first was that they were down two men, and needed to be kept

focussed. The second was that those men were their brothers, and they would want to be a part of bringing revenge
onto the heads of the enemy.

"Jay!" it was the JTAC calling down from the rooftop.
"MERT is five out. Gunship's on station."

As Jay started to run up the steps he could hear it: the
drone of a Hercules somewhere in the night sky.

"Do we need to clear the airspace?" Jay asked.

"The Apaches are in a holding pattern and clear. I've
coordinated with Tricky and the incoming Uglies. They're
well clear. We're good to go."

"Do you want to get the MERT away and then concentrate on the gunship?" the OC asked Adam.

"Trust me, Boss, I can do both."

"OK, then do it."

The JTAC started speaking into his radio, sending positions of friendly callsigns and confirming with an American
voice that all of the friendly positions had been noted.

"Chinook," an American voice said, and then Jay heard
the *whock-whock-whock* of the MERT. A few seconds later,
the HLS team said that they were in position and ready to
hand over.

Jay got onto the company net: "Be prepared for RPGs
onto the HLS, over."

His men would have eyes on the rooftop from all angles.
The JTAC confirmed that the gunship, now circling high in
the sky above, had its miniguns trained on Casino: if any of
the enemy appeared, they'd be running into steel rain.

Jay looked north and saw the Chinook weaving its way
around the high ground and descending quickly. Then,

movement in the compound drew his eye. He looked down and saw Assault Team 1 replening their ammo. Jay wanted to watch his men get onto the chopper, but the dust cloud was already billowing, and he needed to hear what his team had to say. He went downstairs and found that team's commander, Sam.

"Mate, tell me what you could see from inside the compound," Jay asked him, and as the rest of the team pressed rounds down into their magazines, Sam sketched out to Jay how the target building looked from ground level: where the firing points were, what they covered and how he thought they could get around them.

"Honestly, Jay, there's almost thirty metres of space between the wrecked trucks and the front door. It would just take one spray and pray to take out the team as we crossed. We think our best bet is a window on the left hand corner. If we can get fire down on the front door area, and this entrance area, the angle is sharp enough for them that our guys would only be exposed for a couple of seconds. We could expand a breach on that window, and get a team in there."

Jay listened patiently, taking it all in. If life was a computer game he could ask the gunship to keep firing on one part of his building as his men entered a window a little further down, but the margin for error was far too risky. One mistake from the crew and it would be his men on the end of the minigun's bullets. Instead, Jay would use the Spectre to beat up their opponent, and then Jay and his men would slip in to put them down.

"The MERT's away," the JTAC called down, and then the Supacat crew were on the squadron net, confirming the handover.

Just a split second later, and fire began to rain down from the skies.

• • •

Hundreds of years ago, the earliest Royal Marines had stood on the decks of warships that bristled with cannons along their flanks. Tonight, in landlocked Afghanistan, it was an AC-130 Spectre gunship that was bringing the heavy firepower to the battle.

Unlike the warships that had gone broadside to broadside, the AC-130 was only armed alongside its left flank, and it certainly wasn't looking for a fair fight. The idea was that it would circle an enemy area in a lazy left bank, and then – impervious to danger – it would circle and smash the enemy below.

With a 105mm cannon, powerful Gatling guns and an incredible array of weapons sights, it was near impossible to escape from the gunship in the sky. No wonder that many of the American crew wore patches with the slogan: "Don't bother to run. You'll only die tired."

The first shot from the Spectre came from its largest weapon, a 105mm HE shell smashing into the target building. Crouching beside the JTAC, Jay watched a live feed on the air controller's handheld screen. It was like watching a thermal image movie, except that he could feel the concussion of the impact, and hear the roar of the explosion on the other side of the small village.

Jay was amazed at the accuracy of the gunners on the airship: they had put the first round exactly on the area of the target buildings. He watched as another came in, then another. It was like watching a sniper's master class.

"God bless these guys," Corey said, clearly proud of his countrymen. He turned to Jay, then: "I said a prayer for your guys."

Jay wasn't sure what to say to that. He was about to put out his hand, then remembered it was covered in blood.

"I'm Jay," he said.

"Corey. So look, feel free to say this, but if you're two men short, we'd be happy to make up some numbers."

Truth be told, Jay had been thinking about the matter as soon as they went men down. In the battlespace and working in small units, letting men go to waste was not an option.

"I'm down a breacher."

"Jimmy's your man for that. Mind if I work on his shoulder? Bam here can man the pig," he said, meaning the machine gun.

"We'd be happy to have you," the OC said, knowing it was a decision that should come from his rank. There was risk in mixing units, but they might need the use of breachers.

"I'll put you at the back of Assault Team 2," Jay said. "Spectre should open up breaches into the compound and building, but we don't know what's inside. Might need to call you up to put us through some walls."

"Whatever you need," Corey told him. "You want some dip?" he asked, and Jay laughed.

"The one time I tried that stuff I nearly shit myself."

"Oh it's a potent stimulant," Corey said, and Jay decided he liked the man: as one leader to another, the American recognised that Jay was on top of everything. And, in a lull in the battle, he had given Jay an excuse to laugh and relieve the build-up of stress.

"Fuck this crew are good," Adam the JTAC said, in awe of the Spectre's fire, each explosion casting the village orange in a flash of light.

There was nothing the Taliban could do against the bombardment. No thermal shapes of the enemy appeared on the footage. They hunkered down as their stronghold was picked apart around them. After working around the building, the Spectre started blasting chunks out of the compound wall, and then – perhaps hoping to catch the Taliban re-manning their positions – they started smashing the building again.

"That should keep them guessing," the OC said. Like all of them, he knew that a few seconds of delay from the Taliban in getting to their positions could be the difference between his men crossing the open space, or being cut down.

"It won't take long at this rate," Jay said to the OC, and then Major Wood said something that surprised him.

"Once Assault Team 1 have finished bombing up, take them back and prepare to go in again."

Jay had expected to be held back in his traditional role at the CP. He wasn't sure if the OC wanted as many men in the fight as he could, or if he wanted to give Jay the chance to handle unfinished business. Whatever the reason, he was glad for it. Biscuits' blood was still warm and sticky on his gloves. He wanted to pay the enemy back for that.

He wanted Dadullah, dead or alive.

CHAPTER TWELVE

Jackpot

Jay moved quickly through the village, the two Americans behind him, followed by Assault Team 1. Once he'd dropped Sam's team close to the target compound, Jay called all 1 and 2 Troop's commanders to him to issue Quick Battle Orders:

"This is how we're going to do it. Assault Team One are going to breach through this window they identified here, at the eastern end of the building. Assault Team Two will go into the western end. The Spectre should have blown us a hole straight through, but if they haven't, the TF373 guys will be with me, so they can expand the breach."

There was a *whoosh* and then an explosion as another round from the AC-130 smashed into the target building.

"You're coming in, Jay?" Sam asked.

"Yeah, I'll be at the back of Assault Team Two for Command and Control. Assault Team Three, you'll take this stairway here," he said, indicating a narrow stairway that led to the roof, "it might be a bit chewed up from the bombardment but it will get you some elevation, which is all you need to breach onto the second floor. Teams Two and Three will work our way across the building. One will come from the other end. Two Troop, I want you to put cut-off groups here, here and here. With any luck, they'll decide to bolt out of the open door, and you can pick them off as they cross the court-yard. Be prepared to be called forward as assault teams."

"Roger."

"I'm also bringing the two snipers in," Jay added. "Now the gate's out of the way, they've got a good lane down the track, and onto those murder holes by the front door that were giving us trouble. With that being said, no one is to cross in front of the open gates without clearing it with Robbie and JB first."

"Is there any way we can get the Supacat in?" someone asked, adding "that fifty cal might come in handy?"

"I can't think of anywhere to put it where it's not sitting for an RPG," Jay said. "Any suggestions?"

But there were none. As much as they would have liked the fire support of the heavy machine gun, the Supacat was much better suited to engage at long ranges. In a village, the machine gunner and crew would be highly exposed.

Before Jay could say anything else, the OC came onto the net: "All callsigns, be advised that the casualties are at Bastion and stable, out."

It was unusual for a message like that to be passed on in the middle of an operation, but Jay guessed at the OC's intent: there was a lull in the battle, both sides preparing for a final showdown, and Major Wood didn't want even the smallest fraction of his men's mind worrying about their mates in the hospital.

"There's at least fifteen enemy unaccounted for," Jay said. "We don't know how many of them are dead or injured, but we've got to assume they're all fighting, and that there's more S-Vests. You know what to do," he finished.

WHOOSH – BOOM went another round from the Spectre. Even pulled back a hundred metres from the compound, Jay still felt the blast and the concussion wave of the shell. For a split second he thought back to the young Fusiliers he had met at the beginning of the tour, and how they had called in airstrikes as little as thirty metres from their positions.

"I want to get closer to the compound before we call off the Spectre," Jay said. "They've been threading the needle on every shot. If we get in on the heels of one of those rounds, Terry will still be trying to recover from the blast wave."

"105mm flash bangs," someone joked in the dark, and the others laughed.

"Exactly," Jay said. "We've lost the element of speed, and a lot of surprise, so we need to regain it with violence of action."

The words were as much for the Americans as his own men: speed, surprise and violence of action were the three principles of American CQB doctrine.

"Any questions or suggestions?" Jay put to the group. There were none.

"Looking forward to fighting beside you," Corey said to the frogmen. It was a cheesy line, and something that would have got an instant piss-taking if it had come from a Brit, but coming out of the mouth of an American, Jay's men seemed to like it.

"Yeah, you too, mate," one of them said, and there were a couple of brief introductions before everyone went their way.

"Something doesn't make sense to me," Corey said quietly to Jay, and for a moment he wondered if the American was about to pick his plan apart. "Why no reinforcements from Bahram Chah?"

"I've been thinking about that too," Jay said. "In the briefings, it seemed like the Taliban bullied the town into compliance, rather than the town kicking out the ANP by choice. Maybe they're biding their time to see which way the wind blows."

"That does seem the way with the warlords out here," Corey agreed. "All the more reason for us to finish this now, right?"

"Exactly. The longer this goes on, the more likely they are to throw their chips in with him. It's probably the Spectre that's really giving them second thoughts."

"Shit," Corey laughed, "can you blame them?"

As if on cue, the aircraft fired again, and another shell ripped a chunk out of the building's wall.

"Two more rounds," Jay said, "and then we go."

• • •

Jay pressed himself into the cover of the compound wall as the 105mm round exploded fifty metres away. There were metres of mud brick between him and the blast, and that was great protection against the debris hurled in all directions, but it did nothing to stop the blast wave that passed through his body, and shook his guts.

The men in the trenches went through days of this, Jay told himself, *you just have to sit tight through a couple of rounds.*

That was easy to say, but harder to do. Even with all of his training, Jay was still a human being, and it is not a normal human instinct to deliberately put yourself close to big fucking explosions. Discipline, professionalism and a rational mind kept Jay in position: yes, there was a chance that the gunners would make a mistake, and he would be torn apart in a cloud of bloody rags, but he trusted their training as much as he trusted his own. He had weighed up the risks and rewards, and the risk of a stray shell was outweighed by breaching the building while the enemy were still stunned. They'd been pounded by artillery fired from the sky, and he hoped to find them dazed, confused or better yet: dead, or dying.

"Jay, JB," came over the PRR, "we're all set." That meant that Jay's snipers had come in on the bikes that they'd unloaded from the Supacat at the FSG, and were now looking straight down the track that led to the main gate. Jay had considered putting the Supacat and its .50 cal in that position, but his snipers would be just as deadly, and far less exposed.

"All call signs, this is Three Three Alpha. Standby to move after the next round from the Spectre, out."

WHOOSH – BOOM!

"Go-go-go!"

Assault Team 1 were on their feet and moving a split second after the explosion, the two Americans on their heels, and Jay on theirs. There was nothing slick or glamorous about what happened next. The Spectre had chewed pieces out of the wall for them, and just like soldiers had done for thousands of years, Jay and the team scrambled over the broken masonry and went through the first breach. It was tough, physical work, and no amount of SOPMODs or night vision made up for the fact that the work of killing at close quarters required now what it had always done: brute strength, and a brutal mind.

Jay almost lost his footing as he came through the breach in the wall and his boot slipped on a loose piece of brick. It sent a jab of pain through his ankle but there was no time to think about it. This was no slow move with weapons up in the aim, just a sprint to get into the cover of the target building wall as quickly as possible. If any of the teams were caught out in the open, it would be disastrous.

But the "105mm flashbangs" had done their job. Jay could hear shouts coming from inside the building, and though he didn't speak the language, he was pretty sure that he knew what the enemy were saying: "Get into a fucking fire position!"

Fair play to the 055 Brigade fighters. One of them did get to his position quickly, but that didn't do him any good: Jay recognised the crack of one of his sniper's rifles. That would give the other enemy pause for thought, and every pause meant a chance for the assaulting teams to build up speed and momentum. Jay knew that momentum was the key to war, and even life. They had lost it during the casevac, but he could *feel* it now. They had wrested back the initiative, and now they had to keep pushing.

He looked to his right. Assault Team 3 had poured through the breach after him, and had branched off to climb the outdoor staircase that were so common to Afghan buildings. The first man was already moving up it, ready for them to start attacking along the second storey.

BOOM! Jay heard an explosion from the far end of the compound. Assault Team 1 had just remodelled the window at the eastern end of the building. *CRUMP-CRUMP!* They followed it up with grenades, and now they would be moving fast – all that smoke and chaos. Just like that – in an instant – C Squadron had a toehold inside the enemy's stronghold.

Everything was about momentum.

Assault Team 2 were stacking up on a hole that the Spectre had blown clean through the wall. It wasn't the biggest, but Jimmy helped it out by swinging a sledgehammer. He must have been a hell of a baseball player, as half of the damaged wall seemed to come down with the American's hit. The Team Commander decided against grenades, and instead the first men went in, the lasers of their SOPMODs searching out targets. Above them, Team 3 had also been able to make a soft entry.

Jay wanted nothing more than to be inside the building, dropping the enemy, but he held back by the breach, watching until the last of Team 3 above went into the building. Then he shouted back to one of the cut-off groups from 2 Troop:

"Move up to here! Stay on this wall!"

That would allow Jay to push further into the building, right behind the assaulters.

CLAP-CLAP-CLAP! It was the sound of one of his own men firing, and the carbine seemed to act like a referee's whistle: all of a sudden, deafening gunfire burst out along the entire length of the compound building. It was in front of Jay. Above him. The noise was so loud it almost felt like it was punching him.

Jay looked down and saw one half of an enemy fighter. The other half of was in a different corner of the room: a kill for the Spectre crew.

There was no sign of a suicide vest on the body: Jay quickly knelt down and pulled the man's torn clothing back: nothing under the garments either. That was good news. Perhaps the man on the rooftop had been acting under his own initiative.

There was screaming in the building now. Taliban fighters shouted "Allahu Akbar!" Long bursts of fire followed, as the enemy emptied their magazines, contrasted with the *CRACK-CRACK* of double taps of Jay's men, or three shots if they had a clear enough target to put two in the chest and one in the head.

The building stank of cordite, dust, smoke, blood and shit. It was a real butcher's yard, with bits of the enemy smeared against the walls from the gunship's howitzer rounds. Jay had never seen anything like it, but he pressed on, thinking only about the mission. Momentum was slowing as they pressed towards the centre. The enemy were dazed, and battered, but they weren't beaten. Not yet.

His men were shouting:

"Magazine!"

"Doorway to the left!"

"Grenade!"

And then:

"Man down, man down!"

• • •

Major Wood watched from his vantage on the rooftop. He had never felt more useless, or more proud. He desperately wanted to be in there fighting besides his men, but he knew it was his duty to command and control the squadron. He could trust Jay and his team commanders to do what needed to be done.

It was no mean feat to be able to regain momentum in a battle, but C Squadron had done it. The crew of the AC-130 would never need to buy a beer in Poole, that was for certain. Their accurate fire had allowed the assault teams to close the distance to the building, and now Wood's men were working their way accurately and methodically through the building. The fighting sounded savage, a never ending, crashing roar of automatic weapons and grenade explosions, and Major Wood started to fear the inevitable.

That didn't make it any easier when it came over the net: "Man down! Man down! "

• • •

Jay pushed forward into the room ahead of him. There were prayer mats on the floor, and one of the enemy dead had been laid on top of one, his hands folded on his chest. Jay thought about putting two rounds into him, but as he moved further into the room he saw that most of the man's head was missing. He couldn't care less, though. The only thing that mattered was his own men, and one of them was down.

Ahead of him, two of his men were firing through loopholes that the enemy had smashed into a wall before retreating. The wall looked thick, and was doing enough to save the rest of the men from fire. The first man in hadn't been so lucky, taking a round in the shoulder. The accurate fire into the loopholes by the next two men had killed the waiting enemy, and now they were using them as their own cover: the Taliban weren't able to shoot as well as the SBS, but with the amount of fire going back and forth, there was a high chance of a lucky shot. Corey had seen as much, and as Jay knelt beside the casualty, Corey sprung off to the left towards the doorway with a grenade in his hand.

"Frag out!"

He threw it side arm in a whipping motion, like he was trying to strike out a home runner, and the grenade arced around and in through the next doorway.

BOOM!

As soon as the explosion went off Corey and Jimmy, his fellow TF373 operator was pushing forwards into the dust. Corey fired off two rounds at a target out of sight to Jay, shouted "stoppage!" and transitioned instantly to his pistol, firing off several double taps. For a second someone was screaming something in Pashtun, and then they weren't.

One of the Americans had slapped a dressing on the casualty's wound, but they hadn't had time to fix it in place. Jay lifted it off for a split second to take a look: if there was no clear sign of an exit, he would be worried that the bullet could have travelled down inside, hitting internal organs. He breathed a sigh of relief at what he saw, then pushed the dressing back down and began to bind it under the man's arm. Assault Team 2 had taken a battering tonight, but they'd been lucky: nothing about the wound seemed fatal: it had gone in through the front deltoid muscle, hit the scapula, and exited out of the top.

One of the reserve team had taken the initiative to come forwards, and Jay handed the end of the bandage to him so that he could take over the work and let Jay get back to following the assaulting pairs. He got on the PRR and asked Teams 1 and 3 to report their progress, updating the mental map he had built in his mind of the target building and their process.

Suddenly there was a loud explosion that sounded different to grenades:

"S-Vest!" Corey shouted back behind him. "We're OK!"

The SBS pair who had been firing through the loopholes moved up and cleared through Corey and Jimmy: they were glad to have the Americans with them, but Dadullah belonged to C Squadron.

Dust shook from the ceiling as a grenade exploded on the second storey. Jay looked to his left, and saw the firing positions that were around the main entrance.

"JB, Robbie, stop, stop, stop, over."

"Roger, out."

The snipers were now out of the game: any fire from their 7.62mm high powered rifles could pass straight through a target and hit an operator out of sight.

Happy with the progress on the ground floor, Jay turned and started running to the back of the building, telling the commander of the reserve team to push up and relieve the men ahead of them. Every step had been brutal and fought for, and there was only so much of that someone could take before they needed a pause to reset.

Jay exited the building through the breach and scrambled up the stairs to the second storey. He passed over three enemy dead before he closed onto the team commander, who shouted excitedly:

"I think I saw him go into the next room up as we breached, but it's like a fucking bunker," he said to Jay. "The doors are all barricaded and they've got a few murder holes knocked through the walls."

Jay could barely hear the words. The noise was deafening, the situation was beyond dangerous, but the solution was obvious: Jay had seen it six years ago when his Squadron Sergeant Major had taken matters into his own hands, and assaulted the enemy position with grenades.

Now it was time for Jay to do the same. "Keep their fucking heads down! Rapid fire, rapid fire!"

The operators at the loopholes hammered away as Jay passed around their backs, first dropping to a crouch, and then to a crawl. The enemy loopholes were small and tight, making it hard to see the enemy, but making it just as hard for them to adjust their aim downwards: bullets creased the air over Jay's back, and chewed into the wall behind him, but they couldn't get low enough to get him.

Jay crouched back against the wall. If the enemy had any explosive, then their best play would be to lay it against the wall and blow him to pieces. He tried not to think about that as he pulled the pin from the grenade.

"Hit the loophole!" Jay shouted to his men. "Fire me in!"

He needed the enemy away from the hole. Otherwise, his hand would be shot to pieces the moment it appeared by the hole. His men's marksmanship was amongst the best in the world, and supersonic cracks passed over Jay's head as he let go of the grenade's fly-off lever: if he posted it too early, that would give them time to catch it and send it back out of the hole.

Jay counted to one: "Stop!" he shouted, pushing himself to his feet and trusting his men to hold their fire. Jay pulled his arm back, ready to post the grenade through the hole.

But the enemy had known what was coming, and a hand appeared on the other side of the loophole, reaching and wrestling for the device. *This was it*. Combat at its most basic, and most brutal. From Stalingrad to Fallujah, men had fought and died in close proximity, and sometimes at the same moment.

The enemy fighter was ready to hold the grenade, and die for his cause.

Jay wanted to go home, and see his family again.

"Fuck off!" he shouted, pushing with every bit of his strength, and will. He was the bigger man, and he the one who wanted to come out of the house on his feet.

He forced the hand back, and slammed the grenade to the floor the enemy's side of the wall.

It all happened in under two seconds. His hands clear, Jay dropped to the ground.

• • •

The roar of the explosion was followed by the greatest high that Jay had ever known. Everything was crystal clear and razor sharp. He had known adrenaline, but this was something different, the closest of kills.

But the fight was not over. One of Jay's men was now standing over him, emptying an entire magazine through the loophole, the hot brass falling onto Jay's face and singeing the hair on his beard.

The man stepped aside and Jay scrambled to his feet, shouting: "Sledgehammer! Sledgehammer!"

They started battering through the wall. No fire was coming at them. Elsewhere in the house there were gunshots, but then the torrent had become a trickle, and a voice piped up in Jay's head:

We fucking did it.

But Jay told himself to stay focussed. It wasn't over until it was over. Until every one of his men was out of this house, loaded onto the Chinooks, and back at camp.

A double tap rang out downstairs, but nothing more.

A voice came onto the net: "Ground floor, all clear."

There were no longer any enemy left breathing below Jay. All that remained to be uncovered was the room in front of them. Finally, the sledgehammers broke through, and the assaulter used his boot to knock a few more bricks out of the way.

There was nothing moving on the other side. Jay pulled his pistol, and pushed through. A dead fighter in the corner. Another with his arm and head missing: the man who had tried to beat Jay, and lost.

"The room twists around to the corner," Jay said as two of his men followed him in, "push–"

There was no time to say anything else. Mullah Dadullah appeared from behind the hardcover that had saved his life. There was an AK-47 in his hands and a look of rage on his face as the muzzle came up to fire.

Neither phased the operator who was closest to him. He was one of the youngest men in the squadron – a 25-year-old from Plymouth – and he put three rounds into the hardened Taliban leader as though Dadullah were no more than a range target. The first two rounds ripped through his heart and lungs. The third blew out the back of his skull. By the time that Dadullah fell to the floor, he was dead three times over.

"Clear," the young operator said. Jay stood over the body, and gently kicked the Mullah's metal leg: they had their man.

"All callsigns," Jay said into his radio, "jackpot. I say again, jackpot."

CHAPTER THIRTEEN

Aftermath

The job wasn't over with Dadullah's death. The site needed to be exploited, and Jay set the teams to looking for any intelligence that they could find.

"So this is what he looks like," Major Wood said as he entered the room and looked at the Mullah's body. "Good shooting," he noted. "Who got him?"

Jay talked the OC through Dadullah's final moments, leaving out the part where he had posted a grenade, and been a second away from losing his own arm, or more.

"I've told the SFSG to bring the ANA in," the OC said, "they'll want to get some pictures I imagine, and hand the body over to the governor."

Considering what Dadullah had done to the Afghan people, Jay wasn't sure the body would leave the building in one piece, but that wasn't his concern.

"Any word on the casualties?" he asked.

"For now, everyone's stable."

"And Biscuits' leg?"

"Still got it."

Jay breathed a sigh of relief. The adrenaline was wearing off, and the past few days were catching up to him.

"Five more minutes here and then we'll collapse back the HLS," the OC said. "ISTAR say there's still no movement from Bahram Chah."

"They must have hated this cunt as much as we did."

"Seems that way, doesn't it?" Major Wood said, looking down at Dadullah's body. "This is a big win, Jay."

Their win, Dadullah's loss, but Jay wasn't going to give a second of sympathy to a man who had overseen beheadings, rape and torture. He took one last look at the Mullah's body.

"Let's see his PR team spin this one."

• • •

There were no further incidents as the Chinooks flew in to extract C Squadron, or with the 160th SOAR Black Hawk that collected Manc and his team at OP South. Troop 1 and 2 left on the first two birds, then 3, 4 and the HQ Element. It was a tight squeeze, and the Supacat was underslung beneath the powerful helicopter. SFSG and the ANA stayed on site a little longer, then they too were recovered back to camp.

Despite the night's action – or because of it – several of the men fell asleep on the Chinook, and only woke when the wheels touched down in camp. There was no "Top Gun moment" waiting for them. No hundreds of cheering support staff. The night and camp were silent. The men walked down the ramps and towards their admin areas. Staff Jenkins had arranged tea and toast, and then there would be weapon cleaning, kit to square away, and finally, the men would be allowed to wash dirt and blood from their bodies.

First, however, the squadron needed to be debriefed, and every man packed inside of the tight space. Many were standing. The room stank of sweat and cordite, but the mood was jubilant. Best mates who served in different Troops reunited, asking the other about the night. There were jokes, and smiles, and then all eyes focussed on the OC as he took "the stage".

"You just did something that will change the course of this war," he said, and many of the men smiled proudly. "C Squadron has removed one of the Taliban's shura, and the man behind suicide bombings, and the spring offensive. Tonight was, without doubt, one of the most successful operations in the history of the SBS."

Major Wood let that sink in. "Our victory came at a cost. Four of our comrades are in Bastion. The good news is that they are all stable. Biscuits is the most seriously injured. It's going to be a tough road to recovery for him, but I'm confident that all of the men have a path back to their Troops."

That did something to ease the worry for the wounded men's brothers: losing their place in the squadron was considered a fate worse than death by some operators.

"Look around you now," the OC said, "remember the men in this room. You made history tonight. You fought a determined enemy, you overcame them, and British and Afghan lives will be saved as a result. Jay, do you have anything to add?"

All eyes went to Jay. Word had got around, and everyone knew what part he'd played. Jay didn't care about that. His men were alive, and he was proud of them. *So proud*. That was all that mattered.

"Good job, gents," he said. "Let's get a fucking wet."

• • •

Six weeks later

Jay finished pushing the lawn mower and looked at the job he'd done of his garden. The lines weren't quite as straight as he'd like, and his wife would definitely take the piss, but it wasn't a bad effort.

He'd spent a lot of time in the garden since C Squadron had finished their tour, and flown back from Afghanistan. For a start, there was grass here, not dust. Parts of Britain were currently flooding in one of the wettest Junes on record, but Jay's south coast garden was doing alright, and he decided it was time for a beer.

As he sat on the patio furniture, enjoying the cool air, Jay's mind drifted from his garden, to war. He was home, and glad to be with his family, but it would have been impossible for him to completely switch off from what had happened over the last four months, and after Operation Tetris in particular.

For a while, following that night, Dadullah's body had been displayed by the governor of Kandahar. Governor Asadullah Khalid told the assembled journalists that the Mullah's death was a huge blow to the Taliban, and that a "wild butcher" had been removed from Afghanistan. Unfortunately, many other Taliban butchers remained: they took five hostages from the Afghan Health Ministry, and demanded the return of Dadullah's body in return for the hostages' release. When the governor delayed, they beheaded one of the government workers.

With an eye for propaganda that matched Mullah Dadullah's, it didn't take long for the Taliban's associates to issue proclamations about the Taliban commander's death, perhaps trying to reassure the rank-and-file that there was still a viable chance for the more extreme actions carried out by Mullah Dadullah to carry on to another leader. "I announce to you today the passing of a hero among the heroes of Jihad in this era and a knight among its knights," mourned Ayman al-Zawahiri, Al-Qaeda's leader.

"Today," said Abu Yahya al-Libi, his second-in-command, "we take leave of one of these noble commanders, Mullah Dadullah, who has joined the ranks of the martyrs... after having spent his life on the battlefronts fighting the infidels."

The Taliban themselves were, as always, divided on the issue. Taliban spokesman Qari Yousef Ahmadi initially denied Dadullah had been killed, more in hope than expectation that anyone might actually believe him. Once the news was confirmed, for some, it was a time to feel miserable. For others, his death was a cause for celebration, as his brutality had offended many. One Taliban commander, based near Sangin, was delighted by the news that Dadullah had been killed. He said to Al Jazeera that: "the dirty spot on the white pure cloth of the Mujahideen has been wiped away."

Local people in the bazaars and shops of Kandahar were also happy to see him gone, to the extent that many of them were brave enough to put their names to statements about his death, often highlighting his "cruelty". "He did many injustices to people, killed so many innocent people. He was the biggest kidnapper as well," said one, adding that Dadullah's death would improve the lives of Afghan civilians, declaring "it will be more secure than before."

Security was also the focus of another. "When I heard this news I became glad. People will not be scared while going outside of the city to rural areas," while, "in the city, most of the people are very happy, because now business will see progress." A third saw an opportunity for the Taliban to fall apart, saying, "they will not be as superior as they were. Hopefully their union will break down... because they have lost one of their biggest leaders and commanders."

The Taliban leadership, or at least the Quetta shura, did admit that the JSOC policy of capturing or killing the senior Taliban commanders had disrupted their own planned Spring attacks. However, some suggested it was they – Mullah Baradar in particular – who had tipped the infidels off as to Dadullah's whereabouts. Perhaps Gray Fox had a little more help than they'd let on.

The Americans and their Allies were in no hurry to deny rumours that Dadullah had been betrayed by his fellow members of the Quetta shura. A little aggressive finger-pointing and some unhappy insurgents was music to the ears of the JSOC teams.

Jay wasn't sure what to believe. Part of him struggled to buy the idea that Taliban leaders had been so willing to accept electronics given to them by the very people who had held them captive. To him, a good old-fashioned betrayal between political rivals seemed far more likely, despite what the Americans said publicly.

However it came about, the success of Operation Tetris was stated clearly in the public statements of the NATO and ISAF forces: "Mullah Dadullah will most certainly be replaced in time," an ISAF statement read, "but the insurgency has received a serious blow."

"We're having success in killing or capturing battlespace type leaders," American General Dan McNeill added. "I think we're having pretty good success there. It causes some disruption in their ability to prosecute action, and we think as long as we continue with that technique we will severely disrupt them."

Echoing these thoughts was Sayed Ansari, spokesman for the National Directorate of Security, Afghanistan's spy agency, who said Mullah Dadullah was the "biggest Taliban commander ever killed, the commander of commanders."

Some in the Pakistani press echoed that: "It is a big achievement on the part of the US and its allies, because they have been able to eliminate top commanders. The Americans, NATO and Pakistani forces will now try to get the remaining people on the Taliban council, and if that can be done then the back of Taliban resistance would be broken."

Others called it "the biggest setback to the Taliban since they started resistance in 2001. It is clear that for now, at least, that there is no one who can replace him; he was an inspirational and daring commander. I don't see any person of his standing in the Taliban hierarchy." Another writer suggested that the Taliban needed to find someone who could bring together the various strands of the Taliban, someone who could bring a "sense of unity to its eclectic mix of Islamist ideologues, village malcontents and petty criminals."

Dissenting voices suggested that while there was no doubt eliminating Dadullah was a success for the Allies, the Taliban would never be anything other than opposed to the presence of "infidels" in their country. No matter the divergence of opinion amongst the insurgents, at all levels, they still hated the Americans, and the British, and the other "occupiers", more than they hated each other. And they would also say that the Taliban's leadership in Quetta did not run the campaigns in Afghanistan any more, as the local commanders continued to battle against the NATO forces, without much input from those south of the border.

But on the ground, there was a notable change in the Taliban's tactics. They shifted away from direct confrontation with the British and Americans on the ground in Helmand and started to fight a guerrilla war instead. Increasingly, as NATO forces occupied areas of the province, the Taliban would regroup in the areas that the British and Americans had passed, and used roadside bombs and other IEDs. This only spurred on the efforts of JSOC, as getting at the top levels of the Taliban's hierarchy continued to be thought of as the likeliest way of winning the battle against the insurgency.

It was also thought that killing top-level commanders would have a bad effect not only on Taliban morale but equally convince the less extremist fighters among the Taliban to stop fighting with them, and start cooperating with the Afghan government instead.

Jay turned his head quickly as the gate swung open so violently that it almost came off its hinges. Jay's young daughter might have a future as a breacher, and he smiled at his wife as his little girl ran over to jump into daddy's arms.

Jay had done what he did in Afghanistan to make the world a safer place for his family, and now that he had played his part in that, he would put the war behind him, and concentrate on the people he had been fighting for all along.

For Jay, the Global War on Terror was over. For many others, it was only just beginning.

The End

GLOSSARY

SLANG

.50 cal "fifty cal" – Browning .50 calibre heavy machine gun

240 – **"two-forty"** – M240 machine gun, belt-fed, gas-operated, that chambers the 7.62×51mm NATO cartridge. Used by the United States Armed Forces since the late 1970s.

9-Liner – **"nine line"** – term used by medevacs for calling in a combat injury

Bergen – Backpack to carry a soldier's personal and tactical gear

Binos – binoculars

Blades – SAS

Bone – pointless

Bootneck – Royal Marine

Civvie – civilian

Crab – member of the RAF

Danger close – refers to friendly forces in close proximity to a target

Dicked – chosen for a task that isn't desirable

Dit – war story

Fastball – task given at a moment's notice

Gat – gun, usually a rifle

Gen – short form of 'genuine'. Often used to mean "seriously?"

Gonk – sleep

Gray Fox – codename used by US Intelligence Support Agency

Green Berets – A US Army Special Forces Group

Green Slime – Intelligence Corps

Gucci – desirable piece of kit

H-Hour – the hour when a mission is due to begin

Harry Pussers – standard issue naval kit. Also used to mean "by the book"; comes from "pusser" meaning purser or paymaster, the warrant officer responsible for handling money and supplies

Harry von Redders – very, very hot

Headshed – used both to describe where the decisions happen and commanders

Jack – selfish

Javelin – portable anti-tank missile

Jetboil – lightweight gas-fuelled stove that heats water to boiling point quickly

Loophole – protected opening that allows enough space to fire a weapon while also providing cover from return fire

Neggers – negative

Nod – recruit in training

Northern Alliance (also known as the United Islamic National Front for the Salvation of Afghanistan) – the coalition of militias fighting a defensive war against the Taliban from 1996 to 2001

Operation Herrick – codename for British combat operations in Afghanistan from 2002

Pax – passengers

Pongo – slang for a British Army soldier

Pressel – radio switch operated by a button

Quezzie – question

Rahbari shura – Taliban leadership council

Scan – food

Shemagh – traditional large square scarf used to protect the face from sand and heat

Stag – sentry duty

Supacat – high mobility all-terrain vehicle

S-Vest – suicide vest

Swing a lantern – chat

Terry – Taliban

Wets – hot drink, usually tea or coffee

Yomp – forced march laden with kit

ACRONYMS/ABBREVIATIONS

AFO – Advance Force Operations

ANA – Afghan National Army

ANP – Afghan National Police

ATV – Armoured Tactical Vehicle

CAG – Combat Applications Group, also known as 1st Special Forces Operational Detachment–Delta and Delta Force, a special operations force of the US Army; commanded by JSOC

Casevac – short for casualty evacuation

CJSOTF – Combined Joint Special Operations Task Force

CONEX – converted shipping container

CP – Command Post

CQB – Close Quarter Battle

CSS – Combat Service Support

CTR – Close Target Reconnaissance

DA – Deliberate Action

DEVGRU – Naval Special Warfare Development Group, also known as SEAL Team Six, a special operations force of the US Navy; commanded by JSOC

DShK or "Duskha" – Soviet heavy machine gun first produced in 1938; fired from a platform or tripod

EHLS – Emergency Helicopter Landing Site

EKIA – Enemy Killed in Action

FOB – Forward Operating Base

FSG – Fire Support Group

GPMG – General Purpose Machine Gun

HALO – High Altitude Low Opening (parachuting)

HE – High Explosive

HESCO – rapidly deployable barrier system

HLS – Helicopter Landing Site

HUMINT – Human Intelligence

HVT – High Value Target

HWS – Holographic Weapons Sights

IED – Improvised Explosive Device

IR – Infrared

ISAF – International Security Assistance Force, the NATO-led security mission in Afghanistan, established in 2001

ISI – Inter-Services Intelligence (Pakistan Intelligence Agency)

ISTAR – Intelligence, Surveillance, Target Acquisition and Reconnaissance

JDAM – Joint Direct Attack Munition, a guidance system that converts unguided bombs into precision-guided munitions

JPEL – Joint Prioritized Effects List (Capture or Kill)

JSOC – Joint Special Operations Command, the component of SOCOM responsible for planning and executing US special forces operations

JTAC – Joint Terminal Attack Controller, a person responsible for directing aircraft during a military operation

KAF – Kandahar Airfield

LASM – Light Anti-Structures Missile

LEWT – Light Electronic Warfare Team

LUP – Lying-up Point, a position where units can prepare, concealed, for an operation

MERT – Medical Emergency Response Team

MOG – Manoeuvre Operations Group

MSTAR – Man-portable Surveillance and Target Acquisition Radar

MVT – Medium Value Target

NCO – Non-Commissioned Officer

NightMarks – a clear liquid that can't be seen in normal light but shows up under NVGs

NVG – Night Vision Goggles

OC – Officer Commanding

2 I/C – Second in command

OP – Observation Post

PID – Positive Identification

PRR – Personal Role Radio

QRF – Quick Reaction Force

RFID – Radio Frequency Identification

RPG – Rocket-propelled Grenade

RSM – Regimental Sergeant Major

RTB – Return to Base

SBS – Special Boat Service

SFSG – Special Forces Support Group (formed in 2006 to assist the SAS, SBS and Special Reconnaissance Regiment)

SIGINT – Signals Intelligence

SITREP – Situation Report

SNCO – Senior Non-Commissioned Officers

SOAR – 160th Special Operations Aviation Regiment (Airborne), a special operations force of the US Army

SOCOM – Special Operations Command (oversees the special operations of the US Army, Navy, Marine Corps and Air Force)

SOF – Special Operations Force

SOP – Standard Operating Procedure

SOPMOD – Special Operations Peculiar Modification, an accessory system allowing special forces to customise their weapons

SSM – Squadron Sergeant Major

UAV – Unmanned Aerial Vehicle

UGLY – Callsign for Apache gunship

UKSF – United Kingdom Special Forces

USMC – United States Marine Corps

VDM – Visual Distinguishing Mark

VP – Vulnerable Point